Meaningful Work

Practical Ethics
A Collection of Addresses and Essays
Henry Sidgwick
With an Introduction by Sissela Bok

Thinking Like an Engineer
Studies in the Ethics of a Profession
Michael Davis

Democratic Disagreement
Essays on Deliberative Democracy
Edited by Stephen Macedo

From Social Justice to Criminal Justice
Poverty and the Administration of Criminal Law
Edited by William C. Heffernan and John Kleinig

Meaningful Work
Rethinking Professional Ethics
Mike W. Martin

Meaningful Work

Rethinking Professional Ethics

MIKE W. MARTIN

New York   Oxford

Oxford University Press

2000

Oxford University Press

Oxford   New York
Athens   Auckland   Bangkok   Bogotá   Buenos Aires   Calcutta
Cape Town   Chennai   Dar es Salaam   Delhi   Florence   Hong Kong   Istanbul
Karachi   Kuala Lumpur   Madrid   Melbourne   Mexico City   Mumbai
Nairobi   Paris   São Paulo   Singapore   Taipei   Tokyo   Toronto   Warsaw

and associated companies in
Berlin   Ibadan

Copyright © 2000 by Mike W. Martin

Published by Oxford University Press, Inc.
198 Madison Avenue, New York, New York 10016

Oxford is a registered trademark of Oxford University Press.

Library of Congress Cataloging-in-Publication Data
Martin, Mike W., 1946–
   Meaningful work : rethinking professional ethics / Mike W. Martin.
      p.   cm. — (Practical and professional ethics series)
   Includes index.
   ISBN 0-19-513325-0
   1. Professional ethics.   I. Title.   II. Series.
BJ1725.M34   2000
174—dc21   99-27536

9 8 7 6 5 4 3 2 1

Printed in the United States of America
on acid-free paper

For Shannon

and for our daughters,

Sonia and Nicole

PREFACE

Personal commitments motivate, guide, and give meaning to the work of professionals. Yet these commitments have yet to receive the attention they deserve in thinking about professional ethics. As usually understood, professional ethics consists of shared duties and episodic dilemmas: the responsibilities incumbent on all members of specific professions, together with the dilemmas that arise when these responsibilities conflict. More recently, attention has been paid to the virtues, although usually limiting their role to promoting shared duties.[1] I seek to widen professional ethics to include personal commitments, especially commitments to ideals not mandatory for all members of a profession. In doing so, I discuss neglected issues about meaningful work, moral psychology, character and the virtues, self-fulfillment and self-betrayal, and the interplay of private and professional life.[2]

Integrating personal commitments into professional ethics is an ambitious task. Not only does the task concern all professions, each of which is distinctive in many ways, but it also connects with the core issues in professional ethics. Although I range widely, of necessity the discussions are limited to selected topics and professions. Sometimes I find it useful to concentrate on one profession, as in discussing whistleblowing in engineering, while indicating the general implications for other professions. At other times I pursue a central concern through an array of professions and then develop it further with respect to a specific profession, as in the pair of chapters on professional distance and university teaching.

Part I, "Meaning and Personal Commitments," explores the roles of personal ideals in giving meaning to work, interpreting professional responsibilities, and inspiring voluntary service. Part II, "Caring and Client Autonomy," explores ideals of caring about clients and the limits of these ideals. Part III, "Shared Responsibility and Authority," takes up related issues about the interplay of personal ideals and respect for organizational authority, including religious organizations. And Part IV, "Threats to Integrity," explores three dangers: character-linked violations of shared professional norms, betrayal of personal ideals, and loss of balance that causes burnout and harm to families. Chapter 1 further introduces some of these themes.

More fully, chapter 2, "Meaningful Work," examines the role of personal commitments in motivating professionals. Most professionals want their work to be worthwhile beyond the paycheck it provides. In sketching my view of human nature as it applies to professional ethics, I distinguish three groups of motives: (i) personal compensation: money, power, reputation; (ii) craft: technical and creative excellence; (iii) moral concern: caring about and respect for persons, as well as about social practices, organizations, communities, animals and the environment; and concern to maintain integrity rooted in such commitments. From Adam Smith on, economists have been preoccupied with compensation motives, neglecting motives of craft and moral concern. (To be sure, there have been notable exceptions, such as Amartya Sen, who was awarded the 1998 Nobel Prize in economics.) Smith's doctrine of separate spheres—that work is the domain of money and private life the domain of moral motives—contradicts even the consensus paradigm, which regards moral rules as essential in professional life. After acknowledging the predominance of self-interested motives, I attend to how outward-directed ideals make work meaningful and self-fulfilling.

Chapter 3, "Responsibilities," challenges the consensus paradigm on its own terms, arguing that personal ideals shape how individuals interpret shared professional duties. I begin by identifying the large element of truth in the consensus paradigm. Shared values are crucial in promoting public trust, establishing shared understanding among professionals, placing fair limits on economic competition, supporting responsible individuals, and in other ways promoting professionalism. Or rather, these goods are promoted when the shared values are morally warranted, and I comment on how shared professional standards are established as justified. The moral consensus places limits on the pursuit of personal ideals in the professions, but it does not exclude that pursuit. Personal ideals shape interpretations of even fundamental moral responsibilities such as confidentiality, respect for clients, and loyalty to employers. They play an even more dramatic role in shaping career choice, job choice, and supererogatory commitments.

Chapter 4, "Voluntary Service," discusses several (overlapping) dimensions of voluntary service in the professions. One is the possibility of "supererogatory responsibilities": responsibilities acquired through personal commitments that transcend the minimum requirements incumbent on every member of a profession. Another dimension is applying one's professional skills to pro bono philanthropy—voluntarily giving one's time, talent, or money for public purposes. Yet another is accepting lower-paid work in nonprofit organizations. The focus on personal commitments opens the door to exploring these neglected ways to promote professional goods, whether or not doing so is a shared duty.

Chapter 5, "Caring About Clients," highlights the contribution of ideals of caring to helping clients. "Caring" is intended in a strong sense that implies altruism—concern for others for their sake—as a substantial element in motivating helping behavior. Typically, codified duties require only appropriate behavior, not motives. Indeed, some critics argue that substantial altruism is either impossible, irrelevant, or harmful; conduct is all that matters in the professions. In responding to these criticisms, I clarify what it means for professionals to care about their clients as persons, rather than as interchangeable recipients of services. I also suggest that caring implies respect for autonomy and does not imply objectionable types of paternalism.

Chapter 6, "Professional Distance," extends the discussion of caring. Professional distance, which is avoiding inappropriate personal involvements in professional life, combines psychological states (or their absence) with moral requirements. The moral requirements place strong limits on the pursuit of personal ideals, as well as on the range of appropriate emotions, attitudes, and conduct in professional life. The requirements do not, however, banish caring and personal ideals from the professions. Proper professional distance is the reasonable middle ground between harmful intrusions of personal values into professional conduct (underdistancing) and equally undesirable loss of personal caring (overdistancing). Precisely what that means depends on the context, and I take up three such contexts: the psychological needs of professionals in coping with demanding careers, the responsibilities to respect clients' autonomy, and various forms of maintaining objectivity in pursuing truth and exercising professional judgment.

Chapter 7, "Advocacy in Education," deals with the tension between professional distance and advocating values in university teaching, a tension brought to the foreground during the "campus wars." It also illustrates how the shared duties emphasized in the consensus paradigm sometimes imply a direct role for personal ideals. Professors' shared responsibilities make it inevitable and often desirable for them to advocate values pertinent to their disciplines. How they do this is a matter of personal style within the limits imposed by responsibility to respect student autonomy. The primary concern is not overt coercion of students but instead the gray area of undue influence and pressures surrounding grading.

Chapter 8, "Respect for Authority," shifts from client autonomy to employers' authority as limiting the pursuit of personal commitments. Most professionals, including physicians and attorneys, no longer work as independent practitioners. Instead, they work in authority-structured corporations where they are as accountable as any businessperson for the corporate bottom line. Rather than idealizing professions and demonizing corporations, as Alasdair MacIntyre comes close to doing, we need a model of shared agency in which managers and the professionals they supervise share responsibilities. We also need to understand professional autonomy as involving rather than opposing responsible participation within corporations.

These ideas are developed by focusing on engineers, and in particular on the events leading to the explosion of the space shuttle *Challenger*.

Chapter 9, "Whistleblowing," also focuses on engineering while raising issues pertaining to all professions. Pick any major public hazard caused by an organization: Almost invariably salaried professionals are aware of it in advance and must decide whether to make information available to the public. When whistleblowers convey information outside approved organizational channels, they are routinely punished by corporations for disloyalty and lauded by consumer advocates for conscientiously meeting their duties to the public. In reply to charges of disloyalty, I argue that there are professional duties to whistleblow. In reply to consumer advocates, I argue that there are also significant duties to oneself and one's family that need to be weighed. Most important, the public shares responsibility for protecting its members and, until it offers effective support for whistleblowers, there remains a question whether whistleblowing is a paramount duty or supererogatory. I expand "personal commitments" to include commitments to family, as well as to one's career, an expansion that carries into Part IV.

Chapter 10, "Religion Ethics," does two things. First, it amplifies how religious commitments motivate and guide careers, a topic introduced in chapter 1. Second, and more extensively, it explores profession-related issues surrounding organized religions. I attend to clashes between religious and secular authority—for example, concerning faith healing and teaching creationism. Within democracies, these clashes must ultimately be resolved by law, especially where children and other nonconsenting individuals are involved. At the same time, where responsible adults consent as members of a religion, practices such as confidentiality take more varied forms than in secular professions. Most of that chapter is a critique of Margaret P. Battin's *Ethics in the Sanctuary*, a groundbreaking book that nevertheless pays insufficient attention to personal commitments and consent to religious authority.

Chapter 11, "Explaining Wrongdoing," integrates character and social explanations of wrongdoing. Social explanations identify pressures and structures of organizations as well as professions and the wider society. In contrast, character explanations cite general character traits or more situational character failings. Social explanations are now dominant, and character explanations are widely dismissed as naive, subjective, unscientific, and suspect because of their reference to values. In contrast, I seek to renew an appreciation of character explanations by showing how they carry explanatory force and complement social explanations. I return to MacIntyre's virtue-oriented ethics to provide a framework for integrating the two types of explanations. In doing so, I pry apart two important distinctions he conflates: private versus public goods, and internal versus external goods.

According to the consensus paradigm, wrongdoing consists of violating the minimum standards incumbent on all members of a profession. Yet there are many additional threats to personal ideals. Insofar as personal ideals are central to self-identity and self-respect, betraying them constitutes self-betrayal, the topic of chapter 12. That is the only chapter focused entirely on a novel, George Eliot's *Middlemarch*. Themes include self-respect, self-deception, envy and self-righteousness, realism in pursuing ideals, regret, shame, and guilt. But the primary theme is the connection between work and family, a topic continuing into the following chapter.

Do personal ideals unduly add to the already huge demands on professionals, thereby adding to risks of burnout and harm to families? I respond to this objection in chapter 13, "Integrity and Integration." Burnout is often caused by the absence of reasonable moral commitments that give meaning to work. Ideals of caring can serve to bridge work and family life so as to provide coherence overall. Most important, we need a widened conception of professionals' overall integrity as integrating all major aspects of their lives, rather than as simply abiding by shared duties. We also need a pragmatic conception of moral reasoning that appreciates shared duties without reducing professional ethics to them. Such a conception is implicit throughout this book, as I seek to make personal commitments integral to the study of responsible professionalism.

This book developed amid the pleasures and perplexities in teaching professional ethics for two decades. The pleasures came primarily from dialogue with my students, to whom I express heartfelt thanks. The perplexities included frustration at the neglect of issues concerning personal commitments and ideals in most books on professional ethics.

I am grateful for interactions with a number of pioneers in professional ethics, especially Margaret P. Battin, Robert J. Baum, the late Michael D. Bayles, Joan Callahan, Thomas Carson, Elliot D. Cohen, Richard De George, Thomas Donaldson, Albert Flores, Leslie P. Francis, Peter A. French, Charles E. Harris, Deborah Johnson, Kenneth Kipnis, John Kultgen, Bruce M. Landesman, Edwin T. Layton, Jr., the late Martha Montgomery, Michael S. Pritchard, Michael J. Rabins, Stephen H. Unger, Vivian Weil, and Caroline Whitbeck. Roland Schinzinger has been an inspirational coauthor on several projects, especially the several editions of *Ethics in Engineering* (New York: McGraw Hill, 1996). Michael Davis's writings provided an invaluable stimulus in writing several of the chapters, although (or because!) sometimes I disagree with positions he defends incisively. My emphasis on virtue-structured personal commitments is influenced by the works of John Kekes, Bernard Williams, Alasdair MacIntyre, Edmund L. Pincoffs, and Charles Taylor.

Colleagues at Chapman University and other universities helped me, through conversations, critiques, or invited talks. I wish to thank Earl R. Babbie, Kurt Bergel, the late Alice Bergel, Donald R. Booth, Roy R. Bullock, Dennis and Carlene Cada, William and Stephanie Clohesi, James L. Doti, Michelle Dumont, Lawrence Finsen, Herbert Fingarette, Donald L. Gabard, Charles Hughes, Jacqueline Hynes, Craig Ihara, Thomas Jeavons, Kathie L.

Jenni, Terri Brint Joseph, Eva Feder Kittay, Haavard Koppang, Mark Maier, the late A. I. Melden, Marv Meyer, Diane P. Michelfelder, David Morgan, John S. Morreall, Barbara Mulch, Kathryn A. Neeley, Robert L. Payton, Hiêú Trân Phan, Paul K. Predecki, Joseph Runzo, Steven L. Schandler, Ronald L. Scott, Patricia W. See, Cameron Sinclair, Thomas Slocombe, Jimmy Smith, Pennington Vann, John M. Virchick, Virginia L. Warren, and Myron D. Yeager.

Administrative assistants Anita Storck and Katherine Renn provided valuable secretarial help, and Chapman University librarians Sharon Kerr, Claudia Horn, Lana Wong, Susan Schlaeger, as well as University of California-Irvine librarian Eddie Yeghiayan, provided highly professional research assistance. A one-semester sabbatical from Chapman University enabled me to complete the manuscript. In making final revisions, I benefited greatly from the comments of Peter Ohlin and three anonymous reviewers at Oxford University Press.

Several chapters were published in journals and books, and others were given as invited lectures. They are used here with changes that range from minor to major.

Chapter 2, in part, was the 1997 Honors Lecture at Chapman University.

Chapter 3 was published in an earlier version as "Personal Ideals in Professional Ethics," *Professional Ethics* 5 (1996): 3–27. An earlier version was presented at the University of Redlands (March 1996).

Chapter 4, in part, was read at the University of Northern Iowa (March 1997) as "Professionals and Voluntary Service."

Chapter 5, "Caring About Clients," appeared in earlier form in *Professional Ethics* 6, no. 1 (spring 1997): 55–75.

Chapter 6 was published in an earlier form as "Professional Distance" in the *International Journal of Applied Philosophy* (winter/spring 1997): 39–50. (Used with permission of the publisher.)

Chapter 7 was published in an earlier version as "Advocating Values: Professionalism in Teaching Ethics," *Teaching Philosophy* 20, no. 1 (March 1997): 19–34. (Used with permission of the publisher.) An earlier version was read in Pittsburgh at a conference (June 1995) on "The Role of Advocacy in the Classroom," cosponsored by the American Philosophical Association and fifteen additional professional societies.

Chapter 8, section 3, was published in an earlier version as "Professional Autonomy and Employers' Authority," in Wade L. Robison, Michael S. Pritchard, and Joseph Ellin, eds., *Profits and Professions: Essays in Business and Professional Ethics* (Clifton, N.J.: Humana Press, 1983), 265–73. (Used with permission of the publisher.) Sections 1 and 2 were presented as "Professional Ethics, Organizational Ethics, and Safe Technology" at California Polytechnic Institute, San Luis Obispo, in the Forum on Ethics, Technology, and the Professions (February 1995). Some of the ideas were developed in "Moral Character and Shared Responsibility for Safety in Engineering" read at the University of Virginia (January 1990) and Rochester Institute of Technology (March 1990). Section 4 is a condensed version of "Rights of Conscience Inside the Technological Corporation," *Wissen und Gewissen: Arbeiten zur Verantwortungsproblematic,* ed. Otto Neumaier (Vienna, 1986): 179–93. (Used with permission.)

Chapter 9, with minor differences, appeared as "Whistleblowing: Professionalism, Personal Life, and Shared Responsibility for Safety in Engineering," *Business and Professional Ethics Journal* 11 (1992): 21–40. Versions were read as "Whistleblowing in Engineering" in a lecture series on Integrity in Scientific Research, sponsored by the Committee on Ethics in Research at the University of California, Santa Barbara (January 1992), and as "Whistleblowing for the Public Good" at Denver University (February 1994).

Chapter 10, in large part, is from "Religion Ethics and Professionalism," *Professional Ethics* 3, no. 2, (1994): 17–35. An earlier version was read at the American Philosophical Association, Pacific Division, in Los Angeles (March 1994).

Chapter 11 was published in an earlier version as "Explaining Wrongdoing in Professions," *Journal of Social Philosophy* 30, no. 2 (1999): 236–50. (Used with permission of the publisher.)

The earliest attempt to work out the general direction of the book was "Personal Ideals and Professional Responsibilities," an essay invited for the Fifteenth International Wittgenstein Symposium in Salzburg, Austria (August 1991), the first time that Symposium was devoted to Applied Ethics. I thank Edgar Morscher, Otto Neumaier, and Peter Simons for the invitation to participate, and also for allowing me to draw on the essay which was eventually published in *Applied Ethics in a Troubled World* (Dordrecht: Kluwer Academic Publishers, 1998), 167–78. The conference was cancelled when a political furor arose over whether papers concerning euthanasia would be permitted at a time when the rights of the elderly were an especially sensitive social issue. However regrettable, the cancellation attests to the relevance of applied ethics and perhaps also to the importance of personal commitments in philosophy as a profession.

Finally and especially, I thank my wife Shannon for her love and for her gifts of confluence in personal and professional life.

Mission Viejo, California　　　　　　　　　　　　　　　　　　M. W. M.
June 1999

CONTENTS

Meaningful Work

1

INTRODUCTION

In 1983 Dr. David Hilfiker left a comfortable medical practice in
rural Minnesota to work in a ghetto in Washington, D.C. There
he practiced "poverty medicine," not low-paid medicine—although it was
surely that, given his two-thirds cut in salary—but medicine devoted to
patients who lived in desperate poverty. He helped build a housing complex
in which he and his family lived with people who were drug addicts, men-
tally ill, and who otherwise lacked adequate shelter and medical services.
The needs of the community he served were overwhelming, and each day
he confronted frustrations and dangers that few physicians would tolerate.
Hilfiker is not a saint, yet he testifies that his "decision to enter the inner city
was born of a conscious desire to move into a closer relationship with God."[1]
He also reports finding greater happiness than he had experienced before,
including moments of joy in the "miracle" of helping a homeless person return to a "community of hope."

In studying professional ethics, a familiar response to people like Dr. Hilfiker is praise followed by neglect, if not dismissal. The assumption is that personal ideals like Hilfiker's have little or nothing to do with professional ethics
per se. They are "private" matters, regardless of how admirable they may be
or how dramatically they shape careers. Professionalism (as the very term
connotes in some contexts) implies setting aside personal values, feelings,
and interests in order to meet the responsibilities attached to professional
roles. Failure to set aside one's personal life constitutes a lack of professional
distance and creates conflicts of interest. In any case, personal values are
automatically trumped whenever they conflict with the shared duties incumbent on all members of a profession. Those duties alone need to be considered in studying professional ethics.

To expand this response further, professional ethics is reducible to duties
and dilemmas. It consists of (a) identifying the duties that are or should be
standardized within professional codes of ethics applicable to all members

3

of a profession, and (b) grappling with how to apply the duties to particular situations where they conflict or have unclear implications. All professions specify duties: to provide competent care, obtain informed consent, maintain confidentiality, be honest, avoid conflicts of interest, and (collectively with other professionals) provide public access to services. How such duties apply in particular roles and institutional settings is spelled out in each profession's code of ethics. In addition, the law specifies further duties for some professions, such as duties to participate in continuing education and pay licensing and registration fees. Commitments to meet these duties are important, but the duties themselves constitute the content of professional ethics. Any additional personal commitments are, by their very nature, excluded.

I call this dominant perspective the *consensus paradigm:* Professional ethics consists entirely of the moral requirements attached to a profession and imposed on all its members, together with the ethical dilemmas created when the requirements conflict or are too vague to provide guidance. In calling it the dominant perspective, I am not claiming that all professional ethicists avow it. It permeates the literature in professional ethics without being defended or even formulated as a viewpoint. Usually it operates as the unspoken legacy of Immanuel Kant's preoccupation with universal principles, as well as the emphasis on general rules in most human rights ethics, contract theory (which grounds morality in the rules that ideally rational agents would agree upon), and rule-utilitarianianism (the view that right conduct is specified by a code of conduct that maximizes the social good).

I argue that the consensus paradigm is implausible and constricting. It neglects how personal moral commitments and ideals motivate, sustain, and guide professionals in their work. To be sure, the paradigm embodies important truths. There is a vital need for shared standards to restrain greed, secure public trust, and limit personal moral ideals when they become misguided. In addition, professional standards restrict inappropriate intrusions of the personal into public life, as the scandals in Bill Clinton's term as president glaringly remind us. Nevertheless, the consensus paradigm is incomplete. Even questions about the proper demarcation of personal and public life cannot be answered until personal commitments are given their due. Shared duties form the backbone of professional ethics, but a backbone is not a complete anatomy.

In exploring personal commitments, I will often introduce narrative case studies such as that of Dr. Hilfiker and also include portrayals of professionals in works of fiction. Case studies are ubiquitous in studying professional ethics, but almost invariably they consist of episodic (time-slice) dilemmas about how to act when confronted with conflicting obligations. My widened perspective encompasses these episodic dilemmas, but also attends to narratives about how personal commitments emerge, unfold, change, and are put at risk. A diachronic perspective reveals the importance of caring relationships, meaningful work, voluntary service, burnout, self-betrayal, balancing family with other commitments, and other topics examined in this book.

Having started with a religious case study, I should emphasize that I have no ax to grind on behalf of any particular religion or religion in general.[2] My focus is on moral commitments in caring about persons, social practices, organizations, communities, and the environment. Nevertheless, it is obvious that many individuals do closely unite their moral commitments with religious convictions. They also link their moral commitments to ideals of aesthetics, intellectual achievement, technical merit, and physical excellence. We need not share these linkages in order to appreciate their contributions to professionalism.

Because most personal commitments explored here involve commitments to ideals, I will sometimes use the terms "ideals," "values," and "commitments" as stylistic variants. The word *ideals* may give pause, conjuring up images of unrealistic perfection, self-righteousness, and dangerous overreaching. I abjure these images, and I will critique the distortions that generate them. Ideals are commitments to (perceived) forms of goodness around which individual character is formed and which are not reducible to general duties. The ideals I explore are eminently practical. Rather than depicting visionary vistas, they enter into what Bernard Williams calls an individual's nexus of "ground projects" that provide meaning-giving guides and goads throughout long and frequently arduous careers.[3] A sincere commitment to an ideal of justice, alleviating suffering, or promoting learning implies both high aspiration and practical engagement within a set of given constraints. Not only are such ideals achievable in significant degrees, at least with any luck, but the element of high aspiration often motivates greater practical achievement than would otherwise be possible.[4]

An array of commitments to varied moral goods is desirable in the professions, even though one person could pursue only some of these in a lifetime. Given limited time, energy, and interest, professionals tend to focus their endeavors on a few specific ideals of goodness, typically those to which they can contribute creatively. The resulting plurality of goods morally enriches professions and professionals alike. Much the same is true of the virtues that correspond to the goods pursued, for example, the virtue of justice that corresponds to justice as a social good, and the virtue of compassion in alleviating suffering. The varied forms of goods and virtues are not reducible to shared principles of duty, even though they bear on how professionals understand their responsibilities.

Calling ideals *personal* means that they shape the work of individuals without necessarily being incumbent on all members of a profession. It does not mean that the ideals are idiosyncratic or eccentric. Indeed, some of the most important ideals are widely shared among members of religious and moral communities, as in the case of Dr. Hilfiker. Moreover, justified personal ideals typically instantiate general ideals of professionalism, for example, what John Kultgen says is the ideal of being "dedicated to providing proficient service to those who need it,"[5] and what Albert Flores says is "a commitment to the ideal of excellence in the exercise of professional skills and talents as the best way of achieving the ends of a profession."[6] In addition, justified personal ideals usually instantiate ideals attached to particular professions and the type of service each offers, for example promoting health (medicine and allied health fields), serving justice (law), or creating efficient and safe technological goods (engineering). Far from being extraneous to wider professional ideals, justified personal ideals unfold and enliven them.

However, Kultgen's and Flores's talk of "the" ideal of professionalism or of professions can be misleading. With sufficient abstraction, all professional commitments collapse into a few: to serve clients, promote the public good, and advance excellence. Such generic descriptions illuminate the shared elements in professional ethics, but they eclipse the enormous variety of ideals that shape individual lives and careers. Thus, describing the ideal of medicine as the promotion of health conceals the significant differences among health care professionals in understanding exactly what health is, how it should be pursued, and why it is valuable. This is especially true if "health" is understood broadly as the physical and mental capacities needed to function effectively in one's environment. "Effective functioning" disguises moral and social values about desirable forms of behavior and interpersonal relationships. Differences in understanding these values arise at the levels of both individuals and subgroups within medicine such as Catholic physicians, Christian Scientists, and an array of holistic medicine practitioners. The detailed differences influence how medicine is practiced.

The expression "professional ethics" can mean three things, each of which I intend in rethinking professional ethics. First, "professional ethics" might refer to *de facto morality*, that is, a profession's status quo on moral issues, both its professed standards and actual practices. More fully, de facto morality refers to (a) a profession's officially endorsed moral standards as stated in its code of ethics and elaborated in related documents, as well as conveyed symbolically in awards and speeches on official occasions; (b) the beliefs held by most members of a profession about moral issues in their profession; and (c) the patterns of morally relevant conduct manifested by most professionals. In connection with de facto professional ethics, I draw attention to the actual influence of personal ideals in guiding and motivating a great many professionals and professional organizations. The rest of what I have to say would be of little interest without the presence of large numbers of professionals who express moral commitments in their work.

Second, "professional ethics" might mean *justified morality* in the professions, that is, the moral values desirable for professionals. The consensus paradigm restricts these values to the mandatory shared duties incumbent on all members of a profession. In a *conventional* version of the paradigm, the values are equated with the content of current codes of ethics and related documents. In a *critical* version of the paradigm, the values are equated with ideal codes of ethics, the ones that ought to be officially endorsed and promulgated as uniform standards within professions. Regarding the critical version, I urge that many personal ideals are justified because they contribute to the well-being of clients and the general public. For the most part, I am interested in personal ideals that meet minimum standards of decency, respect the voluntary consent of clients, and in some way are morally justified. I seek to explore the interplay between admirable personal ideals and those justified uniform standards emphasized in the consensus paradigm.

Third, "professional ethics" might refer to *moral inquiry* into the professions, especially scholarly activities and their resulting bodies of knowledge. Moral inquiries can be divided into two categories. "Descriptive ethics" studies de facto professional ethics. It describes and explains the actual beliefs and conduct of professionals. As conducted by psychologists and social scientists, typically it strives to be value neutral, although some humanistically minded scientists conduct their studies within a normative (value-laden) framework. "Normative ethics" evaluates beliefs, conduct, and ideals. It is an inquiry into justified professional morality. As conducted by philosophers, religious thinkers, practitioners, and others, it is a value-laden attempt to clarify, organize, and discover the foundations of the values desirable in the professions. This book is a work in normative ethics. Although I touch on theoretical issues about the foundations of professional ethics, I emphasize applied normative ethics: the study of moral issues having practical import in understanding responsible professionalism. My main thesis is that normative inquiries should include the roles of personal moral ideals.

Acknowledging an important role for personal ideals in the professions is dangerous. It could easily be misunderstood by fanatics who pursue ideals without good judgment, in disregard of the legitimate limits established by shared professional duties and legitimate organizational authority. I attempt to avoid misunderstandings by proceeding with caution, sensitivity to context, and ample caveats that block facile generalizations. In addition, such an approach avoids sentimental boosterism while enabling us to appreciate professional ethics as a source of meaning in work, rather than merely a set of onerous requirements.

PART I

Meaning and Personal Commitments

At long last I have been *learning* to work. By that I mean that there is in my daily life a satisfactory predominance of activity over passivity, of reality over fantasy, of creation over conception. It continues to astonish me that this simple human ability to work brings so much additional pleasure, order, solace, and meaning to my life.

> —Sara Ruddick, "A Work of One's Own," in Sara Ruddick and Pamela Daniels, eds., *Working It Out*

2

MEANINGFUL WORK

Kanji Watanabe is a city manager in charge of responding to citizens' complaints. After being diagnosed with cancer, he struggles to reconcile himself to a death only months away. His wife died many years earlier, his son has grown distant, and he lacks other family and friends who could help. Pride in his career might bring some solace, but as he reflects on his job he reaches a sad conclusion: "I've been there almost thirty years and now I can't remember one day, can't remember one thing I did. All I know is that I was always busy and always bored."[1] A short time later his attention is drawn to a citizens' petition to build a playground by draining a polluted and dangerous swamp near a residential area. The petition had languished on his desk after bouncing among several city offices, and he could easily have done nothing about it without repercussions. Working unobtrusively, he cuts through a thicket of red tape to complete the project before he dies. The accomplishment brings him little recognition, yet it means more to him than anything else accomplished during his career.

Assuming it is sufficiently well paid, work that keeps us always busy and always bored has something to be said for it in a world of poverty and economic uncertainty. Like Mr. Watanabe, however, most of us need more from our professions. In addition to earning money to pursue interests outside work, we seek activities and relationships at the workplace that are inherently meaningful in terms of our fundamental values. I will focus on moral values, keeping in mind how they are linked to ideals of religion, aesthetics, intellectual achievement, physical excellence, and technical merit.

This chapter discusses questions about human nature and motivation that underlie most of the topics in subsequent chapters. Is self-regard the only human motive, or are we genuinely capable of being motivated by moral ideals? If we are capable of concern for ideals, is it realistic to expect ideals to play an extensive role in our work, beyond death-bed gestures like Watanabe's? Are there perhaps reasons for restricting personal ideals to private life? I begin by contrasting two sharply opposing views, articulated by Adam Smith and Albert Schweitzer, concerning how personal values relate to work.

Ethics and Economics

According to a doctrine of separate spheres, moral ideals should essentially be relegated to private life, with professional life guided primarily by economic and self-interested values together with minimal moral restrictions. This dichotomy has several variations, but its most dramatic and influential version is found in libertarianism. In the libertarian view, considerations of justice set the ground rules for making contracts and engaging in fair competition. But the justice considerations should be minimal in order to guarantee individuals the right to pursue their economic self-interest without government and social interference.

This libertarian outlook has dominated economic thinking since its first powerful articulation by Adam Smith in the *Wealth of Nations*, published in 1776. In his famous words, "It is not from the benevolence of the butcher, the brewer, or the baker, that we expect our dinner, but from their regard to their own interest."[2] By "benevolence," Smith means desires and emotions aimed at promoting the happiness of others, for their sake rather than solely for ulterior self-interested ends.[3] Smith's sweeping generalization is that merchants seek personal gain *and not* the good of others, certainly not the good of the wider public. To be sure, in order to acquire personal gain, merchants must please customers, and in the long run that means producing quality goods at competitive prices. In this way, self-seeking individuals benefit the wider community without intending, trying, or even wanting to do so. Each merchant is "led by an invisible hand to promote an end which was no part of his intention," certainly no part of an altruistic intention: "I have never known much good done by those who affected to trade for the publick [*sic*] good. It is an affectation, indeed, not very common among merchants, and very few words need be employed in dissuading them from it."[4]

Notice, however, that professionals do claim to trade for the public good. They claim to care about how their services contribute to society and help their clients. Physicians, nurses, and physical therapists profess to be concerned about the health of their patients; attorneys purport to care about legal justice; engineers claim to care about safety of technological products; and educators declare a commitment to student learning. They claim to care about these things, at least in part, for the sake of the people they serve, rather than solely for private gain. In addition, many businesspersons affirm a professional identity and commit themselves to producing quality goods and services in order to benefit the public.

Would Smith say that professionals are engaged in affectation, that is, pretense, insincerity, self-serving sham? Would he view professions as based on affectations and hypocrisies designed to fool the public into respecting them, thereby adding to the high salaries they command as well as the monopoly over services they enjoy? Would Smith perhaps share George Bernard Shaw's cynicism that "all professions are conspiracies against the laity"?[5] Or, if that sounds too strong, would he say that professionals are naively deluded about their motives and intentions?

Smith had ample opportunity in the nearly one thousand pages of the *Wealth of Nations* to take account of any moral commitments that professionals and businesspersons bring to their work. Instead, he repeatedly accents self-seeking. Although he begins his discussion with the promising remark that "the most generous and liberal spirits are eager to crowd into" honorable professions, he drops that theme immediately, as if it were a mere rhetorical flourish, and proceeds to reduce professionals' motives to self-interest.[6] In particular, he highlights two motives. One is to make more money than they could elsewhere. Indeed, the main discussion of professionals is located in the chapter explaining why some forms of work offer more money than others. He adds that young persons are attracted to the professions because of confidence in their ability to become successful enough to make up for lost income during the years of education needed to prepare for their professions.

The second suppportive motive is the desire for "the reputation which attends upon superior excellence" manifested in the profession. By "reputation" he means honor, respect, and fame, although perhaps he also intends the deserved recognition because of one's admirable character manifested in work. Either way, he plainly leaves the impression that money and social esteem are all that motivate professionals. The emphasis in the *Wealth of Nations* is unmistakable: professionals, like merchants, are driven by self-interest and not by moral values of caring about helping people. "Every individual"—*every* physician, pharmacist, and professor, as much as every butcher, brewer, and baker—"is continually exerting himself to find out the most advantageous employment for whatever capital he can command. It is his own advantage, indeed, and not that of the society, which he has in view."[7]

Scholars have struggled with the "Adam Smith Problem": How can the theme of relentless self-seeking in the *Wealth of Nations* be reconciled with the centrality of sympathy in Smith's other major book, *The Theory of Moral Sentiments?* In the latter book, Smith explicitly rejected the wholesale reduction of motives to self-seeking. Indeed, he emphasized that morality requires us constantly to restrain self-seeking by judging our actions from the perspective of a fair and impartial spectator: "The wise and virtuous man is at all times willing that his own private interest should be sacrificed to the public interest of his own particular order or society" and adhere to basic decency and fair play in the pursuit of wealth.[8] On the surface, Smith's two books are flatly inconsistent. Did he simply change his mind during the seventeen years between writing them?

According to some scholars, a closer examination reveals that self-interest is central to both books. They point out that Stoic doctrines of prudence, frugality, and self-command permeate all of Smith's writings. Moreover, when Smith speaks of sympathy in *The Theory of Moral Sentiments*, he usually does not have in mind altruistic motivation. Technically, he means that moral judgments are shaped by what we today call empathy: seeing things from the points of view of others, not only by putting oneself into their situation, but by imaginatively taking on their identity and character so that one's self-interest is indirectly engaged. Moreover, Smith downplays benevolence as being a "feeble spark," suggesting that a desire to promote the happiness of others is something less than a major source of human motivation.[9]

According to other scholars, the books are consistent in the opposite direction of allowing greater room for altruistic motives. Justice and universal respect for other persons are at least as important as self-mastery in Smith's overall outlook. *The Wealth of Nations* shunts themes of justice into the background, but they remain present, nonetheless. Why, after all, would Smith set forth the invisible-hand argument, which defends free markets by appealing to their overall social benefits, unless he believed his readers share his commitment to the good of all members of a society? Additional moral appeals, ones that presuppose a concern for other people for their sake, are implicit in his celebration of liberty, fair competition, and fair play as necessary for maintaining free markets.[10]

In my view, the two books are consistent. Both contain the dual themes of self-interest and altruism, prudence and public good. Nevertheless, they are so astonishingly different in emphasis that some explanation is called for. It will not suffice to say that their subject matter differs: ethics versus economics. Smith's economic theory, just as much as his ethical theory, is rooted in his view of human nature and human motivation. Instead, I believe that Smith is a compartmentalist, someone who embraces a doctrine of separate spheres.

Smith believes that benevolence neither does nor should play a significant role in business and the professions as a major source of motivation, intentions, and commitments for specific actions and activities. Its proper role in motivating specific actions is limited to private life. Or rather, the only role of benevolence regarding free enterprise resides in acts of citizenship that support the system of free enterprise based on self-seeking, for example, voting against laws that restrict free enterprise. Because nonbenevolent, even ruthless, economic competition ultimately benefits humanity, benevolence should lead us to support it as a system. Benevolence and self-interest both recommend laissez-faire capitalism, a system in which individuals' actions are motivated solely by self-interest. As a direct motive for actions supporting others, benevolence should be limited to private life.

Whether applied to the professions or to business, this compartmentalization is a dangerous half-truth. On the one hand, it is accompanied by a profound insight into the importance of vigorous free markets where self-seeking is indeed the predominant motive. Smith writes with a genuinely prophetic voice, anticipating the successes of free-market economies and the failures of Communist, fascist, and other economies controlled from top down. On the other hand, Smith seriously underestimates the harmful side effects of unregulated markets, and he could not possibly have foreseen the scale of threats within modern markets to public safety, the environment, and workers' rights. Ravaging depressions, deadly but lucrative products such as cigarettes, and shortsighted exploitation of the environment make it impossible for us to share Smith's theodicy that God's invisible hand always transforms narrow self-seeking into community goods.[11] A vibrant free market is essential, but so are reasonable laws and regulations. But even government is powerless unless the majority of professionals are morally committed in ways that merit the public trust.

The need for public trust explains why a purely libertarian theory is self-defeating, whether in the version defended by Adam Smith or that of his contemporary disciple Milton Friedman.[12] It is self-defeating to seek minimum government regulation while insisting that profit maximization should be the sole aim of business. When business and professions pursue profit in disregard of wider moral concerns, they eventually cause visible harm. The public then reacts with outrage in forcing legislators to pass overly restrictive laws. The only way to avoid excessive regulation is for business and professions to manifest moral concern, not merely with occasional symbolic acts of corporate philanthropy, but with daily commitment to the good of clients, customers, workers, the environment, and to other constituencies that have a legitimate stake in not being harmed by corporations and individual professionals.

Nowhere is Smith's celebration of economic self-seeking more striking than in his optimism about the effects of greed. Revealingly, his optimism is expressed in a passage in *The Theory of Moral Sentiments* that parallels the invisible-hand passage in the *Wealth of Nations*. "In spite of their natural selfishness and rapacity," the rich make possible jobs for the poor. In doing so, they "are led by an invisible hand to make nearly the same distribution of the necessaries of life, which would have been made, had the earth been divided into equal portions among all its inhabitants, and thus without intending it, without knowing it, advance the interest of the society."[13] Granting the power of the free market to expand and redistribute wealth, the enormous disparities between rich and poor today hardly approximate an equal distribution. Without government regulation, the disparities would be even more enormous. Greed is not good.

Another side effect of unregulated markets, combined with hostility to taxation, is the inability of a society to express its shared moral vision. This consideration led Robert Nozick to express grave concerns about his earlier defense of libertarianism: "The libertarian position I once propounded . . . neglected the symbolic importance of an official political concern with issues or problems, as a way of marking their importance or urgency, and hence of expressing, intensifying, channeling, encouraging, and validating our private actions and concerns toward them. Joint goals that the government ignores completely . . . tend to appear unworthy of our joint attention and hence to receive little."[14] Nozick speaks of a "zig zag" of politics that, through swings and cycles, maintains a middle ground based on common endeavors and shared community, far richer than is possible using a minimal ethic of allowing individuals to act on their rights to liberty. The proper balance between vigorous competition, reasonable regulation, and moral commitments cannot be determined in the abstract; it needs to be continually worked out, revised, improved.

Compartmentalizing has additional harmful side effects, this time within individuals. Some persons develop moral schizophrenia: greed in public life separated from moral engagement with a private circle of family and friends. Others find their entire lives gradually dominated by self-seeking, at enormous cost to their families. Still others suffer damage to their health, physical and mental, as they find it increasingly difficult to integrate their lives in fulfilling ways. This topic of integration is explored in chapter 13, but it also frames discussions in much of the rest of this book.

Personal Ideals

Adam Smith reduced the professions to their economic roles, narrowed professionals' motives to money and reputation, and restricted moral ideals of goodness to private life. As a sharp contrast, consider Albert Schweitzer, a physician, philanthropist, and philosopher who made personal moral commitments central to his life and thought.

Schweitzer regarded his work as worthwhile beyond the paycheck it provided, as meaningful in terms of his ideals of caring for clients, colleagues, and the wider community. When he was a university student, he resolved to pursue his interests until he turned thirty, at which time he would devote himself to helping others. At that time he was already a professor and a religious scholar of some stature, but he kept his resolve. He entered medical school, supporting himself by working as a professor and minister, and, after completing his degree, served the hospital he created at Lambarane for nearly fifty years.

A life is more than outward events, and we understand persons only when we grasp the value commitments embedded in their motives, character, and worldview. Schweitzer's value commitments were complex. He called his outlook "ethical mysticism."[15] "Mysticism" refers to appreciating the interconnectedness of all living things, together with a sense of their sometimes mysterious and extraordinary connections. "Ethical" refers primarily to the moral values that make possible self-fulfillment through service to others. (Hence "ethical mysticism" is opposed to the "passive," otherworldly mysticism that turns away from moral engagement.) Schweitzer's writing sparkles with metaphors of moral unity, of invisible hands quite different than Smith had in mind. Each of us is a wave that exists as part of an ocean; a wellspring of idealism whose reserves are concealed like underground streams; a source of kindness whose roots are joined to those of others.[16] We are not economic atoms; instead we are defined through our relationships with others within communities.

Ethical mysticism underlies three more focused sources of motivation in Schweitzer's life of service: religion, reverence for life, and gratitude. His religious views were strikingly unconventional. Although he was one of the great Christians of the twentieth century, he was probably an agnostic about supernatural beings and life after death. He had markedly pantheistic leanings, as revealed in a letter written at age forty-eight: "Pantheism and theism remain in undecided conflict within me."[17] Again, Schweitzer's ethics of service was rooted in his Christian faith, but he insisted that ethics is justified by reason, not religious authority, albeit reason that culminates in a sense of oneness with all life. Fulfillment consists in joining our lives to others in caring ways.

Ethical mysticism is invoked in justifying reverence for life, the attitude that all life has inherent value and that each of us is obligated to preserve and help develop other life, both human and nonhuman. The crux of the justification is an appeal to empathy, to imaginatively felt kinship with other organisms. Each of us has an "elemental" awareness of our own will to live, our instinctive drive to exist and to develop according to our particular nature. If we are healthy, we affirm our will to live. If we are honest, we are moved by empathy to feel the similarity of our will with the will to live in other organisms. "A thinking being . . . experiences that other life in his own" in a manner that generates a felt obligation to affirm its worth.[18] Schweitzer's sympathy-generating empathy led him to develop an environmental ethic of biotheism: All life is sacred and interconnected.

From childhood on, Schweitzer questioned the right to lead a privileged life without helping to alleviate the suffering of others. "Whoever is spared personal pain must feel . . . called to help in diminishing the pain of others."[19] "I must not accept this good fortune as a matter of course, but must give something in return."[20] Herbert Spiegelberg suggested that this principle of "good fortune obligates" is based upon an egalitarian view of justice that requires the privileged to compensate those disadvantaged by birth or circumstances.[21] But in fact, Schweitzer explicitly renounces a socialist economic redistribution that would leave everyone with the same resources.[22] Instead, he justifies the good fortune principle by appealing to gratitude. For him, gratitude is far more than one among many virtues; it is a "mysterious law of existence" that reveals how each of us benefits from others.[23] When, to cite another famous phrase, Schweitzer speaks of "the Fellowship of those who bear the Mark of Pain"—the communion among individuals who have escaped but understand horrible suffering—he specifies that gratitude is the primary motive in funding global efforts to relieve suffering.[24] And

Schweitzer urges that gratitude is appropriate toward professionals who help us, in part from benevolent motives, for example our teachers and those health professionals who provide us with medical care.[25] Often we cannot fully show our appreciation to individuals who helped us, perhaps because they are unknown to us or dead or do not want what we can give. Even then we should indirectly express gratitude by helping others in the same spirit as our "inaccessible benefactors."

The point in dwelling on these details is not to recommend Schweitzer's particular ideals of compassion, gratitude, and reverence for life, although I personally find much that is admirable in them—once we renounce his involvement in colonialism. Instead, my aims are to illustrate how personal ideals motivate professionals and also to provide an outlook quite different from Smith's. Smith reduces professions to economic exchanges; Schweitzer sees moral values resonating throughout all civilized practices, including work. Smith rightly celebrates the contribution of wealth to nations. Schweitzer appreciates that contribution, but he insists that cultural progress occurs by individuals "thinking out ideals which aim at the progress of the whole, and then so fitting them to the realities of life that they assume the shape in which they can influence most effectively the circumstances of the time."[26] Schweitzer sought to "make his life his argument" for his views, and only cynics would deny that caring about others was a major motive in his profession.[27]

It might be objected that Schweitzer is a special case. Not only were his moral commitments too exceptional to offer a realistic model for others, but he worked within a nonprofit service organization rather than for-profit corporations where most professionals work. In reply, we should not overlook not-for-profit organizations in thinking about professional ethics, as is usually done. Nonprofit service organizations form a vital and creative part of our economy in which moral ideals play a prominent role, and I will have more to say about them in chapter 4.[28] Nevertheless, we do need to broaden the range of examples to include work in for-profit corporations and in government, as well as in nonprofit organizations. In doing so, it will be useful to distinguish several roles of personal ideals in shaping the work of professionals.

Choosing Professions

Ideals contribute to choices of professions, whether directly as with Schweitzer or more indirectly. Frequently a profession awakens, augments, and unfolds patterns of caring already present in personal life. Madeleine M. Kunin, former governor of Vermont and later Deputy Secretary of the U.S. Department of Education, writes that her political career began as a natural extension of her concern for her family and for other children. The same aim earlier led her to start a volunteer organization to sponsor professional theater for children: "I had discovered the political imperative: the desire to expand upon personal experience and transform it into a public agenda, to develop an issue of individual importance and merge it into a generally felt community need."[29] Later, similar aims led her into politics: "Concern for my children's safety enabled me to span the distance between mother-wife and public person, and that is how my political involvement began and how it would continue. As my children's world expanded, so did mine. . . . My priorities became more encompassing: education, the environment, and social services."[30]

Specialization

Most contemporary professions offer a wide array of specializations that individuals select, guided in part by their personal ideals. Gertrude B. Elion chose chemistry as her profession when, as a college student, she visited her grandfather who was dying painfully from stomach cancer. Her goal of doing research on drugs to treat cancer had to be postponed for seven years because sex discrimination prevented her entrance to graduate school and finding a suitable job, but once she found her first research position she worked with great intensity. In her early thirties she began a series of discoveries of powerful new drugs for treating childhood leukemia, making organ transplants possible and laying the foundation for developing the drug AZT, the first serious hope for treating AIDS (and which was later found to be especially effective when used in combination with other drugs). She also helped transform drug research from trial and error to systematic analysis. And she demonstrated differences in how nucleic acid metabolizes in cancerous cells, the work for which she received a Nobel Prize in 1988. As she reports, her research was not narrowly self-seeking: "When you meet someone who has lived for twenty-five years with a kidney graft, there's your reward."[31] Colleagues testify to the genuineness of her social conscience: "Achievement [for her] is finding new medicines to treat medically important indications that aren't currently being met, and there is no other bottom line."[32]

Role Emphasis

Often a profession combines several different types of activities which individuals selectively emphasize. Sometimes the activities are so dissimilar that they seem to be different careers pursued in tandem, for example, the physician who is also a medical researcher or hospital administrator. More often, the activities are interwoven in ways that are mutually supportive, though occasionally conflicting and open to alternative emphases. Thus, the work of professors includes teaching, research, and service, in varied combinations. For example, Katie Cannon is a professor at Episcopal Divinity School in Massachusetts and also the first African-American woman to be ordained a Presbyterian minister. She describes her teaching as the center of her life and devotes enormous time and energy to it. She became a teacher partly because of a natural gift in guiding groups of friends to learn, but primarily because she saw teaching as a way to change lives for the better. Specializing in liberation theology, she feels a responsibility for "imparting values" in a creative way that will improve society. Her teaching embodies her commitments to social justice and liberation: "I used to want to change the world, to get rid of racism and sexism through my teaching. . . . Now I say to myself, if I can change *one* person's perspective so that they leave my course with a changed perspective and ready to be part of the struggle, then I'm satisfied."[33]

Job Choice

Along with the incentives of money and social status, personal ideals guide decisions to accept, retain, or leave places of employment. Robert MacNeil could have made much more money by remaining in commercial news, where he began his career as a television journalist. He took a two-thirds pay cut in leaving NBC to work for the British Broadcasting Corporation (BBC). Later he gave up a comfortable life in London to co-create the MacNeil/ Lehrer Report for the U.S. Public Broadcasting Corporation. That program provided an opportunity for a new type of television journalism having greater clarity, depth, and balance than the brief "sound-bite" approach of commercial news. Together with his colleague Jim Lehrer, he pioneered a new form of telejournalism centered around dialogue between representatives of differing perspectives, allowing viewers to form their own conclusions without the intrusion of a reporter's filtering summations. MacNeil praises the value of greater freedom and fewer frustrations by working in public television, but primarily he testifies to the value of "putting into practice a lot of ideas you believe to be right. . . . It is gratifying not to have anything to be ashamed of when you go home at night."[34]

Personal Style

Ideals influence the style or manner in which individuals pursue their work. For example, architects have responsibilities to meet the needs of their clients and to avoid coercion and paternalistic violations of clients' freedom. Nevertheless, architecture allows flexibility in how far professionals are allowed to assert their own aesthetic and even moral ideals. Thus, Frank Lloyd Wright brought a strong personal vision to his work which some clients resisted and others desired.[35] Although his vision changed dramatically throughout his career, it was largely guided by a Romantic ideal of "organic architecture" defined by simplicity, unity with the natural environment, highlighting the natural qualities of building materials, and achieving multiple unities within the space experienced by occupants. For Wright, these were both aesthetic and moral aspirations toward unity.

These examples, which barely hint at the enormous variety of personal ideals in the professions, invite two observations. First, the guidance provided by personal ideals depends partly on their specificity. Ideals can be described at different levels of generality. Abstractly described, they refer to the generic community goods to which a profession is devoted. For example, at one level MacNeil's ideal is to contribute to an informed citizenry and a more rational society, and Wright's ideal is to create aesthetically interesting and useful structures for human habitation. Even more abstractly stated, the ideals of improving community (Kunin), alleviating suffering (Elion, Schweitzer), and furthering justice (Cannon) have no unique connection with any one profession. Yet these specifications would hardly suffice to convey the personal nature of the ideals in our examples.

Second, even though personal ideals are focused outwardly on public goods, they allude to ideals of character. Sincere commitment to improving community safety, alleviating suffering, pursuing justice, or promoting informed citizenry implies affirming the virtues of caring, compassion, justice, and rationality. We suspect self-righteousness when individuals become self-preoccupied with how well they embody these virtues, rather than remaining focused on helping others. Yet we could not begin to understand the above individuals without understanding how their ideals became central to their character.

In both ways—by providing specific goals and by shaping character—personal ideals contribute to the coherence of entire lives. Personal ideals serve as organizing principles that motivate, discipline, structure, and integrate activities. In doing so, they contribute to the overall coherence and significance of professional endeavors. To be sure, the ideals pursued at work can conflict with other ideals and with personal relationships. They, too, need to be integrated within the complete set of motives guiding our lives.

Mixed Motives

Given the demands of professions in terms of time and energy, most professionals achieve meaningful lives substantially through the meaning they derive from their work.[36] Inherently meaningful work is, by definition, rich in intrinsic satisfactions from goods internal to the work. Some of these goods are public goods linked to the goals of professions, for example, health in the case of medicine and justice in the case of law. Other goods are private or self-oriented goods such as private property and income, power, social reputation, and their attendant pleasures. Usually, though not always, work is inherently meaningful only when something more than money is gained. In this sense we say a job is deeply meaningful despite its relatively low pay, or a job is not especially meaningful even though it pays well.

We might sort professionals' desires, pleasures, and sources of meaning into three broad categories: craft, compensation, and moral concern.

Not surprisingly, these categories correspond to three goods that enter into the very definition of professions: advanced expertise, social recognition, and service to clients and community.

Craft Motives

Professions are based on advanced expertise that combines theory-based understanding, practical know-how, and liberal learning. The expertise is acquired through higher education and developed throughout a career. Craft motives are desires to achieve expertise and desires to manifest technical skill, theoretical understanding, and creativity. When committed professionals meet standards of excellence, they experience satisfaction. When they do not, they are vulnerable to feelings of regret, shame, and guilt.

Two sources of satisfaction stand out. One is related to what John Rawls calls a "deep psychological fact" expressed in the Aristotelian Principle: "Other things equal, human beings enjoy the exercise of their realized capacities (their innate or trained abilities), and this enjoyment increases the more the capacity is realized, or the greater its complexity."[37] Accordingly, individuals will tend to embrace professional ideals that evoke their interests and talents with sustained challenge and complexity. Robert Nozick adds, because meaning involves connecting our lives with wider unities, "We often estimate the 'meaningfulness' of work by the range of things that come within its purview, the range of different factors that have to be taken into account. The (hired) craftsman must take account of more than the assembly line worker, the entrepreneur must look out upon conditions in the wider world, and so forth."[38]

The other source of satisfaction derives from exercising autonomy as part of professional expertise. The relevant autonomy is not complete independence, a notion that lacks relevance in a world where most professionals work in teams within authority-structured corporations. Instead, it is exercising good judgment and sound discretion when providing professional services. This autonomy enables individuals to express themselves far more personally than in routine or assembly-line jobs.

Compensation Motives

As Adam Smith emphasized, professionals typically receive above-average social rewards in the form of income and prestige. This occurs largely because professions establish monopolies or at least dominance over the services they provide. For example, educational certification, licensing, and legal supervision ensure that only physicians can perform surgery. The resulting dominance limits the economic competition professionals must confront and also tends to increase public appreciation of the value of their work, assuming the profession provides a high standard of services. Compensation motives are desires for social rewards, including money, power, authority, recognition, and job stability.

Compensation motives are not exclusively self-interested. They may be linked to desires to support one's family or philanthropic desires to obtain resources in order to help others. Nor are the motives directed toward craft and caring relationships entirely selfless. Nevertheless, the immediate aim of compensation motives is to gain things for oneself, whereas craft motives are primarily aimed outward, toward people and social practices, as is moral concern.

Moral Concern

Professions provide valuable community services, such as health care, legal justice, education, and safe technological products. In addition, delivery of the services involves relationships of trust, trustworthiness, confidentiality, and caring about clients, employers, colleagues, and the wider public. As a result, professions have inherent moral significance, in two ways: (i) Professions provide opportunities to make ongoing contributions to the well-being of others, and (ii) they place special responsibilities on professionals as outlined in codes of ethics. Motives of moral concern fall into two corresponding categories.

First, moral *caring motives* are desires to promote the good of clients for their sake. They are also desires to enter into and sustain caring relationships with clients, customers, colleagues, and the wider community. In addition, caring about animals is important in professions such as veterinary medicine and environmental science. The degree of personal involvement with clients varies greatly, ranging from intimacy (as in counseling) to anonymity (as with public health service) and sometimes a mixture of both (as with teachers who know some of their students very well and others hardly at all). "Relationships" may suggest that caring is two-way, but I will also include relationships in which caring goes in one direction, as when a caring physician helps an unconscious person injured in a car accident. In this wide sense, we speak of parents having a caring relationship with their newborn child who is not yet able to reciprocate.

Second, *integrity motives* are desires to meet the ethical standards governing a profession and in other ways to seek moral aims by working as a professional. Integrity motives include desires to meet professional responsibilities—because they are one's responsibilities—and to maintain personal integrity. They also include desires embedded in particular virtues. For example, honesty embodies a desire to be truthful and trustworthy, justice includes desires for people to be given what is owed to them, benevolence and loyalty imply desires to promote others' well-being, gratitude implies a desire to reciprocate the beneficence of others, and conscientiousness embodies a desire to meet one's duties. And they include the general desire to be an ethical professional and to sustain moral commitments throughout one's career.

These categories of motives are not exhaustive, and certainly many additional factors shape careers. One of the most important is chance; another is temperament. When Schweitzer neared age thirty, the age when he had resolved to undertake a life of service, he experimented with several alternatives, including helping abandoned children, the homeless, and convicts. He went to Africa partly because a missionary brochure happened to cross his desk at the right moment. In addition, the opportunity was especially inviting because he wanted a direct, hands-on form of helping and also a high degree of independence outside formal organizations.

My point is that each of the three categories of motives is a wellspring of intrinsic satisfactions. Perhaps that is sufficiently clear in the case of craft motives, which are aimed at the very activities defining a profession, and in the case of moral concern which is directed toward the people served by the profession. Together they make possible most of what psychologist Mihaly Csikszentmihalyi calls "flow" experiences, in which work absorbs us without thought about money or other extrinsic rewards.[39] Several features are typical of flow experiences: clear goals as one proceeds, immediate feedback about progress, a balance between challenges and our skills to respond to them, immersion of awareness in the activity without disruptive distractions, lack of worry about failure, loss of anxious self-consciousness, time distortions (either time flying or time slowing pleasurably). The defining feature of flow, however, is that the activity becomes *autotelic:* an end in itself, enjoyed as such.

When money is the exclusive motive, work usually fails to be intrinsically satisfying, although it might provide the resources for pursuing meaning elsewhere. Witness the remarks of an investment portfolio manager: "[My job] is not a self-fulfilling job. The financial incentive is really what I'm here for. It gives me the freedom to do what I want, to go places, do things. . . . A lot of people are saying to me, 'You're too money-oriented.' I'm just being honest."[40] For this man—and of course he is not alone—work is no more than a means to gain money in order to buy other things which give life meaning.

Nevertheless, some compensation motives include social rewards that are more deeply rooted in the work itself. One executive comments: "Power is so much more invigorating [than money]. It is so much more fun to believe in, so much more romantic, so much more exciting. . . . The idea of money does not replace emotions, pleasure, the Don Quixote side. It is much more fun to believe that you are the boss, that you have charisma. It's enlivening. It has to do with emotion, with passion . . . with romanticism."[41] The power and authority this executive finds in his work are not mere means to further goals that provide meaning. Instead, they are inherent in the work itself and yield intrinsic satisfactions.

In neither of these examples is there reason to think the individuals described are unethical or violate the standards governing their profession. We might suspect, however, they are missing opportunities for greater meaning offered by caring relationships within their work—caring for the well-being of their clients and communities, as well as for the well-being of their profession.

In practice, all three types of motives are mutually reinforcing, interwoven, fused. In the main, moral concern is perfectly compatible with compensation motives. More interesting, sometimes compensation motives and goods support moral concerns. Consider police officer Sherry Schlueter.[42] Her high-school volunteering at the humane society led to a job as an animal-abuse investigator. After years of work she became convinced that to do the job well she would need professional training as a police officer that provides authority to arrest offenders. In becoming a police officer, she was motivated by moral concern to seek power and authority, thereby blending caring and compensation motives. The new profession brought opportunities and fresh challenges for expanding her expertise. Within four years, she became a sergeant in charge of the nation's first police unit devoted to fighting crimes against animals. She succeeded in convincing Florida legislators to make animal abuse a felony, and her success made her a consultant to other police forces throughout the country. No doubt this brought additional compensation motives of recognition and prestige, but such motives would likely reinforce rather than displace moral motivation.

Even when one type of motive is the sole or nearly exclusive motive for a particular act, motives interweave at the level of *patterns* of work, that is, tendencies, habits, types of activities. Exhausted toward the end of a hectic day, a teacher might resist the tendency to leave work an hour early, motivated by fear that colleagues will view her as a slacker. But fear is hardly the primary motivation for the teacher's overall activities. Instead, a combination of craft, compensation, and moral concern are generally present and interwoven, as they are with most professionals.

Or are they? Unfortunately, a great many psychologists, sociologists, political scientists, sociobiologists, and economists reduce human motives to self-centered ones, in particular to compensation motives. They embrace *psychological egoism*, the view that all people are always and only motivated by what they believe is good for themselves, at least in some respect. In most variations, this view reduces all motives to the category of compensation.

Psychological egoism is false. Far from being proven scientifically, it is a dogma that is uncritically assumed or else argued for using simple (though seductive) fallacies. For example, psychological egoists argue, that because we always act on our own desires, we must always seek something for ourselves, namely, the satisfaction of our desires. The premise is true, of course: By definition, my actions are always motivated by my desires, and your actions are motivated by yours. But the conclusion does not follow. It is muddled to say that we only desire the satisfaction of our desires. If we did not have (first-order) desires for goods, it would make no sense to speak of (second-order) desires to satisfy our desires. And we desire innumerably many goods.

Some are goods for ourselves (for our sake); others are good for others (for their sake). The former are self-interested desires; the latter are altruistic.

Another fallacious argument is that we always seek to gain pleasure and to avoid pain; therefore we only seek something for ourselves, namely our own pleasures. But even if we granted the primitive and implausible pleasure-pain psychology in the premise, we need to recognize many different sources of pleasure, including satisfaction in getting something for oneself (self-seeking) versus satisfaction in helping others (altruism). And even if we supposed that some pleasure seeking (and pain avoiding) is always a motive for any given human action, it would not follow that self-seeking is the only motive for all conduct, for there may be additional motives mixed in.

If psychological egoism is a confused view, *predominant egoism* is a plausible one: Self-seeking is the strongest motive for most people most of the time, and it is a factor in nearly all human conduct.[43] This view, which Adam Smith held, allows that many types of motives play a role in human conduct along with self-interest, and that the precise combination of self-seeking and altruism varies among individuals. The view is also consistent with recent cognitive psychology that documents the existence of altruistic or "pro-social" motives, and it is consistent with developmental psychology that recognizes distinctively moral motives in the higher stages of moral maturity.[44] Even with regard to self-oriented motives, cognitive psychologists acknowledge a fundamental motive of self-esteem that comes from a sense of competence and accomplishment.

In my view, self-seeking and altruistic motives are inseparably mixed in nearly all human activities. How else could we have evolved as complex creatures with multiple needs, interests, and commitments that constantly must be integrated in order for us to function effectively? As Mary Midgley insisted, human nature "must consist of a number of motives which are genuinely distinct and autonomous, but which are adapted to fit together, in the normal maturing of the individual, into a life that can satisfy him as a whole."[45] Specifically, although the self-interested motives of compensation play a predominant role in the professions, as elsewhere, they are continually interwoven with community-oriented motives of craft and moral concern in supporting the daily lives of most professionals. Sometimes this interweaving causes problems, as self-interest distorts moral concern, but in general the interweaving of motives is a matter to celebrate rather than regret. The need to make a living and to avoid social penalties functions as a potent motive for heeding professional standards. Conversely, professions encourage individuals to focus their mixed motives around communal goods— public goods shared by professionals and the communities they serve.

In a similar vein, Daryl Koehn argues that professionals must find self-interested satisfactions beyond money and social recognition, or else their work will tend to become unethical by being "mechanical or sloppy."[46] Some of these satisfactions are profession-generic in that they can be found in all or most professions. They derive from the freedom to work according to professional standards so as to gain significant control over work, in particular to enjoy the right to refuse clients who request services that violate professional standards and to discontinue services for uncooperative clients. Other intrinsic satisfactions are profession-specific or unique to particular professions. They consist in receiving a share of the specific good served by a profession. Thus, physicians' expertise enables them to pay greater care to their own health; attorneys who voice the concerns of their clients benefit from a community governed by law; and clergy pursue their own salvation through furthering their church's mission.

In emphasizing self-interested motives, however, Koehn neglects moral concern. She repeatedly downplays altruism, benevolence, and humanitarian motives: "We must be wary of accepting a professional's desire to be 'giving' as a legitimate professional motivation."[47] Again, the public seek services, not caring: "The sick do not come to the doctors to be loved. They come to be healed."[48] In fact, clients usually do expect or at least hope for caring that is not entirely the product of ulterior self-seeking motives. In going to physicians to be healed, most patients want to feel cared for as persons. While it is impossible for any professional to care deeply about all clients, caring can bring satisfaction to clients and themselves alike.

I endorse Koehn's call for great caution about professionals' claims about altruism, but I reject her cynicism about a role for benevolence. If we are cynical about professionals' motives, as clients we will be far more reluctant to trust professionals who purport to care for us. As citizens, we will be more likely to support strong government regulation of professions. As professionals ourselves, we may even become less responsible: If everyone is exclusively self-seeking, why not attend solely to our own interest, becoming cynically indifferent to ideals of caring for others (for their sake)? We might even abandon our profession in despair, like Jean-Baptiste Clamence in Albert Camus's *The Fall*, an example I will cite several times in subsequent chapters. Clamence ends his career as a respected attorney, renowned for pursuing noble causes, because, "After prolonged research on myself, I brought out the fundamental duplicity of the human being. Then I realized, as a result of delving in my memory, that modesty helped me to shine, humility, to conquer, and virtue to oppress."[49] His corrosive cynicism leads him to become a "judge-penitent" who confesses his duplicity in order, god-like, to obtain the pleasures in forcing others to recognize their own hypocrisy.

We can avoid the extremes of cynicism and sentimentality by recognizing that mixed motives are ubiquitous in the professions, as elsewhere. Work fuses self-interest and moral concern, as does love, friendship, and philanthropic giving. Rarely is caring about clients, colleagues, or the public entirely selfless, but usually it is not wholly self-interested. Craft motives are potent as well, thereby tending to fuse professional excellence with ethics. Only compensation motives are directly self-interested, although even they can become linked to the well-being of family and community.

By taking seriously how motives are mixed, we can also avoid a strict dichotomy between intrinsic rewards and extrinsic rewards of social recognition. Some rewards are both. Thus, when scholars publish articles or books, they derive both social recognition and intrinsic rewards from engaging in their craft. The achievement in the field (publishing) cannot be separated from the social recognition (acceptance by a publisher and attention from peers). Again, achievement in one's field sometimes amounts to being promoted to a position in which one has greater authority (and higher salary). Many professionals do not seek achievement, fame, and power in the abstract (as external to their work) but instead seek these things as defined in terms of their chosen profession. Thus, a biologist seeks recognition as a biologist and, when that recognition is achieved, it may bring both intrinsic satisfactions and social rewards.

Finally, in saying that meaningful work is intrinsically satisfying, are we saying that it produces happiness? Meaningful work does tend to increase happiness, but work (like life) can be meaningful even when it is not completely happy. Happy work, like happy life, is not only rich in enjoyable activities and relationships. It is work that we can affirm overall: "That's the way I want it to be".[50] Happiness requires that intrinsic and other satisfactions "add up" and be part of an overall "package" that we can affirm overall. Happiness depends in some measure on luck, on whether the world cooperates in allowing us to succeed in our pursuit of meaning.

Vocation

Sociologist Robert Bellah and his colleagues distinguished three conceptions of work—as a job, a career, and a calling (or vocation). Although Bellah presents these conceptions as mutually exclusive, I will interpret them as accenting different aspects of work and, as such, compatible in principle. A profession can be a job, career, vocation, or all three, in different respects. Viewed as a job, work is a means to earning money that facilitates the pursuit of meaningful activities and relationships during leisure. Viewed as a career, work is a pathway to achievement, power, and social recognition. And viewed as a vocation, work is a value-laden activity directed toward public goods, those shared by members of a community. By definition, vocations have a moral dimension in linking one's identity to social practices and communities.

> In the strongest sense of a "calling," work constitutes a practical ideal of activity and character that makes a person's work morally inseparable from his or her life. It subsumes the self into a community of disciplined practice and sound judgment whose activity has meaning and value in itself, not just in the output or profit that results from it. But the calling not only links a person to his or her fellow workers. A calling links a person to

the larger community, a whole in which the calling of each is a contribution to the good of all."[51]

The word "calling" is too strong if it suggests a summons from God to pursue a specific task, although it includes work interpreted in that way. Vocations are forms of work that are well-suited to individuals' talents and interests and that are inherently valuable because of the contribution they make to communities. In this sense, there might be alternative callings for each of us. When only one line of work seems uniquely suited to us, it is probably because of circumstances, luck, and previous choices, as much as to our talents and proclivities. But, typically, personal ideals play a key role in establishing and shaping caring relationships with clients, customers, colleagues, and the wider community.

To understand professions as inherently meaningful vocations, we need to clarify the relevant sense of "meaning." Meaning is both subjective and objective. As subjective, it is a "sense of meaning," an enlivening attitude that our activities and relationships are worthwhile. As objective, it refers to justified values, ultimately to what is inherently valuable and worthy of being cared about. Perhaps the professionals who served the Third Reich, including doctors, attorneys, and managers, had a deluded sense of meaning when they committed acts of violence against Jews and other social outcasts, but they were not engaged in work that had objective meaning. They were betraying the public goods and standards of excellence embodied in their professions.

If personal ideals warrant attention as part of professional ethics, they must be compatible with fundamental moral norms such as justice, honesty, and compassion. They must also be compatible with justified professional standards. ("Justified" is not redundant: We should not assume that all the present standards of a profession are warranted.) An enormous diversity of genuine ideals meet these requirements. There are many forms of goodness that individuals can achieve by focusing their endeavors on one or a few ideals beyond a morally mandatory minimum. Individuals are free to give their lives meaning by centering them on some but hardly all of these forms.

Of interest here are personal ideals that allude to goods beyond narrow self-interest. Can it be shown that the values that give life meaning must include public goods, that is, practice-oriented craft goods and community-oriented moral goods? Can we show that meaning-creating values are not reducible to the largely self-oriented compensation goods of money, power, social reputation, and their attendant pleasures?

Perhaps we should first reflect on the aims of such a contemplated argument. When we assess the objective meaning of our lives and others, we are making value judgments. Arguments supporting those judgments can only go so far. Ultimately they depend on some areas of shared values, without which discussion quickly comes to an end. There may be little point in trying to show that public goods contribute to meaningful (valuable) lives, because such arguments are ultimately circular in that they assume the fundamental value of those public goods. Persons already committed to the public goods need no such argument, and people devoted exclusively to private goods are so self-oriented that they will be indifferent to the argument.

Yet recognizing that arguments have limits does not render them futile. At times we become confused about the values to which we are committed, especially about how to pursue them. At these times, ethical arguments play an important role in clarifying how public goods provide meaning.

Consider pleasure. Using a set of provocative metaphors, Stephen L. Darwall explains why meaning is not reducible to pleasures and preferences, as hedonists claim. "Something can give meaning to our lives only if we believe it to have intersubjective value. . . . Values that give our lives meaning both inspire and root our lives. They give our spirits the very air they need to breathe. They give us a rootedness: a place to stand, to defend, and to hold precious. But the value of what both enlivens and supports us [and grounds our responses] cannot itself be based on our own individual responses as such."[52] Notice that Darwall only indicates why a sense of meaning requires a *belief* that our enjoyments and other responses to the world have a foundation in intersubjective values. That is an important first step in explaining why pleasures do not suffice, even for a subjective sense of meaning. Yet can more be said regarding the need for objective meaning?

Robert Nozick's famous thought experiment provides a powerful argument against hedonism. Imagine that there is an experience machine, something like an elaborate virtual-reality device, that enables us to program an array of pleasurable experiences. The experience machine has us float in a tank with electrodes connected to our brain that feed us a series of felt experiences. Periodically the series ends, allowing us to disconnect and arrange for new programs, but while attached to the machine our experiences seem attuned to reality. Few of us would choose to live an entire life attached to the machine, precisely because our values encompass more than pleasant feelings. We discern the objective value in participating in real value-laden activities, in having genuine value-structured relationships, and being a person in contact with reality.[53]

What about a life devoted to private goods themselves, not merely to the pleasures they bring? This is a new question. Power, money, and recognition are genuine goods and in some respects interpersonal values. Can they suffice to create meaning?

According to a traditional faith voiced by Schweitzer and embedded in all major world religions and much secular ethics, the most important private goods—happiness, self-fulfillment, a sense of meaning—are linked to the pursuit of public goods. At least for most of us, it is self-defeating to seek these goods with an exclusive eye on compensation goods of money, power, and fame. As social creatures our well-being is tied to caring relationships with other people and social activities. Or, if some hedonists find a sense of meaning in diligently pursuing pleasures, their self-absorption tends to narrow meaning, isolating rather than connecting them within wider circles of caring. To limit meaning to self-oriented pleasures is to narrow and lessen our identity and self-worth, as measured by objective values. The "real" or authentic self is not an isolated atom, but instead defined and fulfilled through concerns for goods beyond the self.

Recently Charles Taylor offered a version of this argument in diagnosing the "malaises of modernity," that is, the forces causing a widespread decline in meaning. The malaises include the economic pressures that increasingly make money a primary end rather than a means as well as bureaucratic pressures from large government and organizations that restrict personal freedom. The deepest malaise, however, is extreme individualism. In the name of authenticity, persons have become self-absorbed in ways that eclipse wider value "horizons" (perspectives). In particular, professionals lead lives of quiet desperation, owing to an eclipse from their daily work of meaning-giving commitments to public values.

Taylor's diagnosis of our social ills is noteworthy because he takes authenticity seriously as a valid ideal, when properly understood. It is the ideal that "each of us has an original way of being human": "Being true to myself means being true to my own originality, and that is something only I can articulate and discover. In articulating it, I am also defining myself. I am realizing a potentiality that is properly my own."[54] In addition to self-respect, authenticity implies the virtue of accepting personal responsibility for our lives. But it also requires a background of things that matter in their own right. We cannot whimsically create the values that give life, though we have great freedom to choose among alternative ideals of goodness and forms of valuable relationships. We define ourselves in terms of goods that extend beyond ourselves, through common enjoyments and endeavors.

As Taylor also warns, social goods are currently undergoing unprecedented assault and with them the possibilities of fulfilling work, as economic forces increasingly dominate our lives. His hope is that we can nudge economic forces in humane directions that leave room for individuals to find self-fulfillment through participating in communities of caring. I share that hope.

To conclude, Adam Smith presents us with an economic paradox: Pursuing self-interest contributes to the common good. Albert Schweitzer advances an opposing moral paradox: Self-fulfillment comes through moral concern and service to others. Both paradoxes express important though partial truths about the indirect consequences of motives and intentions. The paradoxes coalesce as we understand that professionals typically have mixed motives—personal compensation, devotion to craft, and moral commitment. The motives are not artificially yoked together, but instead find a unified expression in commitments to communal goods such as justice, health, and learning—goods that are neither purely self-oriented (egoistic) nor purely other-oriented (altruistic), but are instead community goods for self-and-other.[55] With these results in mind, we can turn to how personal ideals contribute to professional responsibilities.

3

RESPONSIBILITIES

The consensus paradigm reduces professional responsibilities
to the shared mandatory requirements developed as a consensus within a profession and imposed on all its members equally. Any
additional ideals, commitments, or responsibilities that individuals embrace
are matters of personal morality, not professional ethics, even when the
ideals directly and dramatically affect their work. If anything, personal ideals
are automatically suspect because of their potential to disrupt the workplace and threaten uniform standards. The consensus paradigm contains a
large element of truth, as I emphasize in the first half of this chapter. Nevertheless, the paradigm eclipses the moral significance of personal ideals in
the professions, including their role in interpreting and occasionally challenging current views about professional duties, as I begin to explore in the
second half of the chapter.

Shared Standards

The consensus paradigm has both a conventional and a critical version. According to its conventional version, professional responsibilities are those
stated in a profession's current code of ethics and in supporting documents
such as interpretive guidelines and disciplinary rules. According to its critical version, professional responsibilities are those that would appear in an
ideal or fully justified code of ethics. Most of what I say about the omission
of personal ideals from the consensus paradigm applies to both versions. After all, the broad professional duties—including competent care, confidentiality, informed consent, honesty, and providing access to services—will
appear in virtually any list of codified standards, a list that would then be
fine tuned within a fully justified set of standards. In the opening section,
however, I will concentrate on the conventional version because, in practice,

individuals are held accountable for meeting their profession's currently codified standards. Subsequent sections focus on how the entries in actual codes are endorsed or critiqued in light of justified standards.

The large element of truth in the consensus paradigm arises from the need for shared minimum standards and shared moral understanding. Minimum does not mean low. Instead, it refers to the level of excellence that can realistically be demanded of the vast majority of professionals. Six considerations support the need for this shared minimum. The considerations are too broad to establish specific entries in codes, a matter to which I turn in the next section, but they serve as the rationale for having codes at all.

First, often much is at stake in providing professional services. Individuals and the general public can be harmed substantially, including through loss of life and livelihood. All professions do well to begin with the physicians' motto—"Above all, do no harm"—but they also aspire to a degree of quality care beyond that negative injunction. Codes and accompanying requirements of due care are key elements in assuring a basic standard of due care and avoiding a hit-or-miss approach. Other key elements are self-regulation within professions and legal supervision of the profession, including discipline for noncompliance.

Second, everyday nonprofessional ethics constitutes a morass of clashing viewpoints and languages, a seeming Tower of Babel.[1] Professional norms must be standardized in order to establish a common understanding about what can be expected by way of professional diligence and decency. A code represents the formal and authoritative statement by a profession, through its representative professional society, of the standards for providing services. It constitutes the bedrock for a shared moral worldview within the profession. Even a flawed code is preferable to moral chaos. Without codes, practitioners would have license to make up their own rules, and professions would lack moral coherence. This shared understanding is among professionals themselves as well as between professionals and the public. Indeed, shared understanding among professionals acquires added importance as individuals work in interdisciplinary teams in which they must relate the standards of their profession to those of other professions.

Third, and partly combining the first two considerations, professionals provide important services to clients who must trust in their expertise. Professional groups win the approval of society to exercise a monopoly, or at least dominance, over vital services, based on their particular credentials that establish their singular claim to competence in providing specific services.[2] Once that approval is granted, members of the public have little choice but to depend on professionals in order to gain access to services. Typically that dependency is accompanied by reasonable expectations and trust that shared minimum standards have been established and enforced by the profession. The need for trust becomes especially important as society grows increasingly impersonal, fragmented, and bureaucratized so that often clients must rely on professionals who are complete strangers to them.

Fourth, mandatory and enforced guidelines are needed to create a fair playing (or working) field where professionalism can flourish without cut-throat competition. In addition, the guidelines help control temptations to cut corners in the pursuit of private or corporate gain. Despite an ongoing procession of scandals in the professions, we continue to be shocked upon learning of the latest horror story. Even the most accomplished experts seem vulnerable. For example, the fertility clinics associated with the University of California campuses at Irvine and San Diego involved internationally-renown scientists and physicians.[3] Combining negligence with malfeasance, including fraudulent billing and tax evasion, Dr. Ricardo Asch and his associates used the genetic material from one woman to help other women conceive, without the informed consent of the relevant parties—a gross violation of basic principles of biomedical ethics.

Fifth, the consensus established by a code of ethics provides strong support for the many individuals who strive to act responsibly. Most professionals are employees of organizations in which supervisors might occasionally pressure them to engage in unprofessional conduct. Supervisors might even act with callous disregard of the public good, although they might also fail to understand the codified standards of the professionals they supervise. For example, businesspersons holding MBAs are usually educated in a radically different business culture that does not prepare them to appreciate the professional standards of the physicians and nurses they supervise in managed care organizations. Without a code of conduct to back them up, salaried professionals lack their professions' authoritative collective voice, leaving them stranded with only appeals to private conscience that employers easily dismiss.

Sixth, professional morality includes special standards that are more or less stringent than particular requirements of ordinary morality in other contexts. The expression "ordinary morality" refers to the justified moral principles that apply far more widely, well beyond a particular profession.[4] Professional standards sometimes require actions that clash with elements of ordinary morality in nonprofessional contexts. Both the public and individuals preparing to enter professions have to be educated about, and also arrive at some negotiated agreement concerning, the occasions in which professionals legitimately adopt special standards.

For example, "dirty hands" from engaging in unsavory deeds do not always constitute immorality. Some instances involve justifiable acts of causing specific harms because one's professional, social, or organizational role requires it. The most compelling situations concern fundamental duties common to all professions, such as informed consent, loyalty to clients, and confidentiality. In a famous case involving confidentiality, New York attorneys Frank Armani and Francis Belge were appointed by the courts to defend Robert Garrow against a murder charge. Garrow told his attorneys he committed the murder for which he was charged. He also told them he killed two other women whose bodies he left in an abandoned mine shaft. In order to confirm this information, the attorneys went to the mine shaft and, as documentation, photographed the bodies.

When the father of one of the mine-shaft victims approached Belge to ask him if he knew about any other murders committed by Garrow, Belge told the father nothing. Months later, after these events became public because Garrow confessed to the murders, a local prosecutor indicted the attorneys for failing to reveal information about a crime and for failing to see that bodies were properly buried. The charges failed to hold. Instead, the New York State Bar ruled that the attorneys' confidentiality obligation both permitted and required them to maintain silence. Divulging the information would have established the client's guilt and betrayed their duty to defend him as required by our legal system. The attorneys were neither callous nor driven by narrow self-interest; they were responsible professionals who suffered considerably from obeying their code of ethics.[5]

This is an extreme and troubling case. Ordinary decency requires citizens to tell police and the father about the fate of the daughter. Professional standards forbid doing so. A shared understanding among professionals and with the public about departures from morality in nonprofessional contexts, and also the limits of those departures, is imperative lest professionals and the public alike lose their grasp of the sometimes troubling moral implications of the professions. Clear codified rules help establish that understanding.

For a variety of reasons, then, mandatory minimum requirements have great importance. These requirements, along with more fundamental principles of justice, impose numerous restrictions on the pursuit of individual ideals. Not only do the requirements forbid much outright bad, caused by unjustified personal ideals. They also rule out some forms of goodness in pursuing personal ideals, at least in certain situations. Given how much is at stake, however, professional standards and codes must be well grounded. How are valid standards identified and justified?

Justified Standards

Codified standards sometimes mention virtues and ideals, but they deal predominantly with responsibilities, the focus here. Presumably the content of professional responsibilities will connect in some way to ordinary morality, that is, to the valid moral principles that apply more widely than merely to the professions. Professional duties may not be identical to morality in nonprofessional contexts, and even may sharply clash with some elements of everyday morality, at least at some level, as we saw in the attorney example. But professions do not create their moral worldview from scratch. Hence, our question can be rephrased: How do justified professional responsibilities relate to ordinary moral requirements? In answering this question, philosophers have appealed to promises, codes, community standards, and ethical theories.

Promises

Promises are among the clearest and most basic sources of obligations in ordinary morality, and they seem to offer a solid anchor in a world of moral uncertainty and disagreement. Hence, it is tempting to locate the source and substance of professional responsibilities in promises made by individuals upon entering their professions. Daryl Koehn adopts this approach in *The Ground of Professional Ethics*. She recognizes that the promises made in formal contracts with specific clients cannot provide a foundation for professional ethics. Contracts tend to be overly narrow in detailing services, whereas professionalism requires exercising complex skills that elude specification in the precise language of contracts—skills exercised in identifying problems, redefining clients' needs, recommending a range of solutions, and helping clients decide which solution is best. Even more important, the contract approach wrongly suggests that a professional's sole duty is to the client, thereby neglecting the wider responsibilities to third parties and to the public. In place of a contract approach, Koehn contends that the relevant promise is a general pledge, made when individuals become professionals, to help people. The pledge may be implicit, but more often it is made explicitly in formal vows, ceremonial oaths, and commitments made in obtaining and renewing a license to practice. Either way, professionals "publicly pledge themselves to render assistance to those in need and as a consequence have special responsibilities or duties not incumbent upon others who have not made this pledge."[6]

Koehn blurs two questions: (i) What is the content and justification of the responsibilities incumbent on all members of a profession?; and (ii) How do individuals acquire those responsibilities? Koehn's primary interest is (i), yet the promises she highlights seem to pertain primarily to (ii).

To begin with the content of the promises, presumably promises must be both morally permissible and directly relevant to providing the services the client needs. But if the content of the promise is simply to abide by the standards defining quality services, it is clear that the standard is already specified, independently of the promise. If so, the issue of which content is justified also is unanswered by the appeal to promises. This objection, by the way, would apply equally against the view that a group promise, made by a profession as a whole to the public, is the source of professional responsibilities. Whether made by individuals or groups, promises to meet professional standards cannot themselves establish the content and full justification of the standards.

Even regarding how individuals acquire professional responsibilities, promises made by individuals are at most a supportive consideration, not the primary one. The promises are formal affirmations that one will abide by the relevant standards, standards already requisite for the profession. The promise does not create the obligation to meet the standards. Instead, it formally affirms a commitment to meet the prior obligation to abide by the standards. To see this, consider those professionals who refuse to make a public pledge of service. Are they relieved of responsibilities? Surely not. Individuals acquire responsibilities when they work in a profession, just as parents acquire responsibilites when they become parents. Neither parents nor professionals can opt out of their responsibilities by deciding not to make a promise to meet them.

Interestingly, Koehn considers some of the objections I have raised. In so doing, she places numerous conditions on professionals' pledges. For example, she says that the pledges must embody genuine commitments to the good of clients and to meet the standards of competent service, as well as to minimize harm to third parties.[7] She concludes, "Swearing the pledge and occupying a role are therefore for all practical purposes one and the same in the case of the professions."[8] This comes close to being an admission that roles themselves impose duties, regardless of whether pledges are ever made. In any case, the appeal to promises leaves us without an answer to our central question about which duties should be attached to these roles, and why.

Ironically, Koehn's pledge-based theory helps us appreciate something important. Plausibly, she says that the crux of professionalism lies in creating and sustaining clients' trust that services will be provided competently and responsibly. Implausibly, she contends that trust is secured through individual pledges to provide the services. Think of a client going for the first time to a physician or therapist who is a complete stranger. What reason does the client have to trust the stranger, even in some small degree? Surely not a promise made at the beginning of the stranger's career, a promise about which the client probably knows nothing. And even if the client did know about it, a promise from a complete stranger provides dubious grounds for trust in matters of great importance.

Whatever trust the new client has is rooted in the wider-scoped trust in institutions that structure professions and give assurances that members of a profession will meet appropriate standards—assurances provided by such things as university-degree requirements, continuing education mandates, state licensing, board certification, referral listings, supervision within the profession, and general government regulation, not to mention the possibility of civil suits for malpractice. Additional trust in a particular professional comes later because of the quality of services received.[9] Koehn writes, "Professionalism does not require a supporting institutional apparatus. The profession exists whenever a single individual freely utters the grounding pledge or assumes the role and abides by its terms."[10] On the contrary, institutions are essential in creating professional roles and sustaining public trust.

Codes

A second approach to identifying and justifying minimum responsibilities appeals to the authority of an entire profession in establishing its code of ethics. In this view, the code is essentially self-certifying in that it embodies the official stand on ethics taken by a profession in pursuing its collective interests and aims. According to Michael Davis, a professional code is "primarily a *convention between professionals*" that enables them to coordinate their activities in serving the public good to which the profession is directed, and to do so in a morally realistic way that minimizes the need for individual self-sacrifice.[11] A code provides the coordination within a profession that produces an array of benefits for its members, such as reduced competition created by sharing in a monopoly over professional services, high pay and prestige, being able to appeal to the code when pressured by employers to act unethically, and avoiding undue burdens in acting responsibly while others profit from immorality. Hence, failing to obey the code is immoral because it is unfair to other professionals.

> Those who claim membership in a profession and yet do not adhere to its standards take unfair advantage of those who do adhere. They take the benefits generated by the living commitment of other members of their profession to its standards while refusing to do their share to help maintain those benefits. Unprofessional conduct is, in short, a violation of the moral principle, "Don't cheat."[12]

Davis is partly right. Individuals who violate their professional code in the pursuit of private gain are indeed acting unfairly by becoming free riders on a practice whose benefits they accept voluntarily. However, fairness, like promises, is a supportive rather than a primary reason for why professionals should heed their codes, as well as a reason for establishing specific responsibilities in the codes. The primary reason concerns how justified codes promote responsible service to clients and the public. And the justification of particular entries in codes requires mention of more than the authority of professions, especially in light of human fallibility and temptations to abuse of that authority.

Codes do not always promote responsible service as well as they should, and treating a group's code as self-certifying is an objectionable form of ethical relativism. A given code might be incomplete, inconsistent. misguided, distorted by self-interest, or even unconstitutional.[13] For example, not long ago most codes in engineering, law, and medicine banned competitive advertising of professional services. The professions claimed, usually in good faith but perhaps not without an admixture of self-interest in reducing the burdens of competition, that these bans promoted quality care by preventing cutthroat competition that results in lowering professional standards. The courts disagreed and ruled that the ban on advertising and competitive bidding harm the public by restraining the benefits of lowered costs and improved quality through free trade.[14]

Whatever one's view of competitive advertising, the Supreme Court ruling reminds us that actual codes should not be confused with ideal or fully justified codes. Davis invites this confusion. For the most part he focuses on actual codes—"conventions" among professionals. But in responding to the challenge that some entries in actual codes are not justified, he quickly shifts to ideal codes, presumably as yet unwritten: "When an immoral provision appears in an actual code, it is, strictly speaking, not part of it (not, that is, what 'Obey your profession's code' commands obedience to)."[15] In various other passages he conflates actual codes with those that "rational" persons would accept in serving ideals that are "good without qualification."[16]

This appeal to rational persons is closer to the truth than the mere ethical relativism in affirming the status quo of a profession's code, but it still does not resolve our question of how specific standards are shown to be justified. We must ask, What are the good reasons that would establish responsibilities in the eyes of rational persons, both rational citizens and rational professionals? Presumably those (moral) reasons are themselves the basis for justifying the specific content of codes. In turn, professions should be able to explain the reasons as part of being accountable to the public. Indeed, informed citizens appropriately participate at some level, through their representatives, in an ongoing dialogue with the profession about the appropriate entries in codes of ethics.

Community Standards

A more plausible approach, then, is to appeal to the values of the wider society within which professions function. Both professionals and the wider public share some basic values, and it is these values that professions use in establishing and justifying their codes of ethics. Professionals do have special technical expertise that enables them to provide insight into how to adapt wider moral standards to their particular work, but professionals do not have authority to establish their own moral universe. They should develop their codes in dialogue with the public and modify them in response to reasonable community demands. Adopting this approach, Paul F. Camenisch argues that professions are moral subcommunities that share the fundamental values of society.

Camenisch plausibly argues that although modern democratic societies tolerate a diversity of moral perspectives, they also contain a rough consensus or "lived ethic" that suffices to establish the goods served by professions as well as procedures for delivering those goods. To be sure, at the level of specific guidelines, professional ethics and ordinary morality differ. Professional ethics selectively heightens some everyday standards and downplays others. For example, confidentiality imposes stricter requirements on professionals than do the looser standards applicable in everyday ethics (at least outside close friendships and love), and at the same time it restricts duties to divulge information, as in the Armani-Belge Case. But these departures from elements of ordinary morality are justified only when more fundamental social values require them.[17] Thus, stricter confidentiality promotes such public goods as health in medicine and justice in law by making clients feel freer to divulge all relevant information to the professional.

Once the content of professional responsibilities is derived from a society's wider values, individuals and groups of professionals are bound by those responsibilities for three additional reasons. First, agreeing partly with Koehn's view, Camenisch says that professionals promise to serve the public good, whether their promises are made explicitly as oaths or implicitly by voluntarily taking on professional roles. Second, agreeing partly with Davis's view, professionalism requires "paying one's dues" by meeting shared responsibilities rather than unfairly exploiting other professionals.[18] Third, adding his own emphasis, professionals owe a duty of gratitude to abide by the responsibilities society requires, because they voluntarily accept society's gifts. These gifts include the financial support that underwrites their education through scholarships and general funding. They include the establishment of institutions that support their work. And they include special privileges such as allowing monopolies over professional services, which bring high salaries, job security, and social prestige.

Camenisch's attempt to ground professional norms in wider social values would be more plausible if he stipulated that the social values must themselves be justified or morally reasonable. It is true that society does and should play an important role in authorizing professionals and professional societies to perform their services, and this process of authorization implies that society has a right to demand that professional norms cohere with its basic values. Society's authorization is not a complete justification, however, because the authorization must itself meet additional standards of justice. Otherwise, a society's perverse customs could be used to justify corruption, gross inequality, racism, sexism, and other forms of exploitation. Whereas Davis embraces a form of ethical relativism with regard to particular professions, Camenisch runs the risk of ethical relativism with respect to particular societies.

To cite an extreme example, Nazi Germany authorized its professionals to carry out abhorrent tasks. In the name of promoting health through eugenic cleansing, physicians at extermination camps selected who would live as slave labor and who would die. In the name of discovering new knowledge, scientists conducted horrifying experiments on humans. Lawyers did the legal work in denying Jews and other social outcasts their property, and engineers designed an efficient technology for genocide.[19] As with individuals' promises and professions' codes, a society's lived consensus is always open to critical scrutiny for how well it satisfies basic principles of justice.

Camenisch is aware of the dangers of ethical relativism and, at the end of his book, he seems to admit the difficulties it poses for his view.[20] He concludes rather abruptly with an allusion to religion as an ultimate standard. That will not rescue his overall view, however, since the entire thrust of his book is to justify professional ethics within pluralistic societies where no one religious view is authoritative.

Ethical Theories

Camenisch's approach exemplifies an antitheory movement in philosophy, in that he explicitly sets himself against ethical theory as a basis for critiquing and justifying professional norms. Koehn and Davis also seek to avoid general ethical theories by making piecemeal appeals to promises and fairness. Yet ethical theories have an important role to play in justifying professional standards. After all, ethical theories are attempts to identify, clarify, and systematize the best elements in ordinary or "lived" morality and thereby to reject unjustified elements. As such, they help us avoid harmful forms of subjectivity, relativism, and parochialism. Of course, in arriving at specific professional responsibilities, an ethical theory must take into account the particular context of professions, including the goods to which they are devoted, the organizations in which they are embedded, and even the laws and customs defining their traditions within particular societies.

Which ethical theory should we adopt? No theory has won anything like a consensus. Won't controversies about ethical theories merely compound controversy about justifying professional norms? In my view, we should be more impressed by the shared implications of major ethical theories than by their differences. After all, no theory attains major status unless it successfully unifies a broad spectrum of carefully considered and widely shared moral convictions. These convictions include familiar principles of valuing human life, respecting autonomy, promoting justice, and maintaining reciprocity and human solidarity.

Moreover, major ethical theories have many variations, and it is the detailed variations within each type of theory that matter most. These major theories include rights-ethics which appeals to human rights, duty-ethics which appeals to duties to respect persons as rational beings, rule-utilitarianism which appeals to the set of rules which (if adopted) would maximize the overall social good, and contract theory which appeals to the rules that rational beings would endorse were they placed in a fair contracting situation. The details are what matter. Everything turns on the specification of rights and their relative priorities, of duties and their relative priorities, of goods and how to weigh them, and of emphases in specifying rational contractors and fair contracting situations. In my view, each of these types of theories, when suitably refined based on testing our carefully considered convictions regarding a wide array of cases, can be applied in justifying the primary duties of professionals.[21]

Here I outline only one example of how an ethical theory can be applied in justifying and specifying the content of professional standards. The example is rights-ethics, in a version that recognizes the existence of both human rights to autonomy ("liberty rights") and human rights to the essential goods for exercising autonomy when we cannot acquire them by ourselves and when society is able to provide them without undue burden ("welfare rights").[22] I do not believe that a rights-ethic by itself provides a fully adequate ethical theory, especially if it neglects the personal moral ideals and virtues that interest me throughout this book. Nevertheless, rights-ethics does capture a large and fundamentally important part of the minimal requirements that can be used to justify the shared duties incumbent on professionals.

Koehn objects to making rights prominent in thinking about professional ethics because clients go to professionals to obtain goods and services, rather than to have their rights respected (and rather than to be cared for, as noted in chapter 2): "Patients go to the doctor to be healed, not to have their autonomy respected."[23] True enough, the patient's goal is to be healed or otherwise helped in coping with medical problems, but nevertheless patients do expect their rights to be respected in the course of seeking to be healed. Equally important, rights are intimately connected with goods. Indeed, rights can be understood as the moral authority to pursue one's well-being and one's legitimate interests (within limits imposed by respect for others' rights). There would be no point in respecting rights unless individuals' good was intimately connected with their rights, rights that enter into specifying goals, means, and constraints in the professions.[24]

Goals

The goal of a particular profession can usually be understood in terms of rational goods: the primary goods that reasonable persons seek in exercising their rights.[25] Indeed, the services provided by the professions include fundamental goods essential to meaningful human life: justice, health, financial security, and safe technological products. Furthermore, at least within democratic societies, professions focus on promoting goods within a framework of equal respect for the rights of all persons, not just those of an elite group. Rights also enter at the level of clients' interpretations of exactly which goods are most desirable to them, for example, rights to interpret the value to oneself of a risky operation or an alternative therapy.

Means

The means in promoting the public good include most of the valid entries in codes of ethics. For example, the principle of informed consent, which requires that professionals provide relevant information to their clients and then allow the clients to make voluntary decisions about the direction of services, is required by clients' basic rights to make decisions about their own lives. Again, responsibilities to respect employers and colleagues are ultimately grounded in their rights to be respected as persons having full moral worth, rights which undergird the special rights created by contracts with organizations. And restraints of free trade, such as bans on advertising and competitive bidding, are shown to be invalid by appeals to public rights of access to quality goods and services within free markets.

Side-Contraints

The constraint of avoiding unwarranted harm to third parties is rooted in the rights of other members of the public affected. Most important are rights not to be harmed nor submitted to great risks without voluntary informed consent. Thus, chemical plants are forbidden from providing products to consumers when they threaten the public's rights to a liveable environment. Again, most professional codes now place some limits on the duty of confidentiality in order to protect innocent bystanders. In addition, ethical theories can be used to assess the fairness of general procedures used by societies in establishing their variable professional standards. For example, any sound ethical theory will condemn practices of exclusion from participation on the grounds of race or gender.

Having illustrated how ethical theories can be applied in justifying and criticizing codes of ethics, I emphasize that ethical theories are too abstract to settle many practical controversies in professional ethics, as elsewhere. This is true both at the level of ethical dilemmas about how to act in particular situations and at the level of determining which principles belong in codes of ethics. Thus, rights ethics can help us understand why it is wrong to offer or accept bribes that subvert the rights of competitors to equal opportunity, the rights of employers to unbiased professional judgments by their employees in meeting their duties, and the rights of the public to the benefits of fair competition. Rights ethics cannot, however, tell us how large a gift must be to constitute a bribe. Nor can it establish that all societies should prohibit government officials from accepting even modest gifts from defense contractors (as the United States currently does).

Inevitably and legitimately, professional norms contain a conventional element that emerges from the customs of particular societies (as Camenisch's appeal to a "lived ethics" implies) and from the circumstances of particular professions (as Davis's appeal to codes implies). Indeed, ethical theories invite room for a conventional element as part of respecting a profession's traditions, just as most ethical theories leave some room for respecting a society's laws and traditions. But the search for theoretical understanding is essential in avoiding the collapse of morality into ethical relativism at the level of professions or societies. Values are not merely *relative* in the sense of being determined by the customs and present code of a profession, even though ethical theories are applied *in relation to* practical realities, including a profession's customs, traditions, and social setting.

Personal Commitments

Even fully justified codes specifying mandatory minimum responsibilities invariably contain areas of indeterminacy, vagueness, and lack of clear priorities about what to do when responsibilities conflict. In all these areas, professionals must exercise personal judgment. The consensus paradigm limits the role of personal judgment to identifying the duty of all members of a profession who find themselves in relevantly similar situations; otherwise, individual judgment concerns personal, not professional, ethics. To the contrary, I will next argue that personal moral ideals do and often should play a role in interpreting professional responsibilities.

The relevant personal ideals include all moral aspirations that shape the work of individuals without being embraced as part of the moral consensus within a profession. These ideals might pertain to individual character, social practices, organizations, or entire communities. Because immoral ideals have no place in professional ethics, the discussion is limited to ideals that meet two minimum conditions. First, they are consistent with basic principles of justice, including principles that forbid sexism, racism, coercion, and unfair exploitation. Second, they are compatible with the set of morally justified shared professional responsibilities. As I have emphasized, these responsibilities may not be exact entries in a particular code of ethics. Hence, there can be disagreements about whether a particular personal ideal is more desirable than a competing entry in a profession's code of ethics, a topic to which I will return at the end of this chapter.

Personal ideals enter into understanding professional responsibilities in many ways, five of which I cite here. The first three concern fundamental responsibilities in all professions: confidentiality, respect for client autonomy when engaging in advising and advocacy, and loyal service to clients and employers. The last two concern shaping one's career by taking on special responsibilities and supererogatory responsibilities.

Confidentiality

All professions have a confidentiality requirement, although its scope and stringency varies somewhat. In many professions, such as medicine, law, and counseling, the requirement functions to encourage clients to divulge sensitive information about their problems so that professionals can make accurate diagnoses and recommend helpful solutions. In these fields the requirement is very strict, with only legally mandated exceptions permitted, such as requiring physicians to report gunshot wounds or requiring school counselors to report evidence of abuse by parents.

Yet, laws do not anticipate all situations in which enormous harm to third parties can be avoided by breaking confidentiality. One example is the attorney case cited earlier. Others are a physician who learns that her AIDS patient refuses to tell his spouse, with whom he has unprotected sex (new laws have begun to be passed about this case); an engineer who learns that her company is illegally dumping chemicals; or a defense attorney who learns that her client plans to kill or maim someone.

Consider the last example, to which I refer again in chapter 6. The American Bar Association permits but does not require breaking confidentiality when necessary "to prevent the client from committing a criminal act that the lawyer believes is likely to result in imminent death or substantial bodily harm."[26] In my view, the ABA code should require breaking confidentiality in such cases, paralleling what the courts require for psychiatrists in similar cases.[27] A human rights perspective, or any sound justice perspective, would place the rights of innocent people not to be killed ahead of confidentiality rights. My point, however, is that personal ideals of justice and caring do and should guide attorneys' decisions in such cases, especially given the weak permissibility standard. Hopefully, their personal commitment to justice will lead them to view their profession's standard as below what is needed for protecting public safety. Or they may accept the ABA guidelines but see themselves as required to break confidentiality in order to prevent violence. Either way, their personal ideals shape their understanding of their professional responsibilities.

Advocacy, Advising, and Respect for Autonomy

In addition to resolving special dilemmas such as those involved in confidentiality, personal ideals shape entire approaches to relationships with clients. For example, all professions mandate a strong requirement of informed consent and more generally of respect for clients' autonomy, but usually they leave large areas of professional discretion concerning advising clients and influencing clients' views. That is dramatically true in college and university teaching, as discussed in chapter 7, as well as in the ministry, as discussed in chapter 10.

Here I cite the example of advising clients, whether it is psychotherapists advising about courses of therapy, investment brokers advising about investment opportunities, or attorneys advising about legal representation. Specifically, attorneys differ in how far they find it desirable or obligatory to advise their clients about morally preferable courses of conduct. Growing economic pressures make it tempting to do what their clients request, even at the expense of sacrificing their personal moral convictions. But suppose that an attorney in a custody suit learns that her client is unfit as a parent and poses a danger to the physical safety of his child. Should the attorney zealously continue to do what the client wants? Hopefully, concern for the children will lead the attorney in a different direction.

Anthony T. Kronman argues that although the legal "profession now stands in danger of losing its soul" because of economic and bureaucratic pressures on attorneys, the traditional ideal of the lawyer-statesperson is still viable.[28] According to this ideal, lawyers are public servants who are civic-minded. They also receive extensive training in human affairs through the case-study method used in their education. This combination of civic-mindedness and practical insight provides them with a special talent in discerning the social-political good. The talent extends to the level of clients.

Rather than being a hired gun, the lawyer-statesperson helps clients clarify their genuine good within the wider community. In general, the ideal of the lawyer-statesperson implies that personal character is expressed in work in morally satisfying ways.

To be sure, even the traditional ideal has variations. Insofar as advising is interpreted differently within moral and religious perspectives, there will be different conceptions of the virtues appropriate to professionalism, and these conceptions will shape individuals' understanding of their responsibilities. Robert M. Veatch suggested that the underlying values and beliefs that shape the work of attorneys differ so greatly that "there is no one set of virtues for generic lawyers. Rather, there are different virtues appropriate to the libertarian lawyer, the Talmudic lawyer, and the Buddhist lawyer."[29] Veatch does not elaborate, and his remark is an overstatement insofar as it neglects the virtues needed in meeting the core of minimal duties required of all members of a profession. Perhaps, however, he meant something like the following plausible claims.

Libertarian lawyers construe their responsibilities toward clients as duties to inform them of their legal options, to explain the implications of each option, and then to allow clients to decide without further involvement from the attorney. After providing clients with a survey of options, Talmudic lawyers are far more willing, if not eager, to offer advice about the morally preferable course of action. Buddhist attorneys are perhaps less systematic (if not cryptic) about the range of options, but they are more subtle in helping clients choose for themselves wisely. The respective virtues of these different types of attorneys are the dispositions to avoid pressure on clients, to provide sound advice, and to skillfully set conditions for clients to receive appropriate inspiration. The relative desirability of these ideals should be debated as part of the study of professional ethics. But society is better off when it allows some latitude for individuals to embrace and pursue different ideals.

Loyal Service

Advising clients is one thing; carrying out their wishes is another. Here it might seem that the consensus paradigm is adequate: The professional is permitted to carry out any services requested by the client on the basis of informed consent, as long as the services are legal, the professional is competent, and the services fall within the bounds of the public good served by the profession. Professionals are also permitted to refuse services that conflict with their personal convictions (accepting any financial repercussions), but such refusals are matters of personal conscience rather than professional requirement. Thus, the nurse or physician who refuses on religious grounds to provide abortion services is asserting a religious ideal, not a professional ideal. And except in extreme cases such as abortion, professionals should rarely refuse to provide services, so as to promote clients' access to services over which the profession has a monopoly.

This won't do. Health professionals' views on abortion are not entirely private matters; they enter into their conceptions of who is a person and, hence, to whom professional duties are owed. More generally, personal ideals enter into professionals' conception of the good served by the profession and the degree of their zealousness in pursuing that good. Personal convictions regarding abortion influence how one understands the medical goals of respect for life and concern for the quality of patients' lives. The antiabortion health professional is under a personal obligation to avoid participating in abortions, whereas the health professional devoted to pro-choice ideals may take on a responsibility to help assure that abortion services are made available—an act that in the current climate may require considerable courage.

A related issue from medicine involves personal courage in assuring that quality services are provided, as well as potential conflicts between loyalty to one's employer and free speech in advising clients. Increasingly, physicians are pushed by economic pressures not to provide the degree of zealous service to patients that they once would have provided without question. To some degree, the economic pressures are inevitable and have even been beneficial in avoiding unnecessary tests and expense. But critics warn of genuine dangers that health care services to patients are being compromised by pressures within health maintenance organizations (HMOs) and other managed care providers that have rapidly come to dominate medicine. Sometimes these pressures prevent physicians from speaking freely with their patients and with the public. The duty to speak with patients is central to the basic responsibility of informing patients about their medical needs, but the precise extent to which individual professionals take personal risks in pursuing this responsibility is linked to their personal ideals.

Toward the end of 1995, Dr. David Himmelstein was removed from his job at U.S. Healthcare, which at that time was the largest HMO in the eastern United States. Three days before the firing he appeared on Phil Donahue's television show to criticize health maintenance organizations for cutting medical costs at the expense of quality medical care. He also objected to the gag orders that physicians where then required to sign with HMOs, such as U.S. Healthcare's agreement: "Physicians shall agree not to take any action or make any communication which undermines or could undermine the confidence of enrollees, potential enrollees, [or] their employers. . . . Physicians shall keep the proprietary information and this agreement strictly confidential."[30] Himmelstein refused to sign the agreement, an act that eventually cost him his job. He refused because the agreement would prevent him from communicating with the public, but especially because it could prevent him from speaking freely with his patients. For example, he could not advise a patient to seek an additional test to check for the possible presence of cancer, a test not offered by the HMO, because doing so could be construed as an implicit criticism of the degree of care offered by the HMO. The degree of zealousness in pursuing professional responsibilities at the risk of self-interest cannot be fixed universally for all members of a profession. Here personal ideals play a vital role in keeping alive the highest aspirations of a profession.

Career Choices and Promoting the Public Good

The most fundamental professional responsibility is also the most abstract: to promote the public good. That responsibility is pursued by undertaking specific responsibilities in several ways: entering, remaining in, or changing professions; accepting, staying with, or changing places of employment; specializing in some branch of a profession; devoting one's time and energies to some aspect of one's role or job. In various degrees, professionals have some control in each of these areas, and their choices help shape the specific responsibilities they acquire.

Recall several examples from chapter 2. Madeleine M. Kunin began her career in public service with a special commitment to issues that extended naturally from her previous role as a mother to concern for the safety of all children, and eventually to pursuing wider responsibilities for social goods. Gertrude B. Elion specialized throughout her career in biochemistry on drug research to alleviate suffering. Her humanitarian ideals led her to seek and stay with jobs in research on drugs for childhood leukemia, organ transplants, and precursors for AZT, the first major breakthrough in treating AIDS. And in taking jobs with public television that paid considerably less than his previous jobs in commercial television, Robert MacNeil helped create innovative forms of journalism that pursued a few stories in depth and relied on conversations with experts offering balanced viewpoints.

Supererogatory Responsibilities

Defenders of the consensus paradigm could readily grant that personal ideals play a role in shaping supererogatory conduct, that is, conduct beyond the minimum shared requirements. Thus, they might acknowledge that Albert Schweitzer's personal religious and moral ideals inspired his life of service in the Belgian Congo. But they would consider his service to be optional conduct that is not strictly part of professional ethics. In my view, by contrast, commitments to (optional) personal ideals can generate professional responsibilities.

For example, engineers who make deep personal commitments to pacifism thereby take on responsibilities to avoid military work whenever possible, and this responsibility is clearly a professional one.[31] The commitment to the ideals may be supererogatory but, once made, it generates specific duties to act on the ideal in practical situations. In addition, moral integrity requires, as a matter of responsibility, that one attempt to live up to commitments to ideals that are central to one's moral identity. These considerations explain why whistleblowers often testify that they are morally required to do what they did, lest they destroy their integrity and self-respect, even when they make sacrifices well beyond the minimum standards of professionalism, as I argue in chapter 9.[32] The considerations also explain why Schweitzer and other philanthropists are not merely being modest when they portray their endeavors as matters of duty, as I explain more fully in the next chapter.

Conflicts

Although most of the preceding examples illustrate how personal ideals buttress and expand minimum responsibilities, it is clear that personal ideals and codified responsibilities can come into conflict. Earlier I suggested that personal ideals play legitimate roles in professional ethics only when they are consistent with other justified professional requirements. Yet I also emphasized that entries in codes are sometimes unjustified and that there can be controversy about which entries are justified. What should happen, then, when personal ideals clash with codified professional requirements? Here I offer only a preliminary reply to this difficult question, which can only be answered with regard to specific cases, and a question that forms the backdrop to many of the subsequent chapters, including those on professional distance, advocacy in education, respect for authority, and religion ethics.

The consensus paradigm suggests that codified statements of responsibilities always take precedence: shared minimum responsibilities trump personal ideals. I agree that this is usually true, when the codified responsibilities are justified. One legitimate purpose in having and enforcing codes of ethics, as the consensus paradigm affirms, is to cut through differences in personal moral perspectives in order to establish common ground essential for maintaining a shared understanding between professionals and the public. In turn, this shared understanding is essential if professionals are to remain accountable to the public for meeting shared standards. For example, a high school biology teacher (discussed in chapter 10) whose Christian fundamentalism leads him to downplay evolutionary theory is properly disciplined by profession, school, and courts alike.

Nevertheless, there are rare exceptions to the paramountcy of codified responsibilities. The primary exceptions consist in reasonable challenges, within the bounds of justice and respect for client autonomy, to dubious entries in codes and aspects of current practice. An especially important example is physician-assisted suicide in cases where patients are terminally ill or have severely disabling diseases. The American Medical Association strongly opposes these practices, appealing to the role of the physician as healer. Like most professions, however, medicine has multiple goals and corresponding responsibilities that sometimes conflict with each other. Thus, health professionals should seek to prolong life, but they should also seek to alleviate suffering and to promote quality of life, understood from the perspective of particular patients.

Dr. Jack Kevorkian both helped and hindered discussion of this issue by engaging in about 130 acts of physician-assisted suicide, culminating in 1998 with an instance of active euthanasia (for which he was convicted of 2nd-degree murder). As a crusader for change, he openly defied courts, state legislatures, and the medical establishment. His crusade was enormously controversial, raising much public support and equally considerable opposition by physicians. Did he always obtain voluntary consent, and had his patients been in sufficiently hopeless medical conditions to warrant their choice of an early death? If not, his public crusade raises major concerns about how far personal ideals should be permitted to enter into professional life. Yet, a great many people, including myself, share his desire to overthrow what they see as an archaic and inhumane ban on assisted suicide. Indeed, behind closed doors, many physicians are willing, acting on their personal ideals, to give such patients an overdose of morphine that brings about a peaceful death with as much dignity as is possible under the circumstances.

In more subtle ways, personal ideals influence how aggressively health professionals extend life. Things are changing, if only because of economic pressures, but many nurses criticize as inhumane physicians' traditional approach to extending life at enormous cost in suffering and dollars. The appeal to the codified consensus in a profession is easily abused when it becomes a shield against responsible assertions of ideals that affirm physicians as compassionate as well as preservers of life.[33]

To conclude, despite the great importance of shared minimum standards and the mutual understanding built around them, professional ethics should be widened to pay greater attention to personal ideals in understanding professional responsibilities. Professionalism shapes, transforms, and limits personal ideals, but it does not eliminate their importance in understanding professional responsibilities. Conversely, personal ideals shape, transform, and occasionally limit a profession's codified statement of responsibilities. For the most part, personal ideals and codified standards are mutually reinforcing, but occasionally they conflict in ways that generate both controversy and creative change.

4

VOLUNTARY SERVICE

Voluntary service beyond minimum requirements is an important aspect of professionalism, yet it has received little attention in the study of professional ethics. The dominance of the consensus paradigm partly explains the neglect: If professional ethics is nothing but the duties incumbent on all members of a profession, together with resolving the dilemmas when duties conflict, then optional voluntary service is automatically excluded from consideration. When higher ideals are alluded to in preambles of codes of ethics, they are generally understood in light of the duties listed in the body of the code, assuming that they are more than rhetorical flourishes to elevate the prestige of the profession in the eyes of the public. A related reason for the neglect of voluntary service is the more general preoccupation of ethicists (over the last two hundred years) with universal duties, to the neglect of personal ideals of service. Combined, these influences encourage the view that service beyond what is mandatory pertains solely to nonprofessional, "merely personal," morality.

I will discuss three overlapping dimensions of voluntary service in the professions: pro bono service, work in nonprofit service organizations, and supererogatory commitments. Each highlights personal commitments in professional ethics, but the last topic especially leads into wider issues in ethical theory. Specifically, I try to make sense of how some courses of action can become responsibilities and yet remain supererogatory—how they can be supererogatory responsibilities.

Philanthropy

Voluntary service, or philanthropy, is voluntary giving for public purposes.[1] "Giving" means donating money, time, talent, or other resources without seeking comparable economic benefits in return. "Public purposes" include goals that are humanitarian, environmental, political, civic, scientific, or related to the arts. And "voluntary" means noncoerced, rather than non-obligatory, thereby leaving open the possibility that some voluntary service is a responsibility.

I have in mind all forms of voluntary service, but especially instances in which professionals exercise their professional skills for professional goals. For example, I have in mind physicians who volunteer their time in AIDS clinics, rather than in physicians who make donations to their local ballet company. Similarly, I am interested in architects who volunteer their expertise to help design a building for a church, synagogue, or mosque, rather than architects who make a financial donation to a religious organization.

Pro bono publico service, or, for short, pro bono service, is the traditional term for philanthropic activities connected with professions. The term applies to professional services given at no cost or greatly reduced cost to clients who cannot afford (without exceeding hardship) to pay the usual fee. But the term applies to additional forms of giving, such as providing services to charitable organizations, giving voluntary service to improve one's profession, and even making monetary donations to profession-related organizations that serve the public good.

Hippocrates, writing in the fifth century B.C.E., urged physicians to offer pro bono services:

> Sometimes give your services for nothing, calling to mind a previous benefaction or present satisfaction. And if there be an opportunity of serving one who is a stranger in financial straits, give full assistance to all such. For where there is love of man, there is also love of the art. For some patients, though conscious that their condition is perilous, recover their health simply through their contentment with the goodness of the physician. And it is well to superintend the sick to make them well, to care for the healthy to keep them well, also to care for one's own self, so as to observe what is seemly.[2]

In this passage, Hippocrates offers several reasons for pro bono service. One reason is gratitude for the gifts physicians receive, together with appreciation of their present good fortune. Presumably these gifts and good fortune include the opportunities to become and to serve as physicians, perhaps together with wider benefits from society. Another reason is that voluntary service expresses caring about patients, and such caring not only contributes to healing but reinforces and manifests commitment to one's art (what I call craft motives). Finally, providing pro bono services manifests caring about clients for their sake, rather than solely for economic compensation, and hence directly answers to reasons of moral concern.

It is unclear from the passage whether Hippocrates thought that pro bono service is a physician's duty or a supererogatory ideal that is desirable but optional. If pro bono service is a duty, it is unclear how much service is required, especially when we attempt to transpose his injunction about helping strangers in Greek city-states into modern settings. Moreover, if there is a duty, the passage does not indicate whether it is a general duty incumbent on all people, perhaps a duty of reciprocity (gratitude) and of mutual aid (general beneficence), or whether it is a duty applicable only to physicians because of their role as healers.

The same ambiguities extend to contemporary debates about pro bono services. Are these services supererogatory or matters of professional duty? If there are pro bono duties, are they extensions of universal duties or uniquely tied to professional roles?

Today it is the legal profession, not medicine, that most vigorously debates the question of whether there is a responsibility to provide pro bono services. Probably this is because the government has gone a long way toward providing medical care for the most disadvantaged (although not nearly far enough), while much less has been done by government to ensure legal services for the indigent (beyond criminal defense). Yet, legal services can be as essential to well-being as medical needs. Given that many people are currently not receiving essential legal services, are all attorneys obligated to provide pro bono services, or are these services supererogatory?

The legal profession remains divided on the question. Libertarians argue that mandatory pro bono service is like a special tax levied only on attorneys. As such, it violates attorneys' rights to liberty. It also leads to shoddy work by lawyers who resent this violation and, as a result, work grudgingly. To the contrary, defenders of a mandatory requirement argue that government allows attorneys to have a monopoly over legal services, thereby providing them with high incomes and other social benefits. With these privileges come responsibilities. Government may reasonably require that the legal profession ensure that the legal needs of disadvantaged people are met, and the fairest way of doing so is to spread the burden to all attorneys. As for shoddy services, the same penalties for shoddy work should apply here as elsewhere in the profession. The problem can also be alleviated by allowing a wide range of ways to meet a pro bono requirement.[3] At present, the American Bar Association says that all attorneys "should" engage in pro bono services, but this term (in legal jargon) amounts to a recommendation rather than an obligation, and no penalties apply for noncompliance.

This debate is important, but it has tended to deflect attention from ideals of supererogatory service. Whatever level of pro bono service is established as mandatory, it will always be possible to go beyond that limit, as many professionals do. Moreover, the legal debate has centered on services for the indigent and also on a "billable hours" approach to measuring required service. We need to appreciate the full range of voluntary service to society, while acknowledging the paramount importance of helping the disadvantaged.

Many professionals engage in voluntary service by expanding the usual boundaries of their jobs, providing services to clients and community well beyond what they are paid for. Typically this involves putting in longer hours than required, although nothing as economically clear-cut as attorneys' "billable hours." Consider Eliot Wigginton who, along with his students, created the *Foxfire* magazine and books.[4] After graduating from Cornell in 1966, Wigginton chose to teach in Rabun Gap, Georgia, a poor though beautiful rural area he had visited as a child. At Rabun Gap he was responsible for teaching all ninth and tenth grade English students who, as it turned out, were far more apathetic and undisciplined than he could have imagined. Early in his first year of teaching he knew his classes were unsatisfying, both to his students and to himself. Determined not to give up, he undertook a searching dialogue with his students about what they could do together to make improvements.

The dialogue evolved into the creation of a student magazine that sparked his students' enthusiasm and encouraged varied skills in journalism, fiction writing, research, art, photography, sound recording for interviews, and business skills in raising funding. *Foxfire* differed from other high school journals in emphasizing local folklife and folklore. The first issue recorded for posterity the memories and insights of a retired local sheriff, and subsequent editions dealt with such topics as home remedies, superstitions, and ecology. The magazine nearly ended after a year of cost overruns, but eventually it became a multimillion-dollar enterprise, as the best magazine entries were republished in books that found a wide audience. Wigginton's caring involvement with his students transcended the requirements of his job in teaching English to high school students. At the same time, it was his way of pursuing his job meaningfully.

Other professionals dramatically change the type of work they engage in so as to work full time in a service-oriented setting. In *Working*, Studs Terkel records an interview with an attorney whose career began as defending insurance companies against accident victims.[5] His plan had been to gain some experience in order to switch later to the plaintiffs' side, where the big money is made. But in addition to its intense competitiveness, the job was boring and alienating. He left the company to work for the Legal Aid Society, taking a substantial pay cut. His new clients included senior citizens, Appalachians, inner-city minorities, and the homeless, many of whom could afford to pay only one-tenth of usual legal fees. They were people about whom he cared deeply, and that caring restored a sense of integrity and meaning in his work.

Another example is creating new services, as an organizational and moral entrepreneur. Early in his career as a law professor, Ray Shonholtz learned that metropolitan courts were able to hear only 5 percent of the cases, and the rest were handled informally by attorneys.[6] He envisioned the possibility of communities creating their own conflict-resolution mechanisms that would empower them to resolve their disagreements simply, quickly, and inexpensively. After obtaining initial funding from several foundations, he established Community Boards, a model program in which neighborhoods established systems to resolve conflicts using volunteers who would be trained in the techniques of dispute resolution. The program, first established in San

Francisco, became a new structure for achieving justice, one that empha-sized creative ways of dealing with conflicts as alternatives to going to court. It also helped stabilize neighborhoods and evoke greater civic participation through voluntary service.

Most professionals are employed within corporations that may or may not support pro bono service. Not surprisingly, then, professionals frequently separate their voluntary service from their paid work, even when they ap-ply their professional skills in both contexts. One of many innovative ways to accomplish this is a "volunteer vacation." Medical professionals, for ex-ample, offer their skills for several weeks through a variety of international relief organizations, such as Focus (established for ophthalmologists help-ing sight-impaired people), Direct Relief International (involving all fields of medicine), and an array of religious organizations (such as the Christian Medical/Dental Society). Professionals usually pay their own travel and liv-ing expenses, in addition to offering their services. For example, Dr. Kent Mellerstig spent a summer vacation working in Equador.[7] In one location his group performed two dozen plastic surgery operations, mostly on chil-dren with problems ranging from cleft palates to burn scars. Mellerstig's wife and teenage children accompanied him and shared in the work, as well as made friends and learned from the culture.

Other professionals who separate their paid work and voluntary service are able to coordinate these activities throughout the year. Cabell Brand is a successful businessperson who transformed a small family business into a multimillion-dollar corporation.[8] Throughout his career he devoted sub-stantial amounts of money and time, as much as twenty-five hours per week, to fighting poverty. In 1965 he founded Total Action Against Poverty (TAP), a nonprofit organization devoted to discovering and implementing creative ways to fight poverty using a "hand-up rather than hand-out" ap-proach. The organization developed several dozen programs to help bring people into the economic mainstream. Because children comprise nearly half of U.S. citizens living in poverty, keeping children in school became a primary goal. Additional programs focus on the homeless, drug addicts, and the elderly. To all these programs, Brand contributed his moral commitment, managerial skills, and entrepreneurial leadership.

Nonprofit Organizations

In one way or another, all the preceding examples involve not-for-profit or-ganizations, whether foundations, service agencies, or corporations. Eliot Wigginton founded Foxfire Fund, Inc., supported primarily by revenues from magazine and book sales negotiated as part of a profit-sharing arrangement with Doubleday Press. Ray Shonholtz created Community Boards, an or-ganization providing educational expertise to local community groups and supported by foundation money. Cabell Brand founded Total Action Against

Poverty which initially relied on federal money from the Head Start Program and later garnered more local funding. And the attorney described by Studs Terkel worked for a Legal Aid Society funded mainly by government from a state money Office of Economic Opportunity. As these examples suggest, nonprofits, business, government, and private donations are increasingly interwoven as social problems grow in complexity.

We can distinguish, but not altogether separate, the private sphere of family, friends, and recreation from the public sphere of work, citizenship, and community involvement. In turn, the public sphere (and economy) is distinguished into three sectors: business, government, and nonprofits. The nonprofit sector—whose other names include the "not-for-profit," "third," "independent," "voluntary," and "philanthropic" sector—is associated with philanthropy and voluntary service because much of its funding and workers come through these sources. At the same time, many not-for-profit service agencies depend as much on government funding as on voluntary contributions, and some nonprofits have no connection with philanthropy or volunteers. The defining feature of not-for-profit organizations, as their name implies, is that they do not seek profit; nor are they government agencies. These negative features, however, do not capture their distinctive function: They have a central goal beyond profit, and money is subsumed as the means to that goal.

This primary orientation inspires the sometimes overly glowing characterizations of the nonprofit sector. For example, Robert Payton calls it the "moral sector."[9] He suggests that whereas profit is the coin of the realm in business, and political power in government, moral values are central in nonprofits: "It is within the philanthropic tradition that the moral agenda of society is put forward." Payton acknowledges that moral commitments are to be found in humane government and socially responsible corporations, but he suggests that their presence there is episodic, hit-or-miss. "Philanthropy," under which Payton includes the nonprofits, "is the instrument that societies have used to compensate for the [moral] indifference of the marketplace and the incompetence of the state."[10]

Payton uses an honorific definition of philanthropy: voluntary action for the public good. Technically, this definition is limited to acts and organizations whose goal is "primarily for the benefit of others."[11] The intent, and possibly even the result, must be desirable. If the mission of nonprofits is some genuine aspect of the public good, then claims about "the moral sector" become largely true by definition, because only morally well-directed organizations would count as philanthropic and nonprofit organizations. Nevertheless, Payton is obviously generalizing over a wide territory.

In reply, let us distinguish three levels at which claims about nonprofits' moral commitments might be directed: (i) the nonprofit sector as a whole, (ii) particular nonprofit organizations, and (iii) the endeavors of individuals working in nonprofits, both professionals and volunteers. Payton's main interest is the nonprofit sector as a whole, whereas my primary interest is in individuals serving particular organizations. I agree that a strong case can be made for the moral creativity of the third sector as a whole. That sector is responsible for numerous innovations throughout American history, including government programs and laws that were initiated by philanthropic leaders and causes in public education (Horace Mann), public libraries (Andrew Carnegie), abolishing slavery (abolitionist movement), securing women's voting rights (Susan B. Anthony), civil rights programs (Martin Luther King, Jr.), and the reform of medicine (John D. Rockefeller), to cite but a few examples.[12] Beyond such specific contributions, a vibrant nonprofit sector is essential to sustaining American democracy by providing opportunities for individuals to improve society.

We should be wary, however, of the generalization that the nonprofit sector is "the moral sector." On the one hand, a large number of for-profit organizations also maintain a focus on morally desirable goals. Many for-profit corporations manage to keep paramount the goal of producing useful and high-quality products and services, viewing profit-making as a necessary condition for staying in business rather than as their primary goal. We should not stereotype for-profit corporations as amoral arenas (a topic I return to in chapter 8). Furthermore, government does enormous good, and most of the time government agencies act responsibly in carrying out their public missions.

On the other hand, some voluntary organizations are morally pernicious, especially those devoted to racist, sexist, and other perverted visions of the public good. Others are poorly managed and wasteful of resources, and a small percentage are simply fraudulent.[13] It is also sobering to realize that the enormously expensive culture wars in the United States have largely been conducted by nonprofit groups. Whatever one's views concerning abortion, gun control, or gay rights, there are well-funded organizations whose missions oppose one's convictions about moral decency. Recognizing the value of democratic debate and the right of nonprofits to exist and to pursue their missions does not entail affirming the overall goodness of their missions. Nonprofit organizations are far too diverse in their intentions, methods, and results to warrant moral generalizations that establish a "halo effect" surrounding them.

Having added these caveats, I believe there remains an important element of truth in Payton's characterization of the nonprofit sector as the "moral sector." As a group, nonprofits do have something special to offer morally committed professionals (and volunteers) who seek to pursue moral ideals of service.

Return to the idea of a mission that keeps service goals paramount. The advantage of nonprofits is that they invite moral focus in establishing their goals and simultaneously allow enormous diversity in their missions. Selecting from a vast array of moral goods, nonprofits organize and galvanize the energies of individuals who share a special commitment to a particular goal. As economic institutions that typically must balance a budget, they sometimes fail to keep their mission paramount. But, on average, they often succeed better than for-profit corporations in creating meaningful work by keeping public purposes paramount.

Shifting to the level of individuals, what about personal motivation of both professionals and volunteers working in nonprofits? Establishing that a nonprofit organization has service as its mission is different from asserting that individual professionals who work in the organizations, either as volunteers or as paid employees, are motivated primarily by that mission. Is there any basis for believing that professionals in the nonprofit sector, as a group, are motivated any differently than those working in business and government? This is an empirical question that has not been fully answered in the social science literature. Nevertheless, a recurring theme in that literature is that volunteers have a mixture of motives. It is even more obvious that paid professionals working in nonprofit organizations have a large admixture of self-interest because they earn a living from the organization.

Another question, however, pertains to values: Ought professionals to be motivated more strongly by genuine goods specified in nonprofit organizations' mission statements than by the self-seeking compensation motives encouraged in business? Payton struggles with this issue in an essay entitled "Philanthropy as a Vocation."[14] His main concern is with managers (leaders) and development officers (fund-raisers), but he also mentions other professionals, such as college professors, working for nonprofit corporations. Payton notes that working in a foundation or nonprofit can be quite profitable, rich in pay and benefit packages. On average, however, pay and benefits are significantly lower than what might be gained by working in another sector. Payton also frankly acknowledges the role of personal ambition, presumably in seeking to make an impact on program goals within a nonprofit organization. And he warns of the danger of self-righteousness that arises when individuals perceive themselves as pursuing service goals. Professionals' arrogance can damage organizations when it spreads to relationships with nonprofessional volunteers. Moreover, Payton acknowledges that creating jobs in the for-profit sector is as vital a public service as anything the nonprofit sector has to offer, as long as those jobs produce products and services that are socially valuable.

Optimistically, we might hope for only minor differences of degree in the range of motives of most professionals working in the three sectors. Inevitably there will be some sharp contrasts, such as Terkel's lawyer encountered. But more often we can hope that many professionals will make relatively smooth transitions between the for-profit and nonprofit sectors over the course of their careers. Consider the career of Jack Coleman. After nearly two decades as a professor of economics, he worked as an executive at Ford Foundation, then served as president of Haverford College, next became president of the Edna McConnell Clark Foundation whose mission is to help the disadvantaged not helped by other organizations, and now owns and manages a small Vermont country inn. In each role he sought "to fulfill his most cherished dreams, to be personally fulfilled, but to do it all in a way that is thoroughly imbued with moral concerns that become for him the pursuit of personal *moral* integrity."[15]

Many others, however, find it increasingly difficult to achieve the relatively smooth transitions Coleman found possible. Pressures from global competition and rapid technological development cause ever greater preoccupation with profit. Similar pressures have also hit nonprofit organizations which still must balance a budget, and certainly the "downsizing" of government funding has added new demands on nonprofits. Moral values must permeate all sectors of our economy and our lives, and hence we should not single out any one "moral sector."

Supererogatory Responsibilities

Acknowledging an important place for personal supererogatory endeavors generates a powerful criticism of the consensus paradigm. But there are puzzling features of supererogatory conduct, especially in the professions but elsewhere as well. How should we understand supererogatory service within a general framework of moral theory?

In a famous paper, "Saints and Heroes," J. O. Urmson objected to the narrowness of ethicists' threefold classification of actions as right, wrong, or indifferent.[16] Right acts are required by obligations (duties, responsibilities); wrong acts are forbidden by obligations; indifferent acts are morally neutral, neither required nor forbidden, neither right nor wrong. This classification, which reflects ethicists' preoccupation with universal duties, omits supererogatory conduct: morally praiseworthy acts that are not mandatory for everyone in a given situation or role. Supererogatory acts are not universally obligatory, nor instances of wrongdoing, nor morally neutral. They transcend obligation in morally desirable ways, at least in some respects.

Michael S. Pritchard is one of the few philosophers studying professional ethics who takes supererogatory conduct seriously.[17] By *good works,* in an essay of that title, Pritchard means morally good conduct that goes beyond the basic duties incumbent on everyone or on everyone in particular social roles such as professions. His examples include professors who serve their universities by working on an extraordinary number of committees, engineers who pursue safety beyond the standard specified in the law, and statisticians who turn down more lucrative work in order to engage in low-compensated projects aimed at a community good. Pritchard points out that special duties arise once such projects are undertaken. That is, the act of taking on responsibilities generates duties to carry through in appropriate ways, or at least not to withdraw from them until giving proper notification so as to allow time to find a replacement. But there are no duties to undertake the projects in the first place.

Pritchard interprets responsibilities to do good works as created at the moment of committing oneself specifically to them, and I agree that is often the case. However, as will become clear, I also believe that many commitments to specific "good works" are implied by prior commitments to moral ideals. Devotion to an ideal embodies a moral mandate to take on specific responsibilities in appropriate circumstances. I will also explore another interesting result implied by both commitments to ideals and to specific courses of conduct: The same line of conduct can be both supererogatory and a personal responsibility.

According to the usual assumption, the same course of action cannot simultaneously be supererogatory and a responsibility. Urmson agrees, which leads him to sharply separate the obligatory from the supererogatory. But this assumption generates what I call the *volunteer paradox*. Bring to mind any paradigm of supererogatory conduct: acts of service that are (a) morally desirable, admirable, and praiseworthy in a high degree and (b) not morally mandatory—not required by duty, obligation, or responsibility—for everyone in a given situation or role. Now imagine that the agent makes a promise to engage in the envisioned conduct. It seems that the promise automatically renders the conduct *non*supererogatory, contrary to the initial hypothesis, because it creates an obligation to provide the service, in the same way any bona fide promise creates an obligation. This is a paradox in the logician's sense of a formal contradiction: The same conduct is supererogatory and not supererogatory. Alternatively, it is a paradox in the looser sense of a puzzling and counterintuitive conclusion: What first appeared to be a paradigm of supererogatory conduct turns out to be nonsupererogatory, indeed merely a routine instance of a promise-created obligation.

Here are some examples: You pursue a self-sacrificing life in order to donate most of your income to world hunger causes (without violating other important duties); throughout your lifetime you donate large amounts of time to charitable organizations; you risk your life to save a perfect stranger (and you are not a police officer or other professional with a duty to do so); you are a professional who pursues ideals of service with a zealousness far beyond what could be required of all members of your profession. Before embarking on any of these courses of conduct, you promise to perform the service. Perhaps the promise is made to a philanthropic organization, an intended beneficiary, or your dying parents. Because the promise creates an obligation, we seem to have a contradiction: The conduct is both supererogatory (according to the initial stipulation) and not supererogatory (because of the promise). Alternatively, it seems we must admit that what appeared to be a paradigm of supererogatory conduct is not really supererogatory at all. Either result is problematic and counterintuitive.

The volunteer paradox is not a trivial conundrum. It bears on the meaning, possibility, and moral significance of service beyond the call of duty, both within professions and elsewhere. Hence, we should be wary of hasty and ad hoc solutions. One such solution consists in citing the time differential: The imagined service is supererogatory before the promise is made and not supererogatory afterwards. According to this proposal, there is no contradiction because we are not talking about morally equivalent conduct before and after the promise. This proposal succeeds in avoiding logical paradox, but it does nothing to remove the air of paradox in the looser sense. Surely a soldier who pledges to engage in an exceptionally dangerous service beyond the call of duty deserves the same praise as a soldier who undertakes the same dangers without making an explicit promise beforehand. If anything, sometimes the promise adds to the deserved praise because it provides valuable assurances to comrades who can then form strategies based on it. We need to find a way to understand how the promise can create an obligation without cancelling out the genuine supererogation.

A second, related, proposal is to distinguish two actions (or courses of action): (i) the act of making the promise, or related acts of undertaking an obligation to provide a service and (ii) the act promised, that is, the service to which one commits oneself. The first act is supererogatory; the second is not. This is Gregory Mellema's approach, although he sees only irony where I see paradox:

> An ironic feature of volunteering is that it often creates an obligation to do that which one volunteers or promises to do. Thus, the act which one volunteers to perform cannot in typical situations qualify as an act of supererogation. I might volunteer to perform an act of great self-sacrifice, and by doing so I might transcend the bounds of duty. But having done this, other things being equal, I am arguably duty bound to perform the act. At the very least, other things being equal, my subsequent failure is morally blameworthy.[18]

As Mellema defines them, supererogatory acts are morally praiseworthy, do not fulfill a moral duty or obligation, and do not make one blameworthy for failing to perform them. The promise to engage in self-sacrificing service meets this definition. The actual acts of self-sacrificing service do not fit the definition, however, both because the promise creates an obligation to perform the service and because the agent is blameworthy for failing to keep the promise. Hence Mellema's proposal: The act of promising is supererogatory, but what is promised is not.

Mellema's dichotomy is unsatisfying. On his view, we would have to say that even the most heroic rescuers who risk or sacrifice their lives are merely doing their duty, nothing more, because they are required by their promise to do so. Thus, soldiers who die while pursuing an extraordinary service, well beyond what their duties specify, are doing nothing supererogatory at the time of their death; they are merely keeping a promise (although their promise is supererogatory). Again, Mellema's view implies that we should restrict praise to the promise to serve (or to the person-as-promiser) and withhold praise from the actual service (or to the person-as-giver). Yet surely we need to find a straightforward way to describe both the actual service and the promise as supererogatory.

Mellema tends to conflate volunteering, promising, and other ways of creating obligations, and before proceeding we should distinguish them. Volunteering is donating one's time, talents, money, or other resources, whether or not one promises to do so. Promising is the speech act of explicitly committing oneself to a course of conduct, typically by uttering or writing the words "I promise" in appropriate circumstances. Finally, obligations can be created in other ways than by making promises, for example by undertaking commitments in situations where our conduct causes people to depend on us. In becoming a parent, I acquired responsibilities to raise my children even though I never explicitly promised to do so. Similarly, a soldier can volunteer without promising, simply by undertaking a course of conduct and thereby taking on a responsibility. In this way, the volunteer paradox applies to a wider array of responsibility-creating commitments than those made by promises.

David Heyd defines volunteering as supererogatory: "Volunteering is a paradigmatic example of supererogation," where volunteering is "the offering of one's services (help, etc.) to do something which is collectively required of a group."[19] This definition is unhelpful. Not all volunteering is supererogatory because not all volunteering is praiseworthy—whereas supererogatory conduct is praiseworthy, at least in some respects. Volunteering one's time and money to immoral groups such as the Ku Klux Klan warrants blame, not praise. Moreover, some volunteering is a duty. For example, I recently served on a university personnel committee in which all members were expected to write the first draft of some letters evaluating colleagues, although members volunteer to write particular letters. There I had a duty to volunteer sometimes, though not on any particular occasion. To cite a more significant and controversial example, it might be argued that some voluntary service is morally obligatory, either because of duties of mutual aid (beneficence, justice) or because of duties of reciprocity (gratitude, fairness), although individuals are not obligated to engage in any specific service.[20]

A third, quite radical, approach to the volunteer paradox denies that supererogatory conduct exists. This approach has several variations, each of which establishes extraordinarily high moral requirements. One variation is theological: Morality is specified by God's commandments, and those commandments are so stringent that it would be impossible for humans to transcend them. Another variation is act-utilitarian: Each of our actions ought to aim at generating the most good for the most people, and hence it makes no sense to exceed this maximum. Still another variation is Kantian: All acts that at first appear to be supererogatory turn out to be required by an imperfect duty, that is, a duty to pursue a moral ideal (or "maxim") which allows room for discretion but not laxity in choosing the occasions for service.[21]

In all its variations, this third approach is radical in that it overthrows the commonsense conviction that at least some conduct is supererogatory. As such, it is neither ad hoc nor easily refuted without setting forth a complete ethical theory. This much can be said, however. The primary appeal of the third approach is practical: It sets a tone of moral rigor designed to provoke greater moral effort and to discredit shallow excuses for selfishness. Yet, setting moral standards too high can be self-defeating. Instead of increasing moral effort, excessively high demands lower the moral enthusiasm of most of us who find meaning in an array of additional nonmoral (not immoral) pursuits—in the arts, science, religion, recreation, and so forth—that require some of the money and other resources for meeting the rigorist's stringent moral standards for helping others. The rigorist's standards might even dampen the moral enthusiasm of some people who are inspired by ideals partly because they believe they are transcending the routine minimum requirements. In any case, an adequate moral theory must be realistic and aimed at human beings rather than angels.[22]

How, then, is the volunteer paradox to be resolved? My solution combines three observations. First, we need to pay closer attention to the ordinary contexts in which the terms "supererogatory" and "beyond the call of duty" are used. Philosophers use these terms too abstractly when they stipulate that supererogatory conduct must transcend all the moral requirements that would be specified by a fully comprehensive and adequate ethical theory. In everyday discourse the terms are applied contextually, relative to standards for mandatory conduct that are considerably more focused, limited, and nuanced. Thus, "supererogatory" ordinarily means morally valuable in ways that go beyond what is morally required of everyone *in* particular situations or roles and *as* those requirements are specified by contextually nuanced standards applicable in those situations or roles.

Jumping on a grenade to save one's comrades is supererogatory because it transcends the role responsibilities of soldiers. That does not mean it is beyond the commandments of God or surpasses the duties specified in a fully adequate philosophical theory—as if we all knew what those things are. Again, when we say that a volunteer has gone beyond the call of duty in devoting fifteen hours a week for twenty years to working with disabled children, we allude to what is ordinarily expected or required by way of such service. We do not refer to esoteric theories about maximum utility or imperfect duties.

Ordinary usage does not preclude, of course, that actions which are supererogatory relative to contextual standards may turn out to be mandatory when viewed from a broader perspective. The point is that our practical moral judgments about supererogatory conduct do not make reference to the widest possible moral horizon. Given our practical interests in recognizing moral excellence and in increasing moral motivation, we legitimately praise conduct as beyond the call of duty when judged within less-than-cosmic perspectives. These practical interests are as important as those served by the rigorist's demand for high moral standards. In fact, our practical interests in praising people using context-oriented standards are in tune with the rigorist's concern to evoke greater moral commitment, insofar as that praise generates self-esteem that reinforces moral commitments.

The second observation, alluded to earlier, is that many exemplars of heroic and self-sacrificial conduct regard their actions as morally required rather than morally optional.[23] Urmson suggests that such individuals are unduly modest when they say they are only doing their duty, but this suggestion does not ring true. Albert Schweitzer repeatedly portrayed his service as something he "must" pursue, that he "must not accept this good fortune as a matter of course, but must give something in return."[24] His good fortune was not vastly different than that of innumerable other middle-class individuals, and he affirmed that all people have obligations of gratitude and reciprocity for their good fortune. He never suggested, however, that there were universal duties to engage in degrees of service on anything like the scale he undertook. The "must" signalled his sense of a personal responsibility, in light of the wider ideals to which he was committed.

Turning to saints, A. I. Melden suggested that saints are wholly unlike the rest of us in that their religious beliefs lead them to regard all humanity as brothers and sisters, quite literally as children of God.[25] More than that, they believe they are God's intermediaries charged with special responsibilities to care for other people as if they were members of their own families. Acknowledging Melden's insight, I am nevertheless struck by the continuities between saints' caring and the innumerable other varieties of caring beyond the minimum duties incumbent on everyone. I agree that special religious beliefs and their accompanying commitments do yield special responsibilities to help, based on genuine caring about and even for others. But saints and moral heroes like Schweitzer are at one end of a spectrum, followed by individuals like Dr. Hilfiker, Madeleine M. Kunin, Gertrude B. Elion, and so on. Moreover, the differences among saints themselves is too great to allow generalizations that they are all wholly unlike other people, and Melden's isolation of saints invites rationalizing away our own modest inclinations to help others beyond what is required.

Third, it is both intelligible and plausible to affirm that people like Schweitzer actually do have special responsibilities. Moral paragons are neither muddled nor falsely modest when they insist that they are only meeting their responsibilities. It is entirely natural to say that Schweitzer had a personal responsibility, one that not everyone is obligated to pursue, at least not in a comparable degree. His service was beyond the general call of duty, but it was not beyond *his* duty. In this way, supererogatory conduct can be one's responsibility because one undertook it as such.

Sometimes responsibilities are undertaken by making a promise or commitment to do a specific act, as Pritchard notes. Perhaps just as often they are formed more indirectly, by gradually forming commitments to morally justified ideals or causes that imply specific commitments. In turn, the moral commitments to ideals imply particular courses of action in specific situations where one has the opportunity and resources to pursue the ideals or causes. To fail to act in these situations might undermine the commitments to the ideals, perhaps undermine one's integrity as a person whose character is formed around the commitments. To be sure, individuals remain free to reshape their character in other directions, and hence the supererogatory commitments to the ideals or causes remain morally optional. Yet, once made, the commitments to ideals imply actions that become matters of personal responsibility.

We can draw these observations together in two ways. On the one hand, we can affirm the commonsense belief that not only heroic individuals and saints but also many other moral exemplars engage in supererogatory conduct which is morally admirable and beyond what is required of everyone in their situation and roles. On the other hand, their conduct may well be their responsibility—not something that they are confused or overly modest in thinking is their responsibility, but that is their genuine responsibility. Their conduct is supererogatory, and it is their responsibility. It is a *supererogatory responsibility*. I hasten to add that questions of fault and blame for not meeting supererogatory responsibilities are another matter altogether. I may be in no (moral) position to criticize you for not fully meeting a supererogatory responsibility, especially if I have done nothing by way of supererogatory service myself. Nor do supererogatory responsibilities always create rights, at least where no explicit promises of service are made.

It might be objected that I have resolved the volunteer paradox only by introducing a new paradox. A supererogatory responsibility is a contradiction in terms: It is both obligatory (as a responsibility) and nonobligatory (as beyond what is required), something like a square circle. This objection, however, fails to take seriously the three observations made above. There is no contradiction in saying that the same conduct is supererogatory in the ordinary sense of going beyond the general duties of everyone in a situation or role (relative to contextually attuned standards) and also the special responsibility of individuals who voluntarily commit themselves, either by virtue of their promises to engage in the conduct or their special commitments to ideals and causes which indirectly imply commitments to the conduct.

It might also be objected that I have replaced a paradox with an oxymoron, "supererogatory responsibilities." But oxymorons are not such dreadful things. As expressions combining incongruous or seemingly clashing terms, they need not imply self-contradictions or counterintuitive conclusions. Apt oxymorons are paradoxical only in the literary sense: statements or phrases that at first glance seem absurd but upon closer scrutiny may insightfully highlight complex realities. Calling love "bittersweet" conveys how love is joyous in some respects and painful in others. Similarly, the expression "supererogatory responsibility" conveys how conduct can be beyond the call of (general) duty and yet required by personal responsibilities.

To conclude, voluntary service beyond the explicit requirements of shared professional duties is a valuable dimension of professionalism and deserves more attention in the study of professional ethics. It is valuable because of the meaning it adds to professionals' lives. It is also valuable because of the contributions it makes to communities, whether through nonprofit organizations, corporate philanthropy, or general philanthropy. Appreciating how service can be both supererogatory and a responsibility acquired by caring professionals overthrows the core of the consensus paradigm—the idea that professional responsibilities are reducible to duties incumbent on all members of a profession.

PART II

Caring and Client Autonomy

How does one live a decent and honorable life, and is it right to separate, in that regard, a person's "private life" from his or her working life?

—Robert Coles, *The Mind's Fate*

5

CARING ABOUT CLIENTS

rofessionals might be competent without caring very much about their clients. To be sure, professional services typically require a show of personal concern, but it might be only a show. Skillful professional detachment, softened by good bedside manners, usually suffices to create an illusion of caring while concealing indifference, dislike, and contempt. As long as due care is taken in providing services, there would seem to be no basis for complaints, assuming we can tolerate the ritualized hypocrisy when organizations that care only about profits advertise them- selves as caring deeply about clients. After all, clients purchase services, not emotions and attitudes of caring. Adam Smith would find much to celebrate in all this. Guided by the invisible hand of the marketplace, professionals pursue their self-interest while pretending to care, thereby benefitting every- one involved: Clients receive the services they need, professionals make a comfortable living, and stockholders enjoy their profits.

Although it contains a substantial element of truth, this perspective on professional-client relationships is one-sided and distorted. It eclipses the extent and significance of professionals' caring. Caring about persons, in a sense that refers to motives and attitudes as well as conduct, permeates the meaning-giving commitments that sustain professionals throughout demanding careers. Because it involves motives and attitudes, as well as con- duct, caring about clients cannot be part of the uniform duties demanded of all members of a profession. Nevertheless, it is a fundamental ideal that should be promulgated within professions, and interpreted and applied within the specific value perspectives that individuals bring to their work.

The first two sections below clarify what it means to care about clients as persons, highlighting how caring professionals relate their services to clients' wider good, which is affirmed as such. The last two sections discuss some connections between caring and respect for autonomy, the most widely dis- cussed procedural norm governing professional-client relationships. Rather than sufficing as a full moral perspective, caring is guided and limited by respect for autonomy. Conversely, respect for autonomy implies caring. In general, caring and respect are interwoven within a complex web of moral values.

Whole Persons

The word "caring" unites a cluster of meanings connected by what Wittgenstein called family resemblances, that is, overlapping similarities among key features without a core of essential properties. Many of these meanings are relevant to professional ethics. Thus, professionals have duties to provide appropriate *care* (services). They must *take care* to meet their responsibilities (be competent, exercise caution, avoid carelessness). Court-appointed guardians of juvenile delinquents *have care of* clients whom they supervise or have legal authority over. Unfortunately, many professionals are *care ridden,* burdened with anxiety and worries. Most professionals *care to* (want to) maintain their jobs and reputation. They *show care* for their clients by presenting themselves as considerate and concerned to help. Professionals might do all these things motivated solely by economic gain and a devotion to their craft, without *caring for* their clients—in the sense of liking, loving, or otherwise feeling deep affection for clients. They can also do these things without *caring about* clients as persons, the sense on which I focus.

Caring about clients implies a significant degree of altruistic motivation. "Altruism" does not mean self-sacrifice, although self-sacrifice is occasionally required. Rather, it refers to positive attitudes toward people, desires for their well-being, and wanting to help them for their sake. "For their sake" implies valuing clients as "ends in themselves," as persons who have inherent worth rather than as "mere means" to personal gain, to use Kant's language. I do not follow Kant, however, in affirming an ideal of purity of motives, neither the ideal of pure respect for moral duty which he affirmed, nor the ideal of spontaneous benevolence which he renounced. Almost always, caring is motivated by additional motives beyond altruism, including self-oriented compensation motives (money, power, recognition) and technical-oriented craft motives (commitment to profession, respect for professional standards, pride in a job well done). Sometimes these motives conflict, but for the most part they are mutually reinforcing. That explains the truth in Adam Smith's invisible-hand doctrine: In matters of business, pursuing enlightened self-interest usually points in the same direction as moral concern for social well-being.

Three additional applications of "caring about" will be alluded to in what follows. One meaning is caring about (loyalty to) groups of persons affected by one's work, including colleagues, communities within organizations, and the wider public. A second is caring about (commitment to) ideals and standards that guide professionals in caring about individuals and groups. A third is being a caring person, that is, having the virtue (desirable disposition) of wanting and seeking the well-being of others. Each of these senses refers indirectly to caring about persons.

We commonly distinguish between "purely professional relationships" and personal relationships such as friendship and love. Personal relationships imply emotional involvement and professional distance requires avoiding inappropriate kinds of personal involvements with clients (as I emphasize in chapter 6). Does it follow that professionals do not and should not care about their clients as persons? Jeffrey Blustein suggests it does: "The participants in [professional] role relations do not matter to each other in their own right, as particular persons, but insofar as they fulfill certain functional norms" that specify role-appropriate behavior.[1]

Blustein notes that our physician or attorney might also be our friend, in which case we have both a personal and a professional relationship with him or her. He also acknowledges that some job descriptions require professionals to be "warm, friendly, and caring," although he seems to have in mind outward behavior designed to create a mere appearance of caring attitudes and emotions. Thus, he says that in order for clients to feel cared for, "The institutional character of the relationship [with professionals] should remain in the background for the client," but "professionals do not lose sight of the fact that a particular client is only one of many actual and possible beneficiaries of their attention" as they seek to "make *every* client feel special."[2]

Presumably clients can be "made to feel special" by a professional who engages in appropriate role behavior while lacking the attitudes and emotions of caring, as noted at the outset. To cite an extreme example, in Camus's *The Fall*, Jean-Baptiste Clamence recalls how, during his former career as an attorney, he made each client feel uniquely valued, but he did so as an elaborate game of ego gratification: "I, I, I is the refrain of my whole life"; "When I was concerned with others, I was so out of pure condescension . . . and all the credit went to me."[3] After scrutinizing his own motives, Clamence concludes that all professionals, indeed all people, are egoists who lack genuine concern for each other. Unlike Clamence, Blustein does not ascribe purely egoistic motives to professionals, but then what led him to conclude that clients do not matter to professionals "in their own right, as particular persons"?

Blustein reminds us that professional role relationships lack several defining features of friendship and love, in particular mutual intimacy, two-way sharing of personal information, and wide freedom to shape the relationship as partners choose. By themselves, however, these elements do not preclude caring about individuals as whole persons. Indeed, as Blustein acknowledges, these elements are largely absent in one paradigm of deep caring: parental love of infants who are too young to reciprocate. Quite apart from the above features, Blustein thinks two other aspects of professional relationships establish the nonpersonal nature of professional-client interactions: replaceability and segmental interactions. Professionals and clients "encounter one another as segmental persons, and are more or less easily replaceable by others who fulfill the same [relationship-defining] norms as well or better."[4]

On the one hand, Blustein reminds us that occupants of professional roles are "easily replaceable by others." From a client's point of view, one physician or teacher will do as well as another, as long as they are competent and meet other professional standards. From a professional's point of view, clients are replaceable as long as they have problems the professional is trained to deal with (and money to pay for services). Thus, "the relationship between, say, a lawyer and a client, as a role relationship, is not materially affected by changes in the individuals who occupy these positions."[5] This aspect of professional-client relationships stands in sharp contrast with relationships of friends and lovers who are irreplaceable to each other, such that changing the persons changes the relationship.

In reply, note that although the general *type* of relationship with a client remains unchanged when occupants of roles change, the *token* or instance of the relationship does change. It changes in exactly the same sense that friendships and love relationships change when the individuals are changed. More important, even when professionals and clients regard each other as interchangeable sources of goods, they can and should treat each other as persons, with respect and caring. Obviously, those professionals who do not care a whit about clients, except to get their money, will tend to reduce their clients to interchangeable sources of income. But that is morally objectionable, both because it fails to show moral respect for persons and because it runs the risk of eroding professional standards when preoccupation with money leads to cutting corners. If Blustein is offering an empirical claim about professionals' actual attitudes (given the restrictions imposed by their particular roles) rather than a normative claim about what is morally permissible, then he should cite supporting studies. Most of us have encountered professionals who treat their clients as interchangeable objects, but we have also encountered deeply caring professionals.

On the other hand, Blustein says that "role relationships are relatively inflexible and limited interactions that engage only well-delineated segments of persons."[6] Professional interactions call upon restricted aspects of individuals as defined by a client's specific problem, the type of services offered, and the duties and rights governing the relationship. As a result, the participants are not fully engaged as persons and hence cannot care for each other as complete individuals.

This conclusion, that professionals cannot care for their clients as complete individuals, does not follow. Even outside role relationships, situations often restrict the appropriate extent of involvement, even though genuine caring is present. When we take time to help a stranger fix a flat tire, the requisite form of help is clearly delineated, but it does not preclude caring about the person we help. Similarly, the fact that professionals provide role-delineated forms of help does not entail an absence of caring. On the contrary, justified professional restrictions facilitate caring by providing a moral structure that protects against inappropriate manifestations of caring. As I suggest later, professional norms of respect for clients protect against paternalism, exploitation, and dominance over vulnerable clients, in ways that support rather than negate caring.

Unified Good

Blustein leaves us with this challenge: Clarify what it means for professionals to care about their clients as persons, rather than as segmental and replaceable sources of benefits. That is a large task, ultimately best accomplished through attention to the case studies found throughout this book. Here I pursue one major theme: Caring professionals are prepared, when appropriate, to connect (a) the profession-specific good they provide with (b) clients' general or unified good.

Clients' *profession-specific good* is defined by the relevant professional service being sought and provided: for example, medical goods (health), educational goods (growth in understanding), or legal goods (justice). Clients' *unified good* is their overall well-being as persons, taking into account all major aspects of their lives. What this amounts to, of course, is not altogether clear. Certainly, clients' beliefs about what is good for them may differ from what is actually good for them, according to an objective conception. At the same time, beliefs and objective truths are intertwined here: Our objective good implies acting on our justified value beliefs, and our value beliefs are justified in part by what is objectively good for us.

The important point is this: A strong indicator of caring is that professionals are mindful of how clients' profession-specific good connects with their unified good. When the connection is clear, professionals communicate their insights to clients; insofar as it is unclear, caring professionals are willing to help clients clarify it. Either way, clients' autonomous views about their good guide the professional-client relationship.

Consider a young female nurse assigned to help an exceptionally difficult patient.[7] The man is uncooperative, his personality is off-putting, and he is physically repulsive. A diabetic weighing 350 pounds, he lacks even basic hygiene and, as a result, develops the gangrene that brought him to the hospital for amputation of his leg. He is verbally abusive, makes sexist and racist remarks and insults, and yells at the nurse. Given her responsibility for many additional patients, the nurse could not be faulted for providing only the minimal care required by professional duties, at most pretending to care about the man while camouflaging her contempt for him. On one occasion, however, the man's hostility subsides and the nurse heard him refer to himself as "a mess." Rather than brushing off the remark or spitefully enjoying it, the nurse interpreted it as a clue to his personality, an indication that his hostility was largely motivated by self-hatred. She convened a staff conference and invited a psychiatric nurse specialist who suggested that the man was frustrated by his dependency in the hospital on a group of women, whereas in his work he had been a construction foreman accustomed to being in charge. The staff decided to afford him greater freedom to make decisions, however minor, about the schedule for his therapy. A gradual but noticeable improvement ensued. As the man came to feel greater respect from the hospital staff, he began to do more for himself and his hostility subsided. Although the nurse never grew to like the man, her commitment to understanding his medical good within the wider perspective of his unified good revealed that she cared about him.

In the same vein, Edmund D. Pellegrino and David C. Thomasma urge physicians to be mindful of how their services impact patients' overall good. Physicians "should attempt to place the medical good within the larger context of the patient's total good, his value system, way of life, life history, spiritual and temporal commitments."[8] Not only do people deserve care-oriented respect; medical services often fail when they are not related to a person's wider good. In routine cases, patients' choices based on informed consent suffice to indicate their view of their general good. That is because the medical procedure relates to overall good in a fairly straightforward manner: A surgery or drug prescription is essential to return the patient to normal functioning. In some cases, however, patients need help in arriving at a reasoned conception of their good in a medical situation, and they may request special help from the physician. The caring physician then makes an effort to understand the patient's attitudes and way of life.

As a further illustration, consider what it means for teachers to connect the education-specific good of learning with their students' unified good. During the time when Herbert Kohl taught secondary school, some parents asked him to tutor their fourteen-year-old son who was both illiterate and rebellious.[9] Kohl was not obligated to provide the tutoring; it was not part of his job description. Yet, viewing the boy as a challenge, he agreed to meet with him after school twice a week. Throughout this time, Kohl remained focused on the service offered—literacy—and on his student-as-learner. Nevertheless, he developed a strong interest in the boy's progress and conveyed to him the importance of literacy to his overall development. Instead of regarding the boy merely as an interesting guinea pig or a source of extra income, Kohl valued him as an individual, even though he found himself unable to like him.

Reflecting on this example, Lawrence A. Blum pinpoints the difference between teachers who care solely about providing services and those who also care about clients as persons.

> If the *only* object of a teacher's concern is making sure that a pupil understands a certain subject matter, then this teacher does not exemplify teacher caring [about students]. To be caring, the concern must involve some regard for the pupil's overall good and a sense of how the good of learning the specific subject matter fits into the pupil's overall good. With-

out this, one can infer that the teacher values her subject matter but does not seem to have a clear sense of the value of her pupils as persons in their own right.[10]

Caring attitudes are important in marking Blum's and Kohl's distinction. Professionals who care only about providing competent services that pertain to one aspect ("segment") of persons might be motivated by a mixture of compensation and craft motives. Professionals who care about clients typically have these motives mixed together with attitudes of concern for the overall good of clients—as persons having inherent value.

It might be objected that many professional interactions preclude the detailed understanding of clients' well-being involved in the preceding examples: for example, professors teaching large lecture classes, investment brokers helping hundreds of clients, and engineers serving clients they never meet face to face. In reply, it is true that different professions and jobs limit opportunities for caring relationships. Nevertheless, even when interactions with clients are restricted, caring is still possible. Many professors with large classes genuinely care about students and about how the educational experiences they offer connect with students' overall good. The caring is conveyed in how they teach—for example, by trying to connect course topics with their students' lives, by offering an invitation for personal dialogue after class and during office hours, and in general by conveying a sense of shared humanity with them. They are mindful of the overall good of their students as persons, even when they must understand that good in somewhat general terms. In addition to caring about their students as a group, they maintain a sense of their students as individuals. Similarly, investment brokers and engineers can work with a sense of how their profession contributes to their clients' overall good.

A more sweeping objection is that it seems possible for professionals to relate their clients' profession-specific good to their general good without caring very much about them as persons. I agree. Hence, relating profession-specific goods to unified goods is not sufficient by itself to establish caring. What is?

A good pretender can fake any attitude, including caring, and hence no particular behavior provides an absolute proof of caring. But we always live without absolute proof and for practical purposes overall patterns of behavior count as decisive evidence. The evidence for genuine caring is as varied and complex, but also as familiar and commonplace, as the evidence for any other mental state. In distinguishing genuineness from pretense, we look closely at detailed patterns of conduct in their full context. We also take account of a variety of overt or covert giveaways that call into question someone's sincerity: for example, less than complete conscientiousness in providing professional services, degrading jokes told behind a client's back, or dumping a destitute client who fails to pay bills promptly. These are signs, not proof, but they usually suffice to distinguish professionals who genuinely care and those who are "playing a game" as did Clamence.

In any case, the possibility of pretense does nothing to refute our main argument. We should renounce the generalization that professionals respond to clients merely as segmental and replaceable persons who do not matter "in their own right, as particular persons." Roles limit but rarely extinguish possibilities for caring. Roles delineate the content and manner of providing services, but professionals can respond to roles in various ways.[11]

One way is to regard the role is as a mere job description specifying what one must do to serve the profession-specific good of clients. Thus, to be a professor is to prepare for and conduct classes, give tests and assign papers, grade fairly, keep office hours for students who need help, and so on. These duties apply to everyone who holds the job so described. A person holding this conception might be a competent professional, motivated by a combination of self-interest and devotion to professional standards defining competence, but have no significant degree of caring about clients. A quite different way is to embrace the role as a vocation, as a set of activities one is well suited to, strongly identifies with, sees inherent value in, and affirms with commitment, enthusiasm, and caring—in light of personal ideals. Unlike fixed duties and rights governing job descriptions, personal ideals of caring differ considerably among individual professionals, but they are vital sources of meaningful work.

Caring and Justice

I am not suggesting that caring suffices as an ethical theory, with regard to the professions or in general. Caring about clients has great importance, but it is balanced by and even partly understood in terms of other key values. Rather than an independent norm, caring acquires its normative force within a web of moral values that structure, guide, limit, augment, and define each other. Certainly this is true of how caring is related to justice and, in particular, to clients' rights to autonomy.

Carol Gilligan's book *In a Different Voice* engendered an extensive interdisciplinary debate about whether an "ethics of caring" is independent from and preferable to an "ethics of justice."[12] According to Gilligan, caring-centered ethics emphasizes concern for the needs of others, responsiveness to them as individuals, maintaining personal relationships, and engaging in contextual moral reasoning. In contrast, a justice-centered ethics focuses on exercising and respecting rights, being independent and autonomous, and following a hierarchy of universal rules of conduct. Applied to professional-client relationships, the emphasis shifts the locus of moral understanding away from respect for clients' rights and toward caring about their well-being.

Despite Gilligan's insights, we should reject her bifurcation of ethics into caring and justice perspectives.[13] One difficulty is that she attempts to reduce an array of moral perspectives to just two, disregarding the many varieties of virtue ethics, rights ethics, duty ethics, utilitarianism, religious ethics, and other theories expressed inchoately by the people she interviews. Another difficulty is that, however vaguely, she links an ethics of caring to women and an ethics of justice to men in ways that empirical studies have not supported. My primary concern, however, is with the attempt to separate caring and justice.

Rather than constituting a stark contrast between caring and justice, the different patterns of reasons identified by Gilligan are better understood as contrasting ways of caring and interpretations of justice. Consider her example of Amy and Jake, two eleven-year-olds who were asked to respond to Heinz's Dilemma. The dilemma (borrowed from Lawrence Kohlberg) asks whether a man named Heinz should steal a drug necessary to prevent his wife from dying. Jake responds confidently that Heinz should steal the drug on the grounds that a human life is more important than money or property. Amy, who is less confident about what should be done, urges the exploration of alternatives, including further conversation with the pharmacist who refuses to lower the price of the drug.

Gilligan concludes that Jake is arguing according to abstract rules of justice, ordered within a hierarchy of rules, with "save life" being paramount over "respect property." By contrast, Amy is more concerned to preserve caring relationships with the pharmacist and others involved. It is just as accurate to say, however, that Jake and Amy have different conceptions of justice and different ways of manifesting caring in the situation. Or, if that implies too much theoretical sophistication on their part, it is more accurate to conclude that they give different weights to conflicting considerations of justice—respect life, respect property—and they also apply different emphases in understanding what caring for one's wife implies.

Thus, in ascribing a rule-oriented morality to Jake, Gilligan seizes on his comment that "a human life is worth more than money." Yet, she neglects Jake's explanation of why a life is worth more than money: "Because the druggist can get a thousand dollars later from rich people with cancer, but Heinz can't get his wife again." Here Jake seems to say that Heinz should care about his wife more than about money. Far from ignoring personal relationships in favor of abstract rules of justice, Jake has a particular attitude about which caring relationship has priority in the situation: Heinz's relationship with his wife has greater moral significance than the relationship with the pharmacist (whom he sees as price gouging). Again, Gilligan portrays Amy as thinking in terms of caring rather than justice because of her concern to maintain a moral relationship with the pharmacist. Yet, she can just as well be interpreted as applying a conception of justice that seeks to maintain respect for property while valuing human life.

Jake and Amy might also differ in their interpretation of the facts. For example, Amy observes that Heinz might get caught and then be unable to save his wife should she get sick again. This suggests she values life more than property, just as Jake does, but she has a different interpretation of the risks involved in stealing.

Perhaps aware that she went too far in separating justice and caring, Gilligan in subsequent writings suggested that caring and justice perspectives are both applicable to most moral situations, much like two visual perspectives in duck-rabbit perceptual shifts.[14] This proposal, however, does not correct the fundamental error in severing the concepts of justice and caring. It leaves the two conceptual schemas unrelated, whereas neither caring nor justice can be understood in isolation. Caring is interwoven with concern for justice. Thus, some acts of caring are bad, at least overall, precisely because they disregard justice—namely, the individual rights to exercise autonomy—so as to cause objectionable forms of paternalism and dependency. Rights to autonomy constitute a large part of what we ought to attend to in caring about persons. Autonomy is not something separate from persons' needs and well-being; it is central to shaping and defining their happiness.[15]

Caring and justice are connected in many ways, two of which have special relevance to professional ethics. First, justice, which includes respect for rights of autonomy, implies an obligation to care about clients. Second, respect of persons both guides and limits how professionals manifest caring.

To begin with the first connection, the duty to respect persons implies a duty to care about them. To be a moral agent is not merely to manifest respect in outward conduct, but to do so on the basis of attitudes of valuing persons. Some minimal degree of caring is inherent in respect for persons, insofar as respect is an attitude and virtue rather than mere outward conduct. In William Frankena's words, to adopt a moral point of view "is or includes a kind of direct Caring about or Non-Indifference to what goes on in the lives of people and consciously sentient beings as such, including others besides oneself."[16] And as A. I. Melden pointed out, respect for others' rights would have no point unless we cared about their good as persons: "Far from it being the case that a consideration of rights of persons occupies a separate moral domain from that of benevolence, it *depends* upon it; for in the absence of a concern with the well-being of others there could be no sense of the important role that the rights of persons, our own and those of others, play in our lives."[17] To respect persons implies appreciating how their autonomy shapes their lives, self-fulfillment, and happiness.

It might be objected that there cannot be an obligation to care, because caring implies attitudes and emotions not directly under our control. Ethics must be realistic, and Kohl is unrealistic when he suggests that "a teacher has an obligation to care about every student as a learner."[18] We all agree that professionals are obligated to show care, provide appropriate care, and exercise due care, but to require that they do so from any particular motives is unrealistic.

In reply, it is indeed impossible for professionals to care for each client, in the sense of liking, loving, or feeling affection for them. Few, if any, humans are capable of such universal affection. Because "ought implies can," in Kant's words, there is no point in saying that everyone ought to feel affection for all his clients. Nevertheless, caring is a matter of attitudes of valuing, rather than emotions of affection, even though the attitudes are on occasion appropriately expressed in emotions. As the examples of Kohl and the nurse made clear, one need not like clients in order to care about them.

In addition, we can distinguish between (a) the motives for a particular act and (b) the patterns of motivation underlying long-term habits or dispositions to provide competent services. Even if caring about each client were impossible, it would remain possible to cultivate attitudes of caring that become embedded in habits of conduct. Attitudes shape conduct. At least for a great many professionals, dispositions to provide competent services are sustained by attitudes of caring about clients. Many professionals are best able to persevere in demanding careers by maintaining attitudes of caring. To that extent, their professional obligations imply an obligation to cultivate attitudes of caring. The caring enriches the meaning they find in their work, and that meaning is a wellspring of continued commitment.

Trust and Respect

As a general duty, respect for persons might seem too abstract to carry much weight in thinking about professional-client relationships. But although the duty is general, it has special implications within relationships of vulnerability and trust. This brings us to the second connection between caring and respect: Respect for clients guides and limits how professionals manifest caring, and effective caring implies respect for autonomy.

Philosophers have been preoccupied with respect for autonomy. Michael Bayles is typical in this respect: "The central issue in the professional-client relationship is the allocation of responsibility and authority in decision making—who makes what decisions," and hence it is essential that each party in the relationship should respect the other's autonomy (self-determination).[19] Centrality is one thing, however, and completeness something else.

Bayles objects to several general normative models, that is, perspectives delineating morally appropriate roles of professionals and clients, although he admits that the models may apply in special situations. In the "agency model," clients have primary authority; professionals act as hired guns in carrying out clients' directives. This model is objectionable because it disregards other professional responsibilities, including obligations to third parties, obligations to clients to exercise independent judgment about what is good for clients, and responsibilities concerning one's own integrity. In the "paternalism model," professionals have primary authority and act for clients' good without their permission. This model may be appropriate when clients are unable to give consent, for example because an automobile accident left them in a coma, but if embraced as a general model it would violate the rights of autonomous adults. In the "contract model," professionals and clients have equal authority in negotiating their relative roles. This model is flawed because the dramatic inequality of expertise makes equal negotiation unrealistic. The "friendship model" also emphasizes equality but advocates more personal aspects of cooperation and mutuality. This model fails to take seriously how friendships involve "affective commitment" and two-way concern between equals that is atypical of professional relationships.

The appropriate model, according to Bayles, is a trust-oriented or "fiduciary model" in which both professionals and clients actively exercise autonomy and responsibility, albeit in different ways. Clients are vulnerable, both because of the problems they suffer and because they lack the technical understanding possessed by professionals. Nevertheless, they retain the moral authority to guide their lives. Owing to their expertise and institutional roles, professionals often have greater power, authority, and control than do clients, thereby generating temptations to exploit, dominate, or be paternalistic. As a result, it is crucial that professionals be trustworthy in providing competent services while respecting the autonomy of clients. They are obligated to avoid conflicts of interest, supply the client with relevant information, offer competent advice about alternative courses of conduct, and then carry out the express desires of clients based on their informed consent. Clients have the moral authority to consent or refuse consent to professionals' recommendations. This model "allows clients as much freedom to determine how their life is affected as is reasonably warranted on the basis of their ability to make decisions."[20]

At first glance, the fiduciary model seems to generate the same hired-gun problems found in the agency model. Later, however, Bayles emphasizes that professionals have additional responsibilities to third parties, including the general public, that place limits on the extent to which they may follow clients' directives. Of more interest, the fiduciary model creates the impression that the autonomy of competent patients is a fixed given, an authority which the professional reponds to in an encounter without influencing. Professionals supply information and expert advice about the various options open to the clients' choice; clients then opt for a choice suitable to their preferences. (To be sure, the client may lack a capacity for autonomy, as with children and comatose adults.) Yet, despite the appearance of fixity, autonomy can be understood as rational agency that professionals support and strengthen. Caring professionals help empower clients, as the examples of the nurse and teacher illustrate.[21] Paternalistic interference and passive acquiescence to a client's choice are not the only possibilities. In this way, effective caring implies respect for autonomy.

Caring does not enter explicitly into Bayles' fiduciary model. That model requires professionals to provide competent services guided by honesty, candor, diligence, fairness, and discretion (respect for privacy). In addition, they must be loyal to clients, but only in the sense that they "act in behalf of some of their interests," namely, those interests connected with the relevant services—what I call the client's profession-specific good.[22] This minimal notion of loyalty need not involve caring about persons. Indeed, Bayles alludes to caring only negatively, for example when he rejects the friendship model and cautions against loss of professional distance by overidentifying with clients.

I am not rejecting the fiduciary model. Respect for clients' autonomy must indeed remain central in professional-client relationships, given that the dangers of exploitation and misguided instances of paternalism are real. I am suggesting, however, that we understand respect more broadly, as interwoven with caring. Professionals should respect the rights of clients because they should care about their clients as persons.

If respect implies caring, and caring implies respect, perhaps we should develop a Janus-faced conception, "care respect," as Robin Dillon suggests. In explaining this idea, Dillon invokes a distinction between two forms of respect, recognition and appraisal.[23] Recognition-respect is the notion of respect I have been using up to this point: recognition of the moral worth of persons as such. In contrast, appraisal-respect is valuing individuals because of their particular features. Traditionally, recognition-respect has been understood as altogether independent of the particular features of individuals, unlike appraisal-respect. Dillon points out, however, that recognition-respect requires responding to persons as individuals: "We respect persons by caring for them as the particular individuals they are."[24] To emphasize this particularity, Dillon recommends viewing recognition-respect as "care respect."

Dillon's insight is that persons are not mere placeholders in abstract duties to respect autonomy, unrelated to caring about them as persons. Instead, we should respond to them as only partly defined by their social roles and relationships, as persons who substantially define themselves through their interest, attitudes, and values. What counts as respecting one's spouse is different from respecting a colleague, and acting respectfully toward a grocery clerk is different from respectful conduct toward a judge in a courtroom. So, too, showing respect towards clients takes many different forms, depending on the kinds of relationships appropriate within a particular profession and workplace.

To conclude, professionalism does and should evoke personal commitments to caring about clients. These commitments are compatible with the traditional emphasis on respect for clients' autonomy, for caring and respect cannot be understood independently. Respect for clients' autonomy implies caring, even though it also guides and limits how caring is expressed. More needs to be said, however, about the interplay of caring and professional distance, a topic taken up next.

6

PROFESSIONAL DISTANCE

Professionals are criticized for being too detached and also for being insufficiently distanced. On the one hand, physicians are denounced when their clinical detachment leads them to become impersonal toward patients, and engineers are blamed when they grow indifferent to the public affected by their work. On the other hand, partisan journalists are reproached for lacking critical detachment, and therapists are reviled for losing therapeutic distance when they become romantically involved with their clients. What is professional distance (or detachment), when is it desirable, and what are its proper limits? In particular, does it require setting aside all personal values in order to be guided solely by the minimum duties incumbent on all members of a profession, as the consensus paradigm might suggest?

Professional responsibilities do call for some forms of distance that limit the expression of personal values in professional life. Distance does not, however, imply the absence of caring and personal involvement. On the contrary, limited detachment often promotes ideals of caring that are simultaneously personal and professional. After clarifying the concept of distance, I discuss three functions of distance in professional life: coping with difficulties in helping clients, respecting clients' autonomy, and maintaining objectivity. These are not its only functions. For example, much could be said about the dangers of excessive distancing that occurs under the influence of authority (a topic in chapter 8).[1] Nevertheless, the functions discussed here suffice to illustrate its importance and its basic compatibility with personal ideals of caring in professional life.

Moral Psychology

In the present context, distance is not physical or temporal separation, but what then is it? Specifically, is the separation a psychological detachment consisting of attitudes and emotions, together with their behavioral expression? Or is it a moral distance (difference) between the requirements set forth in professional codes of ethics and moral requirements in everyday life? Usually it is both.

Psychological distance refers to the presence or absence of mental states such as emotions, attitudes, motives, and habits of attention, together with their expressions in conduct. For example, Perri Klass reports how she and her fellow medical students acquired self-protective habits. In addition to developing strong self-control over their emotions and liberally enjoying medical humor ("sick jokes"), they established a "linguistic separation" from patients by using medical jargon in their presence, not merely for precision but to keep their patients' suffering at arm's length by concentrating on physical problems. In general, physicians use euphemism and understatement to lower their anxieties: "'This is a not entirely benign procedure,' some doctor will say, and that will be understood to imply agony, risk of complications, and maybe even a significant mortality rate."[2]

By contrast, *moral distance* concerns responsibilities. Specifically, it refers to the requirement that professionals adhere to standards more or less stringent than everyday moral principles, concerning such things as confidentiality, conflicts of interest, caring, and helping. Thus, in "Ruthlessness in Public Life," Thomas Nagel reminds us that public officials are required to separate themselves from some values in their private lives. In part, this "personal detachment in the exercise of official functions" is to ensure that they do not use their power to enrich themselves or their families at the public expense.[3] That implies avoiding conflicts of interest in which private interests (or competing professional interests) threaten professional responsibilities. In part, the detachment consists in heeding standards that are more impartial and impersonal than those in everyday life, standards that heighten concern for overall consequences of social policies regardless of harm to specific individuals. For example, a secretary of defense is duty bound to follow orders from a president, even when the orders have unintended side effects of killing innocent civilians during a war.

Psychological and moral distance can be distinguished but not separated. With regard to Klass's concept of psychological distance, we can ask: Which mental states (attitudes, dispositions) are appropriately cultivated or avoided? The answer is, those states which, respectively, help or hinder professionals in meeting their responsibilities. Klass indicates that physicians use psychological distancing in order to meet onerous duties and to deal with the "terror of responsibility" in matters of suffering and death.[4] Although in this instance the psychological distance is not morally obligatory per se, it does help many individuals in meeting onerous duties. In this way, psychological distance links to moral distance.

With regard to moral distance we can ask: What is the psychological impact of acting on impersonal standards that depart from ordinary morality? At its best, moral distance implies setting uniform standards that ensure quality services to the public. At its worst, moral distance generates dangerous psychological tendencies. Nagel warns that public roles and offices "get between" officials and their actions to diminish moral sensitivity and a sense of personal responsibility: "The combination of special requirements and release from some of the usual restrictions, the ability to say that one is only following orders or doing one's job or meeting one's responsibilities, the sense that one is the agent of vast impersonal forces or the servant of institutions larger than any individual—all these ideas form a heady and sometimes corrupting brew."[5] The corrupting brew helps explain why it is public officials who have committed "the great modern crimes," such as the Holocaust, Soviet oppression, and the Vietnam War.

Because psychological distance alludes to responsibilities, and because moral distance has psychological effects, I will employ a hybrid or Janus-faced concept. Professional distance is psychological insofar as it refers to mental adjustments; it is morally resonant insofar as it refers to professional standards, especially those which depart from ordinary moral standards. In this way, professional distance is a concept in moral psychology—a concept useful in understanding the psychology of professionals in pursuing their responsibilities.

Who or what are professionals distanced *from?* They might be distanced from any of the following: clients, customers, colleagues, the wider public, situations, aspects of situations, a job in its entirety, their own actions, their emotions and interests, their personal life, and elements of ordinary morality. Is there a unifying meaning running through these various types of detachment? In each instance, professional distance is selectively withholding expression of personal values in professional life, whether the values are embodied in emotions, preferences, relationships, conduct, or ideals. Personal values include the widely shared standards of ordinary (nonprofessional) morality applicable in everyday life as well as individual ideals of caring for community, social causes, family, and self-interest. Withholding expression of personal values might imply avoiding particular actions, habits, intimate relationships, emotions, or biases.

The expression "professional detachment" is sometimes used in an honorific way, to imply that withholding personal involvement is desirable. At other times, "detachment" carries pejorative connotations, to imply that professionals are failing to accept responsibility for the immorality in which they collaborate.[6] In contrast, I employ a value-neutral definition that leaves open the questions of how much and what kinds of detachment are desirable in specific contexts. When detachment is appropriate I speak of "proper distance," when it is inappropriately absent I speak of "underdistancing," and when it results in objectionable moral dissociation I speak of "overdistancing."

These terms are borrowed from aesthetics. Aesthetic distance is distance from works of art and other objects of aesthetic appreciation. Like professional distance, aesthetic distance can be understood in psychological or value terms, but typically both. These analogies merit a brief comment.

In a famous essay, Edward Bullough develops a concept of psychological or "psychical distance." Aesthetic enjoyment, he suggests, involves putting a work of art or object in the world "out of gear with our practical, actual self; by allowing it to stand outside the context of our personal needs and ends—in short, by looking at it 'objectively.'"[7] The disengagement is not impersonal and emotionless. Instead, it filters and transforms emotional reactions to aesthetic features. For example, terror caused by encountering fog while at sea can transform into intense enjoyment if we distance ourselves from our usual concern for personal safety and attend to the perceptual features of the fog. At the same time, aesthetic appreciation increases if we maintain some sense of the danger of the fog, thereby enriching its emotional and symbolic meanings. Analogously, limited and selective distancing from everyday values, without complete disengagement, can augment professional commitments; it can promote effective caring.

Although Bullough begins with psychological distance, he quickly invokes the values defining aesthetic appreciation. Conversely, Allan Casebier begins with a value-oriented concept centered on aesthetic sensitivity (a value-laden term) and then shifts his discussion to psychological states. In Casebier's view, distance is a matter of the "appropriate aesthetic feelings [and other responses] that a sensitive observer would have in response to the art object."[8] To distance oneself aesthetically is to attend to the aesthetic features and value of an object, but that involves psychological maneuvers such as avoiding distractions, subduing disruptive passions, or cultivating appreciative feelings. Distancing is value oriented in that it is defined in terms of aesthetic appreciation; it is psychological in that it alludes to mental states and activities that facilitate appreciation. Like professional distance, aesthetic distance is Janus-faced.

To be sure, aesthetic and professional distance differ in significant ways. Most noteworthy, aesthetic distancing frequently disengages practical agency, as an object of beauty engrosses our attention, whereas professional distance furthers the very practical aims of meeting responsibilities to clients, employers, colleagues, and the public. Nevertheless, moral and aesthetic distance are sufficiently analogous to shed light on each other, in particular in thinking about under- and overdistancing.

Both Bullough and Casebier draw this distinction. Underdistancing occurs when personal factors play an excessive or inappropriate role, intruding to disrupt aesthetic appreciation. For example, terror prevents appreciation of the beauty of fog at sea, or jealousy toward a spouse prevents appreciation of a performance of *Othello*. In contrast, overdistancing occurs when aesthetic objects are altogether severed from our interests, rendering them alien objects that fail to engage our emotions. It also occurs when distance is inappropriate, for example when an aesthete contemplates the hues of splattered blood and mangled forms at the scene of a car accident rather than offering aid. Proper aesthetic distance is a mean, in the Confucian-Aristotelian sense: the reasonable middle ground between extremes of excess and deficiency in which we respond appropriately.

By analogy, proper professional distance is a reasonable response in pursuing professional values by avoiding inappropriate personal involvements while maintaining personal engagement and responsibility. In contrast, underdistancing is the undesirable interference of personal values with professional standards. And overdistancing is the undesirable loss of personal involvement, whether in the form of denying one's responsibility for one's actions or in the form of failing to care about clients and community.

Precisely what this means varies according to the role played by distancing. When the role is to assist professionals in coping with difficult situations, underdistancing amounts to inappropriate intimacy or loss of emotional self-control; overdistancing is excessive impersonality. When the role is to support respect for clients' autonomy, underdistancing is an objectionable form of paternalism; overdistancing is the moral dissociation of hired guns who disavow moral responsibility for collaboration in wrongdoing. And when the role is to promote objectivity, underdistancing is allowing biases to have inappropriate influence; overdistancing is loss of commitment to the full array of applicable values.

Coping

The first role of distance centers on the needs of professionals in coping with demanding careers—their needs to maintain self-control, persevere under hardship, sustain good relationships with clients and colleagues, and simply survive throughout decades of challenging work. The distancing is from clients, as well as from particular aspects of work and from their own emotions, and yet distancing is justified by how it enables professionals to help their clients. Hence, a paradox arises: Professionals need distance from clients in order to serve them, detachment in order to care. The paradox is only superficially puzzling, however. As will become clear, the requisite detachment is limited and selective in ways that leave ample room for caring about clients.

I begin with a few illustrations of coping-oriented distancing, in addition to those already mentioned from Perri Klass.

Distress and Self-Control

Distancing might be episodic (occasional) or dispositional (habitual). In addition, dispositional distancing can be context-specific (limited to particular types of situations) or global (habitual across many types of situations throughout a career). Either way, professionals are distanced from specific features of work that cause distress. For example, physicians do best to focus on technical procedures when performing dangerous surgery rather than being engulfed with compassion for their patients. Emergency room attendants cannot do their job if they lose clinical detachment by fainting at the sight of blood. Nurses cannot be supportive if they grimace in horror at patients' disfigurement. And forensic pathologists might be unable to perform autopsies properly if they are thrust into deep depression at the sight of a dead infant who reminds them of their own child. In all these situations, clinical detachment is a prerequisite for helping patients or for doing one's job competently. The detachment consists in avoiding, subduing, or withholding expression of potentially disruptive emotions.

Stress and Perseverence

Some professionals, including nurses, teachers, and social workers, are at special risk of burnout from long hours, low pay, and lack of recognition. They need to maintain balance in their lives in order not to become overly involved in jobs that do not suffice to bring self-fulfillment. Avoiding overinvolvement with work means not allowing one's job to consume so much time and energy that one is left continually anxious, angry, or psychologically numbed. Here the distancing is from one's role as a professional or from a job in its entirely.

Decorum

Professionals need to maintain a sense of decorum that elicits respect and confidence from clients. Not only must they be competent and in control, they must appear to be so to clients. Underdistancing occurs when professionals fail to withhold disruptive expressions of emotions, such as anger, hatred, or blame toward a client.

Appropriate emotional expression has a highly personalized dimension. For example, psychiatrist Robert Klitzman reports that early in his career one of his patients asked to dance with him at a hospital party. He declined, worrying that boogying with a patient, especially in front of other patients, might blur perceptions of his authority as a therapist: "I would have liked to participate. I generally liked dancing but felt constrained in my white coat. Somehow dancing with patients went against the sense I had been given of how a psychiatrist was supposed to behave."[9] Klitzman's reaction was not idiosyncratic, nor was it strictly required by his professional role. Faced with the same situation, another psychiatrist might have a different sense of role-appropriate behavior, and perhaps at a later, more confident, stage of his career Klitzman himself might respond differently.

Teamwork and Collegiality

Attempts to maintain respect from colleagues sometimes lead to distancing from clients. Increasingly, professional activities are carried out in concert with other professionals, thereby requiring sensitivity to the subtle interplay of group dynamics. Physician Melvin Konner suggests that team play can dampen some desirable responses to patients, as it strengthens social organizations by encouraging the flow of genuine feelings among a hospital's team members. He draws attention to the sense of comfort and protection in knowing that patients' dependency and fears are "dispersed among the team members." Furthermore, "disloyalty to the team is always dangerous, and it can be remarkably subtle. Too great an involvement with patients can in itself be sufficient to suggest it . . . through an implied accusation leveled against the other team members: I care more than you do for patients, therefore you do not care enough."[10] In acknowledging the legitimate role of team play in distancing behavior, Konner also notes how excessive (over-) distancing can "suppress at least some nurturing impulses toward patients."

Taken together, these illustrations suggest three conclusions. First, within proper limits, emotional distancing contributes to helping clients by enabling professionals to do their jobs competently and efficiently. Episodically, professionals cannot provide help if they are emotionally overwhelmed at the moment when bleeding must be stopped or encouragement offered. Dispositionally, energy and commitment cannot be sustained throughout a career when underdistancing causes burnout, constant friction with colleagues, or loss of respect for clients. The primary justification for professional detachment, then, is in terms of the professional responsibilities it serves. A supporting consideration is professionals' self-interest and satisfaction in their jobs.

Second, overdistancing can harm clients and professionals alike. If unrestrained, habits of distancing acquire a momentum of their own that diminishes caring for clients and lowers quality of services. These habits also erode the pursuit of personal ideals of caring that give meaning to work. That is especially true when the habits are reinforced by impersonal bureaucracies and economic forces. As Chekhov cautions in "Ward No. 6," "People who have official, professional relations with someone else's suffering—judges, authorities, physicians, for example—become so inured in the course of time, from force of habit, that even should they want to be sympathetic, they are incapable of any but a formal concern for their clients."[11] To do their jobs, as well as to find their work rewarding in terms of their ideals of caring, professionals need to maintain an active capacity for empathy.

Third, both in theory and in practice we should avoid confusing proper distance with overdistancing, where overdistancing suggests a loss of caring and the absence of integration of professional life with personal values. Episodic detachment, by definition, is contained and limited to particular situations. It does not require refraining on other occasions from experiencing and expressing emotions subdued earlier. For example, medical students doing their first autopsies must learn to steel their emotions.[12] Before or after, however, they may do well to talk about the experience, either informally with friends or during therapy if the experience proves especially distressing. Dispositional distancing implies more extensive and systematic control over emotions. Nevertheless, appropriate habits of subduing emotions and their expression remain limited and focused on particular aspects of work, or on the overall role of work in a balanced life, rather than requiring the complete absence of emotional involvement. Neither episodic nor dispositional distancing requires the absence of personal caring and ideals.

Consider an objection. Howard J. Curzer contends that health care professionals should not care, in any emotionally resonant sense, about their patients. Although he limits his thesis to professionals working in major medical centers within industrialized nations, his arguments, if sound, would seem to apply more widely. Physicians and nurses, he claims, should take care of (minister to) patients by providing competent medical care, but they should not care about (take an interest in) them, care for (have a liking for) them, nor have emotions of caring toward them. They should be benevolent, but only in the semitechnical sense of providing care in a spirit of general good will, without having emotional responses of caring. They should maintain a comforting bedside manner by *pretending* to have emotions of caring while avoiding compassion for patients' terrible suffering, sadness when they die prematurely, and regret for their tragedies. They "should act *as if* they are significantly emotionally attached, but in fact should involve their feelings relatively little. They should be no more emotionally attached to their own patients than to someone else's patients or to the proverbial man on the street. . . . They should hug patients who need to be hugged. But they should not really care."[13]

In my terms, Curzer defends overdistancing as the remedy for underdistancing. He argues for systematic emotional detachment (overdistancing) by claiming that inappropriate emotional attachment (underdistancing) causes a host of problems: burnout, paternalism (as caring slides into control over patients), unwarranted intrusions on patients' privacy, favoritism of one patient over another, loss of objectivity in making diagnoses, and increased health care costs when caring leads physicians to order too many expensive tests in an all-out effort to help each patient. Of course, by definition, excessive emotional involvement can cause problems: "Excessive" implies placing at risk sound judgment and successful coping. The alternative to inappropriate emotional involvements, however, is not emotional indifference, but instead proper distancing.

In citing every possible way that emotions undermine helping, Curzer neglects the contributions of emotions to good medical care. Systematically stifling emotional responses to patients would render physicians insensitive to their patients' suffering, or at least would erode their capacities for empathy that are vital in making accurate diagnoses and providing appropriate services based on a nuanced understanding of their patients' suffering.[14] In addition, systematic emotional indifference to patients can carry over to relationships with colleagues, patients' family members, and one's own family.

Even with regard to death, complete detachment is usually not the best way to cope. Nurses report that helping a person to die at the right time can bring positive emotions of peace and acceptance of death as a natural process. Some nurses report a sense of privilege in comforting people during their final hours.[15] Their deep frustrations do not arise from patients but instead from physicians who aggressively provide medical intervention when there is no hope of benefit to the patient. Here, as elsewhere, healthy emotions are sound guides to providing good medical care.

Personal ideals of caring greatly enrich the meaning of work. In the helping professions, a sense of meaning is sustained through caring relationships with people helped. As one nurse states, "The people I've cared about, felt something for, become close to, the people I've invested a certain amount of myself in—these are the people I've learned something from. They are the reason I stay in nursing."[16] Additional personal values play a supportive role; for example, religious and humanistic attitudes concerning death enable health professionals to avoid being paralyzed by grief when patients die.

In short, professionals need to find the reasonable middle ground ("golden mean") between the excess of inappropriate involvements and the deficiency of being callous or indifferent. The middle ground is not an average on a scale, but instead the contextual understanding of when emotions should be blocked and when they should be fully experienced, and that understanding must be tailored to one's own personality. Physician Eric Cassell sees this balance between involvement and detachment paradoxical: "The painful paradox of the relationship between doctor and patient is that for it to be employed to the fullest in the care of the patient, maximum possible openness to the patient must be present—but to be open is to be physically and emotionally endangered."[17] Mitigating the sting of paradox, Samuel Gorovitz speaks instead of "a tension between detachment and sensitivity that calls upon the physician to strike a balance between letting emotions run rampant and suppressing them to a point that dehumanizes the physician beyond the point of successful interpersonal interactions."[18] As this language of paradox and tension suggests, finding the appropriate middle ground can be difficult, even if we allow substantial room for differences among reasonable persons. It is especially easy to slide, in theory and in practice, from selective detachment to full-blown separation.[19]

Client Autonomy

The second role of professional detachment shifts the focus from professionals to clients, as well as to employers, consumers, and others served by one's work. Detachment fosters and partly constitutes respect for others' autonomy. Insofar as this respect is delineated by professional standards, moral distancing—as opposed to psychological distancing—concerns the gap between professional and ordinary moral standards. Clients have the authority to seek, accept, guide, and withdraw from professional services concerning such things as legal help, financial services, technological products, and what is done to their bodies. Professionals sometimes disagree with clients about the most desirable course of action, whether because of differences in values or understanding. But, after offering education and counsel, they must either withdraw their services or accede to clients' judgments, thereby distancing themselves from their own judgments about desirable conduct.

Emotional distance might be involved, but what is primarily at stake is agental distance: the distance of actions grounded in the requirement to act on clients' decisions—as the client's agent—rather than on a professional's value judgments. Within limits, agental distance is required by the shared professional standards that assure the public a minimum standard of quality in professional services, maintain trust between professionals and the public, and create rules for fair competition among professionals. Yet, although shared standards limit the expression of personal ideals in professional life, they do not banish them.

Two dangers arise: underdistancing in the form of objectionable paternalism (Curzer's concern) and overdistancing by becoming a hired gun who disavows moral accountability for the goals pursued by clients (Nagel's concern). Both dangers generate a host of complicated issues that can be framed in terms of distance.

Paternalism

Paternalism (or parentalism) is intervening in others' exercise of autonomy with the aim of promoting their good but without their voluntary and informed consent. Objectionable instances of paternalism constitute underdistancing, in a moral sense: They fail to properly separate the professional's values from the clients' legitimate moral authority to guide their own lives. Not all paternalism is objectionable, however, and paternalism can even be obligatory when clients are unable to give consent. Examples range from an emergency room physician's temporary control over a person who is temporarily incapacitated from injuries in an automobile accident to a guardian's permanent authority over a legally incompetent individual.

Exactly when paternalism occurs is a matter of dispute. There are different meanings of the terms used to define paternalism, and not everyone agrees on which definitions to employ: autonomy, voluntary and informed consent, intervention, and a person's good. In particular, autonomy (self-determination) can be understood in either a weak or strong sense. In a weak sense, it means opting for something without being coerced by others. In a strong sense, it means that a person makes decisions from a satisfying array of desirable options, does so voluntarily, and proceeds in a rational way on the basis of full relevant information and reasonable preferences. Patients who opt for suicide might act autonomously in the weak sense (uncoerced choice), but they may be too depressed to act rationally and hence autonomously in the strong sense (rational choice). There are two corresponding senses of paternalism. The physician who prevents the suicide may be paternalistic if the weak sense of autonomy is used to define paternalism, but not paternalistic if the strong sense is used. To complicate matters further, autonomy admits of degrees according to the extent of voluntariness, rationality, and options. Paternalism is a matter of degree along these same dimensions.[20]

Assuming we could agree about what paternalism is, complicated issues remain about when it is justified, and those issues bear directly on what proper distance is. Within the Western tradition of individualism, voiced not only by libertarian rights ethicists but also by some utilitarians such as Mill (in *On Liberty*), paternalism toward competent adults is justified only in rare and restricted situations, primarily those that support a client's overall autonomy. Professional services often play that supporting role, for example, in restoring the health of patients who are temporily incapacitated. Yet abuses are all too common as professionals exceed their proper authority. "Proper authority" means their morally justified social and institutional authority, but the problems are also linked to their expert authority (expertise). Typically their expertise extends to making diagnoses of problems and offering recommendations, the justification of which clients may be unable to assess. As a result, it is a constant temptation for professionals to assume they know what is best for clients, not only in light of technical data but in value terms. To cite a familiar example, physicians trained to extend life may take for granted that an operation is mandatory and pressure a patient to sign a consent form against her deepest desires.

To use another example, social workers and counselors confront a variety of situations in which their personal values differ from those of people they serve. Consider a caseworker at a family social service agency whose clients include college students.[21] One client is a nineteen-year-old who seeks help in adjusting to his emerging sexual orientation as a gay man. If the caseworker holds religious views strongly opposed to homosexuality, is he justified in discouraging the young man from pursuing a gay orientation, motivated by a concern for his spiritual welfare? Decidedly not. Doing so would violate two fundamental professional standards, each of which is justified by basic respect for persons: (i) "The social worker should make every effort to foster maximum self-determination on the part of clients"; (ii) "The social worker should not practice, condone, facilitate, or collaborate with any form of discrimination on the basis of race, color, sex, sexual orientation. . . ."[22] When social workers feel unable to distance themselves from their religious beliefs so as to be able to provide help (without violating their integrity), they should refer the client to another professional who can help.

In short, respect for clients' autonomy makes agental distance morally mandatory. It places strong limits on how far professionals are permitted to act on their own value perspectives even in seeking to promote the good of clients. But it does not follow that professionals should altogether abandon their personal value perspectives when helping clients.

Hired Guns

Hired guns will do whatever clients request, even when the request is morally objectionable. Typically, compliant professionals will disavow responsibility for how they contribute to a client's wrongdoing, excusing or rationalizing their conduct as required by professional detachment and respect for clients' autonomy. Yet, usually the real motive is self-seeking—to please clients in order to maximize income. For example, many cosmetic surgeons are willing to perform any service in return for large fees, rather than candidly tell a client that their services are not worth the cost in money and suffering.[23] Even without self-interest as a motive, professionals are tempted to adopt attitudes of hired guns when they function as the agents of their clients. For example, when properly authorized, insurance agents and stock brokers perform acts that are regarded by law as the acts of their clients; managers' actions count as the acts of the corporation; and perhaps most dramatically, attorneys' acts in representing clients count as clients' acts.

To pursue the last example, attorneys cannot be expected to agree with all the moral choices made by their clients. Within wide limits, it is both legally and morally desirable for professionals to respect the autonomy of clients who employ professionals as their agents to do what they cannot do themselves, at least not conveniently or competently. To that extent, professionals are permitted to distance themselves morally from the goals pursued by their clients. Here, moral distance consists in not being fully responsible for the consequences of clients' decisions; psychological distance consists in not regarding oneself as being responsible. The American Bar Association goes further, however, encouraging complete detachment by insisting that attorneys have no responsibility for their clients' decisions, as long as they act within the bounds of the law.[24] The American legal tradition encourages defense attorneys to be guided by two key values, once a client is accepted: neutrality in representing and promoting clients' interests regardless of the merits of clients' character or specific objectives, and partisanship in aggressively pursuing the client's interests (within legal bounds).[25]

Taken to an extreme, neutrality and partisanship encourage attorneys to disavow personal accountability for helping their clients pursue immoral goals. In practice, however, attorneys differ considerably in the degree to which they endorse partisanship and neutrality. Rand and Dana Jack conducted a survey of attorney responses to the following case: "Suppose that you are an attorney in a divorce proceeding, and your client seeks custody of the two young children of the marriage. In the course of your representation your client gives you a bundle of documents that inadvertently contains a letter bearing on the fitness of your client to have custody of the children. . . .

In your own mind the information clearly makes your client a marginal parent and the other party a far superior parent."[26] In a variation of the case, the letter contains a threat of bodily harm to the children. The Jacks learned that some of the attorneys they interviewed were willing to represent their clients regardless of even severe damage to the children, but most felt that the children's welfare should be taken into account, at least in trying to counsel the client against pursuing his custody battle.

As noted in chapter 3, the ABA code permits—but does not require—attorneys to break confidentiality in order to warn third parties of severe dangers. Hence the code permits attorneys to make their own decisions regarding the Jacks' case, presumably taking into account their personal convictions and ideals.

Moving from what attorneys say they would do to what they ought to do, there is a significant middle ground between (a) being completely responsible for clients' goals and choices, and (b) having no responsibility in doing whatever clients request. Despite economic and organizational pressures, attorneys retain substantial freedom to reject cases on moral grounds. They also have the opportunity to offer moral as well as legal counsel. As David Luban argues, there is a strong moral presumption against attorneys furthering immoral ends (bearing in mind that defending a clients' basic rights can be a good end regardless of whether overall utility is promoted).[27] In offering counsel, attorneys must avoid objectionable forms of paternalism by respecting clients as people who have moral authority over their lives, while at the same time providing calm and reasonable perspective on their clients' problems.

The same is true with regard to other professions. Elizabeth Wolgast warns that we have gone too far in establishing institutions and practices that authorize professionals to speak for others without themselves being accountable for what those others do. We have created far too many "responsibility-free zones" which "obscure the determination" of who is to be held to account for actions.[28] Wolgast urges us to stop thinking of managers as mere instruments of corporations, government officials as mere tools of bureaucracies, and professionals in general as hired guns. While acknowledging the validity of pursuing justified responsibilities attached to social roles, individuals are accountable both for choices to pursue professional roles and for not abusing those roles. In respecting their clients' autonomy, professionals must be accountable for finding the reasonable middle ground between objectionable paternalism and reducing themselves to mere instruments for achieving their clients' immoral ends.

Objectivity

A third role of professional distance is to maintain objectivity, that is, critical detachment, impartiality, the absence of distorting biases and blinkers.

Underdistancing occurs when professionals allow biases to distort their judgment. Overdistancing occurs when they become disengaged from the wider set of values that should guide their work. These values include justified personal ideals whose pursuit is consistent with professional objectivity. Because all professions require skilled judgment, objectivity is a universal professional virtue, yet its focus and appropriate standards vary. In particular, its focus might be truth, adjudication, evaluation, or conflicts of interest.

Truth

Objectivity is central to intellectual honesty in each of its two dimensions: (i) truthfulness, which is commitment to standards of inquiry that define an unbiased search for truth, and (ii) trustworthiness, which is conscientiousness in pursuing and reporting truth.[29] Negligently allowing biases to operate violates truthfulness; it also betrays the trust of colleagues, the public, and institutions that conduct or rely on the results of science.

Objectionable biases take many forms. For example, in science, objectivity and intellectual honesty are understood as following appropriate scientific methodology. The motives for dishonest science, at the level of either individuals or institutions, range from personal ambition and greed to wider social and economic pressures. One form of dishonest science is deliberate fraud, whereby a scientist is fully aware that the data recorded or reported is falsified, misleading, or plagiarized. Another form is preventable self-deception and wishful thinking in which a scientist slants or misinterprets data without consciously intending to, but does so in ways that should have been prevented. In between deliberate fraud and negligent self-deception is sheer sloppiness.[30]

An interesting and complex historical case involves personal commitments that clash with scientific commitments. Today, one cannot be a reputable biologist while repudiating evolutionary theory, the foundation of modern biology. Things were less clear in the nineteenth century. Philip Gosse was one of the nineteenth century's most distinguished marine biologists.[31] He was also a Christian fundamentalist. The publication in 1859 of Darwin's theory prompted a major intellectual crisis that led him to write a book arguing that God created the earth about six thousand years ago but with the appearance that it existed much longer. It is clear that Gosse's fundamentalist beliefs overrode his standards as a distinguished scientist. Was he guilty of bad faith, self-deception, and lack of integrity?

His son, Edmund Gosse, offers a more subtle analysis that suggests his father's integrity was both substantial and flawed. His father was a person of conscience even though he lacked the full set of intellectual virtues necessary for maintaining complete integrity as a scientist. His mind was too narrow. He lacked imaginative vision and the humility to remain open to the scientific evidence even when it conflicted with his cherished personal convictions. Ultimately, he lacked self-knowledge of how his religious dogmatism distorted his commitment to scientific standards. The case indicates the limits placed on personal commitments that conflict with professional standards of excellence.

In journalism, to consider another example, the question is more complex because the standards for honesty are not as sharply delineated as in science. Journalism is driven by newsworthiness, that is, having sufficient importance and interest to warrant reporting.[32] At the same time, journalism is something more than profit-producing entertainment. Stephen Klaidman and Tom L. Beauchamp argue that journalists ought to publish reports answering to the needs of "reasonable readers."[33] What those needs are depends in part on targeted audiences but, in general, journalists ought to provide adequate amounts of relevant information, offer substantial understanding of events, remain balanced by providing a fair presentation of the main competing interpretations of events, achieve accuracy through precise wording and meticulous references to sources, and remain unbiased. Objectivity is lost when these virtues are absent.

As a final example, objectivity plays an important role in the humanities, including philosophy, history, and literary criticism. These value-oriented disciplines have less precise standards and methodologies than does science. Nevertheless, at their best they maintain high standards of clarity of thought, rigor of argument, respect for evidence, self-scrutiny in uncovering and removing biases, openness to alternative reasonable views and to criticism, willingness to engage in critical dialogue with other investigators and submit one's work to peer review, respect for free speech, and tolerance of diverse views.[34]

With regard to all the above professions, the ideal of objectivity has been under assault for some time. The assault comes from many directions, including Marxism, cultural relativism, postmodernism, and some versions of feminism. A central criticism is that objectivity is presented as an ideal of value-neutrality, whereas in fact the standards of objectivity are established by and used to the advantage of groups in power. The interests of the privileged, not a disinterested pursuit of truth, lie just below the surface of pretensions of objectivity.

Replying fully to these forms of skepticism would take us too far afield, but this much can be said here (and more in chapter 7). It is a confusion to think that objectivity requires complete value-neutrality of the sort involved in overdistancing: severing one's work from personal commitments.[35] The confusion arises from equating values with biases and then inferring that, because objectivity requires avoiding bias, it thereby requires complete value-neutrality. But values are not automatically biases. A bias is a belief, emotion, desire, or value that, if unchecked, distorts the truth and undermines the honesty of inquiries and inquirers. In contrast, justified and relevant values enable investigators to discover truth and maintain objectivity. That is obvious when the value is honesty, understood as truthfulness (as well as trustworthiness), but it also applies to other justified moral values. For example, we are not biased when we condemn Nazi Germany or American slavery. On the contrary, this value judgment provides the interpretive framework for understanding the meaning of what occurred.

In fact, many personal values are compatible with and promote the objective pursuit of truth. Thus, a scientist like Gertrude Elion might be driven by her strong social commitments to pursue selective lines of drug research without being biased in how she pursues the inquiry. Or a journalist can be strongly partisan and acknowledge as much openly in an editorial column (an appropriate forum for partisanship) without being biased. Honesty requires acknowledging one's values openly, but it does not require removing their influence in situations where value-guided interpretations further moral understanding. Those values include commitments to an informed citizenry, the public's right to know, the legitimate interests of specific audiences, but also more specific ideals about morally good communities.

Similarly, in critiquing public institutions and policies, intellectuals have the responsibility to develop and present their value-laden interpretations. In doing so, they must sustain a critical detachment that enables them, in the words of Edward W. Said, "publicly to raise embarrassing questions, to confront orthodoxy and dogma (rather than to produce them), to be someone who cannot easily be co-opted by governments or corporations."[36] The requisite detachment is not from all personal values but instead from narrow biases and self-interest. Said's career illustrates the virtues he praises, frequently speaking truth to power in defending unpopular causes such as restoring the rights of disenfranchised Palestinians.

Adjudication

Impartiality enters prominently into resolution of disputes. For example, in law the disputes might concern distributing limited resources or assigning punishments and penalties. Here, justice and fairness are the central values, although their requirements overlap with honesty. Thus, judges must uphold laws rather than base their rulings on direct applications of personal conscience. In distancing themselves from their individual vision of what the law ought to be, judges have less room than many professionals for integrating their personal values into their work. The justification for this restriction is clear: A legal system is morally justified only if it respects individual rights in ways that are at least roughly consistent and predictable. That implies not only restricting bias but also limiting the expression of personal values.[37]

It does not follow that personal ideals should play no role whatsoever in the professional lives of judges. We can distinguish between (a) applying personal ideals to justify participation in a social practice such as judging, and (b) applying personal ideals directly to particular situations.[38] Americans affirm their basic social practices of law, politics, and economics because of a diversity of moral and religious views. The moral views include arguments that are more or less sophisticated versions of human rights ethics, social contract theory, utilitarianism, pragmatism, and nationalism. Religious arguments include those rooted in all the major world religions as well as in innumerable smaller sects. Although it is usually inappropriate for judges to apply these moral and religious values directly to particular cases before them, it is legitimate for the ideals to undergird their commitments to the system of justice in which they participate (a topic to which I return in chapter 10).

Moreover, even the most restrictive professional roles leave some room for personal discretion. For good reason, judges are usually allowed discretion in assigning punishment and tort liabilities. When discretion is altogether removed, both mercy and justice are compromised. For example, California's "three strikes" law, which mandated lifetime jail sentences for third felony convictions, resulted in numerous injustices in assigning excessive punishment to nonviolent offenders, as well as inforcing the release of some earlier-convicted violent defenders because of jail overcrowding. In very rare instances, judges should subvert mandatory-sentencing laws, as illustrated by the following statement by a judge concerning a drug law:

> This is ridiculous law, passed in the heat of passion without any thought of its real consequences. I absolutely refuse to send to prison for twenty years a young boy who has done nothing more than sell a single marijuana cigarette to a buddy. The law was not intended for such cases. . . . I simply will not give excessive sentences and where the legislature leaves me no alternative, I will lower the charge or dismiss altogether.[39]

In any case, within the legally allowed areas of discretion, personal values sometimes legitimately influence judges' verdicts. That is why society needs to select judges who combine compassion, social conscience, and toughness.

To balance the preceding example, consider an instance of toughness undergirded by personal ideals. Before she became a supreme court justice, Sandra Day O'Connor was elected to an Arizona County Superior Court in the early 1970s, running on a law-and-order platform. In one case she had to sentence a woman who pleaded guilty to kiting $3,500 in bad checks.[40] The woman had two small children and had been abandoned by her husband. O'Connor assigned a 5–10 year sentence, which would mean 1.5 years in prison before parole. O'Connor was not callous. Reportedly, she broke into tears in her chambers following the sentencing and the mother's plea, "What about my babies?" We can disagree about whether the sentence was unduly harsh, but in doing so we should acknowledge that O'Connor's personal ideals that had won her election were legitimately exercised on that occasion.

Evaluation

Objectivity plays an important role when managers evaluate subordinates, judges evaluate contestants, and teachers evaluate students. For example, teachers' grading scales differ, not only by level of education (elementary, secondary, undergraduate, graduate) and at different schools, but also among individuals working in comparable settings. Professors, in particular, have considerable discretion in establishing their grading scale, in line with their educational philosophy. Once set, however, standards require impartiality in distributing grades. Teachers cannot avoid liking some students more than others, but professionalism requires setting aside these attachments when assigning grades. In many professions—especially psychiatry, counseling, and social work—sexual relationships with clients pose too great a risk to the professional detachment essential in helping.

There is no contradiction in saying that evaluations should be unbiased while allowing a role for personal ideals in guiding attitudes toward practices of evaluation. In general, we need to distinguish (a) the motives and goals pursued and (b) the procedures and critical standards of analysis. Professional norms do and should dominate procedures and standards and thereby require setting aside any conflicting personal values. But motives and goals are legitimately guided by values that are simultaneously personal and professional.

Conflicts of Interest

Nowhere are questions about objectivity of greater concern and complexity than in dealing with conflicts of interest. In a wide sense, conflicts of interest occur whenever professionals or other persons in official roles have interests that pose a significant threat to meeting the responsibilities attached to the roles. Official roles are those defined by rule-structured activities within groups or organizations. Hence, conflicts of interest were involved in many of the cases already discussed, including scientists who allow desires to publish to slant their interpretation of data and counselors who have sexual affairs with their current clients.

Some conflicts of interest are unavoidable. In particular, it has been argued that the standard system of accepting fees for service embodies the temptation to provide unnecessary services in order to maximize payments.[41] Most conflicts of interest are prima facie objectionable, but some of them are tolerable when openly acknowledged and when permission is granted by clients or employers. For example, a professor who takes on additional teaching at another university ("moonlighting") divulges this information to a department head who may give it her blessing, seeing the experience as valuable to the faculty member professionally, without posing unacceptable threats to departmental duties.

In general terms, the explanation of why conflicts of interest are usually objectionable follows from their definition: They threaten professional duties. But determining precisely when they pose unacceptable threats to specific duties, all things considered, is a task that needs to be explored within the contexts of particular professions. Most often the source of objection involves some personal benefit, such as money or power, that in no way justifies risking one's service to clients or employers. At other times personal ideals, including altruistic-oriented ideals, threaten professional duties in unacceptable ways. That was illustrated by the social worker whose objections to homosexuality distort her interactions with gay clients and their family members. Professional distance requires taking special precautions to prevent such biases from undermining professional duties. Nevertheless, far from threatening professional duties, justified personal ideals often support them.

To conclude, I have argued that professional distance limits but does not outlaw personal ideals from professional life, and that distance becomes morally objectionable when it leads to wholesale loss of personal involvement. In doing so, I made sense of why professionals are sometimes criticized for being too detached and at other times for lacking sufficient distance. Appropriate distance is a reasonable mean lying between the extremes of too much and too little influence of personal values and passions. The delineation of those extremes differs according to whether the focus in understanding distance is (a) emotional self-control, limits on intimacy, and other tools for coping with challenging careers, (b) respect for clients' autonomy that limits paternalism without sanctioning hired guns, or (c) preventing biases from operating in seeking and communicating truth, adjudicating disagreements, making evaluations, and causing harm through conflicts of interest. Whatever its focus, professional distance leaves room for and even supports personal ideals of caring.

7

ADVOCACY IN EDUCATION

Should professors advocate their views on controversial moral issues in the classroom, or should they try to be value-neutral, leaving promotion of their values to extracurricular activities such as publishing, scholarly presentations, public service, and private conversations with students? This *advocacy issue* became urgent during the recent "campus wars" in which the liberty of professors and authority of universities was challenged on several fronts, but it should not be dismissed as a red herring invented by conservative politicians and journalists who used it to their advantage.[1] The advocacy issue raises perennial concerns about good teaching and professional ethics in higher education. It also provides an interesting area in which to explore how the personal ideals of professionals shape their daily work.

I argue that professional responsibilities justify advocating personal ideals and value commitments pertinent to a professor's discipline (which includes its interdisciplinary dimensions). These responsibilities are precisely the ones emphasized in the consensus paradigm, namely, the shared duties incumbent on all professors. Accordingly, shared duties can actually imply personal commitments in professors' work rather than ruling them out. If much advocacy is both desirable and inevitable, the challenge is to distinguish acceptable from unacceptable forms, especially in the gray area of undue influence where inappropriate pressures distort the learning process without amounting to overt coercion, indoctrination, or proselytizing.

Truth, Autonomy, and Authority

In a wide sense, advocacy is publicly asserting one's views about any controversial matter concerning facts or values, but I will focus on advocating values. Thus, citing statistics about abortions is not advocacy unless it is done in a context of expressing approval or disapproval of abortion (or policies and laws about abortion).

Advocacy takes many forms. *Conscious* advocacy implies self-awareness of the advocacy, and *unconscious* advocacy occurs without that awareness. *Direct* advocacy is overt affirmation of one's values, and *indirect* advocacy is implicit or disguised expression of them. *Strong* advocacy is endorsing values with the intention of getting others to share them; *weak* advocacy is endorsing values without deliberately trying to influence others; and *moderate* advocacy is conveying hope that students will share one's value perspective, without actively seeking to persuade them. I will have in mind all these forms, aware that the campus wars center on conscious, direct, strong advocacy whereby professors deliberately try to get students to share their value perspectives.

Where to begin? Civil libertarians rivet attention on professors' academic freedom and affirm a virtually unlimited right to advocacy in the classroom. By itself, this appeal to academic freedom is one-sided and perhaps self-defeating within the context of the culture wars. It merely reinforces the charge that "tenured radicals" are avoiding public accountability for how they pursue their political agendas in the classroom. Academic freedom includes students' rights of inquiry and free speech that limit professors' academic freedom.[2] Most important, professors' academic freedom is justified by more basic professional responsibilities to serve the goals of education.

What are those goals? Any detailed answer will be contested, especially if it is rooted in a fundamental vision of desirable ways of life promoted by education. The same is true, perhaps in a lesser degree, regarding goals in other professions. To repeat an example used earlier, everyone agrees that promoting health is the goal of medicine and providing justice is the aim of law, but the precise nature of health and justice are disputed. Is health entirely a matter of physiology, or does it include mental and social well-being as well as moral or spiritual health? Is justice solely a matter of liberty rights, or are welfare rights equally essential?

I have argued against reducing professional ethics to codified principles developed as a consensus within a profession and incumbent on all its members. At the same time, I have emphasized the importance of codified principles in establishing a shared framework, indeed a backbone, for professional ethics. With regard to university teaching, the codified shared duties actually imply a role for personal commitments. The American Association of University Professors' (AAUP's) Statement on Professional Ethics specifies the goals of higher education as "using, extending, and transmitting knowledge." It also specifies that in pursuing these goals professors have two responsibilities, which I label as follows: (i) the *truth responsibility* to advance and disseminate knowledge, and (ii) the *respect responsibility* to respect students' autonomy within authority-governed relationships. The crux of the advocacy issue is the interplay of these responsibilities. The truth responsibility invites advocacy; the respect responsibility limits it.

To begin with the truth responsibility, professors' "primary responsibility to their subject is to seek and to state the truth as they see it."[3] This duty makes some advocacy inevitable and obligatory. At the very least, advocacy is essential in affirming the procedural values that govern responsible research and teaching in all disciplines. Thus, the truth responsibility requires advocacy of the basic values and standards governing the search for truth in one's discipline, not in the abstract, but in the course of teaching and research. The pertinent values vary among disciplines, but always they include the virtues of academic integrity: clarity, honesty, rigor, and fairness.

The truth responsibility implies additional forms of advocacy when reflective assessment of values is a central part of a discipline, for example in the study of normative ethics, social and political philosophy, and aesthetics. If there are truths to be found in such disciplines—and there are!—then the ongoing attempt to discover and convey the truths requires advocacy. Skeptics charge that value judgments are neither true nor false, and instead mere expressions of feelings, power, and so forth, but even that charge constitutes an act of advocacy. The truth responsibility also requires advocacy in structuring courses dealing with values: deciding which topics to cover, which books to use, how much class time to allocate to particular authors and viewpoints, which assignments to make, how to respond (supportively or not) to students' questions and comments, and how to grade. These pedagogical judgments and accompanying skills are guided by the values of academic integrity.

Advocacy occurs at many levels, however. The truth responsibility is far too abstract to entail an obligation to engage in classroom advocacy about controversial moral issues. Even if it did, such an obligation would be at most prima facie—limited and with justified exceptions—if only because it would need to be balanced against the respect responsibility.

The respect responsibility is the duty to respect students' moral and intellectual autonomy. In the words of the AAUP, it is professors' responsibility to "encourage the free pursuit of learning in their students." Its foundation resides in the right of students, as with all adults, to develop and exercise their moral agency without being coerced.[4] The relevant concept of autonomy is Kant-inspired and Janus-faced: rational self-determination in freely guiding one's own life *and* responsiveness to moral reasons. The respect responsibility clearly rules out indoctrination (using nonrational means to instill values) and proselytizing (dogma-based preaching), but it also pertains to more subtle pressures arising from the authority that professors typically have over students.

Like all professionals, professors have *expertise authority,* which their clients usually lack, that combines theoretical knowledge and practical know-how. Equally important, they have a unique type of organizational or *executive authority* over their clients: the authority to grade and evaluate.[5] Insofar as grading contributes to students' learning, the authority is grounded in the truth responsibility. Insofar as grading is necessary in ranking students who apply for higher levels of education or for jobs, the authority derives from a social mandate to academic institutions.

Classroom advocacy raises difficulties primarily because it occurs within authority relationships in which professors simultaneously respect and contribute to the development of their students' moral and intellectual autonomy. College students are adults who should be free to express their own reasoned convictions. At the same time, a crucial part of the college experience is the continued development of moral and intellectual autonomy. Courses on values contribute to that development.

Temptations and possible abuses arise when vigorous advocacy interacts with the authority to grade. Consider a professor in a philosophy of religion class who awards high grades only to students who both argue effectively and share his views about whether there are good reasons to believe God exists. Apparently, Hugh T. Wilder became such a professor, although he began his career with a more desirable approach. He reports that he once accepted a "principle of liberal tolerance" expressed in the following promise made to his students on each syllabus.

> In evaluating papers, I care more about the arguments you give than the conclusions you defend. Although I care about what you believe, my immediate concern is with *why* you believe what you believe. Papers will be graded more on cogency of argumentation than on the substantive claims made. And of course, students don't have to agree with me on substantive issues in order to get a good grade.[6]

I make a similar promise to my students and make every effort to keep it. Routinely I give comparable grades to students who argue effectively on opposing sides of issues concerning religious faith, abortion, affirmative action, the death penalty, and a host of other controversial issues. As I see it, this impartial grading is a professional duty, analogous to physicians' duty to provide medical care regardless of whether they disapprove of their patients' views. Hence, I am alarmed when Wilder explains why he stopped making his promise.

A student convinced him that he couldn't make the promise in good faith. A sound argument, which is both valid and has true premises, will have a true conclusion. Now, Wilder was convinced there are no good reasons nor sound arguments for believing in God. Hence, the student inferred, Wilder would always be biased against any student paper that attempted to offer a sound argument for believing in God. More generally, matters of truth and argument cannot be separated in the way suggested by the principle of liberal tolerance. Stunned, Wilder abandoned the principle of liberal tolerance and began to tell students he would not tolerate false beliefs. This meant "explicitly stating to the student that I believe his or her claim is false, explaining why I believe it is false, arguing with the student about its truth value, and finally giving a low grade if necessary."[7] This is coercion! It violates both the respect responsibility and the truth responsibility. Far from encouraging students to share one's commitment to truth-seeking, attaching grades to agreement with one's perspective can only pressure students either to drop the course or lie about their beliefs. The student's error, which Wilder embraced, was that strong personal convictions are incompatible with grounding education in fundamental democratic virtues.

When advocating personal values, professors should manifest the same democratic virtues they hope to inspire in students: open-mindedness, broadmindedness, tolerance, respect, and intellectual humility. *Open-mindedness* is receptiveness to new ideas and willingness to consider viewpoints and customs that are unfamiliar and perhaps opposed to our own. *Broad-mindedness* is a tendency to affirm as reasonable a wide range of behavior and viewpoints, even though we disagree with them, based on affirming diversity as healthy (within wide limits). *Tolerance* is the refusal to coerce others or to overthrow practices, conduct, or convictions that we find objectionable, except when they cause substantial harm to others. *Respect* for a position that we disagree with is a stronger attitude: "I disagree with your position, but your way of arriving at it is such that, unless I can change your mind, I think you ought to (try to) do what you think is right rather than what I think is right."[8] *Intellectual humility* is having a reasonable estimate of our own capacities for achieving truth, together with some appreciation of the general limits of human reasoning. These virtues constitute a "spirit of free and open inquiry," which is "the spirit of both democratic citizenship and individual freedom."[9]

Exactly when is advocacy within authority contexts incompatible with these democratic virtues, so as to threaten students' autonomy? The AAUP Statement on Professional Ethics leads us to this reformulation of the advocacy issue by juxtaposing the truth responsibility and respect responsibility, but it provides little guidance in resolving it.

Reason, Commitment, and Influence

In *Neutrality and the Academic Ethic,* Robert L. Simon sets forth a more promising, albeit still incomplete, response to the advocacy issue. According to Simon, universities should be guided by the ideal of "critical neutrality" in pursuing truth. That does not mean they should be value-neutral. Indeed, the ideal of critical neutrality is itself justified by values, most notably the values of respect for truth and respect for students' moral autonomy.[10] Instead, critical neutrality means being guided by standards of rational inquiry that "constitute a court of appeal independent of the personal preferences of the investigators whose inquiries they govern."[11] Those standards include "not only noncoercion, but respect for evidence, obligations to consider criticism, and willingness to test one's view against those of others."[12]

Furthermore, the standards of critical neutrality require that students "be given a fair representation of opposing views on controversial issues" and that universities create "an atmosphere in which expression of diverse viewpoints is encouraged and welcomed."[13] And the standards forbid "using one's status as a professor to impose one's values on students through nonrational means."[14]

Simon's ideal of critical neutrality moves in the right direction, although I will continue to speak of academic integrity rather than "neutrality," a term that inescapably suggests avoiding values. Simon succeeds in delineating most of the primary features of academic integrity. Nevertheless, he provides only a sketch of how the ideal applies to the advocacy issue. Individual faculty, he writes,

> have the right to advocate positions in class that are relevant to their academic expertise and the course material with which they are concerned, as long as they do so in a manner compatible with canons of critical inquiry. That is, at a minimum, they must be open to objection, consider contrary positions and evidence fairly, and provide to the best of their ability a fair and accurate account of alternative views.[15]

Simon leaves the impression that professors may and sometimes should assert and argue for their views in an impartial manner, perhaps a dispassionate and impersonal manner, so as to avoid preaching and indoctrination. Although he does not define indoctrination, he apparently means using nonrational techniques that prevent students from fully using the skills and meeting the standards of rational inquiry.[16] The most common and controversial cases of advocacy, however, concern undue influence and inappropriate pressures falling in between indoctrination and dispassionate argument.

In particular, what about passionate argument? Surely it is desirable for professors to manifest passion—commitment and enthusiasm—in acting on the moral values comprising the ideal of academic integrity. But is the same fervor desirable in advocating views on controversial ethical issues? Does it constitute undue influence that distorts the learning process by intimidating students?

Without some emotional involvement, teaching about moral issues could not be authentic. Yet, rarely is such involvement accompanied by completely impartial assessments of all opposing views. Especially with regard to social injustice, it is desirable for professors to have and manifest strong (and reasonable) convictions, even if doing so precludes dealing with all sides of an issue with complete balance and fairness.[17] In addition, many professors enter and are sustained in their professions by commitments to ideals of justice, the environment, animal welfare, technology, feminism, multiculturalism, religion, beauty, and meaningful communities.[18] Inevitably those commitments direct their work in the classroom so that they give more time and energy to some viewpoints and arguments rather than others.

The same is true regarding more theoretical matters, which are themselves grounded in a personal search for moral understanding. A. I. Melden, in graduate seminars I took from him, spent most of his time on human-rights ethics and gave short shrift to utilitarians. Again, the eminently fair-minded John Rawls devoted most of a course on political philosophy to unfolding his own moral perspective rather than giving equal time to all reasonable options in political theory. These were not impoverished courses. They were stimulating and successful seminars partly because of their powerful focus and depth. An egalitarian distribution of time to all major views is only one way to be fair, and frequently not the best way. In any case, deciding what constitutes a fair representation of opposing views on controversial issues is itself partly a value judgment expressing advocacy.

More generally, what about the impact of a professor's character and personality? Good teaching is more than presenting and evaluating arguments. It involves teaching the intellectual virtues of honesty, precision, reasoning, curiosity, concentration, effort, perseverance, and passion, together with an array of skills, attitudes, sensitivities, and forms of creativity.[19] For the most part, these values are not taught directly, through formal arguments for them; instead they implicitly guide the direction of all effective reasoning. As Michael Oakeshott observes, values are "implanted unobtrusively in the manner in which information is conveyed, in a tone of voice, in the gesture which accompanies instruction, in asides and oblique utterances, and by example."[20] That explains why professors are not interchangeable, either with each other or with computers. Simon's specification of the "principles of rational inquiry" fails to capture this vital personal dimension of education and rationality.

Inspiration is a type of personal influence deserving special mention. Great teachers inspire in students a dedication to an area of inquiry,[21] to inquiry in general, and to intellectual and moral values. They evoke and arouse enthusiasm for a subject, activity, standards, and for life itself. Like advocacy, inspiration takes many forms, ranging from exuberance to patient conscientiousness, from nobility of intellectual vision to depth of caring for students. Is inspiration a rational or a nonrational educational tool? It can be either, depending on its tendencies in particular contexts. It does not fall neatly under Simon's ideal of critical neutrality, but neither is it coercion. The person inspired is an active participant, willingly open to being influenced—occasionally in emulating specific conduct, but more often in approaching particular activities or entire ways of life "in the spirit" of another person's commitments and ideals.[22] To be sure, inspiration does great harm when it conveys immoral views. Yet, a campaign to minimize inspiration would be pedagogically disastrous and remove a vital stimulant to students' exercise of moral autonomy.

With or without inspiration, good teaching requires motivating students through emotional expression, whether subdued or impassioned. As cognitive psychologists, philosophers of mind, and feminists have argued for some time, emotions must not be dismissed as irrational or nonrational forces.[23] Instead of standing in opposition to rationality, they comprise the very heart of moral sensitivity and responsiveness to moral reasons. Our ideal of academic integrity needs to give full recognition to the *rational passions* that guide effective teaching and careful argument. These passions include love of truth, indignation at injustice, disgust for shoddy thinking, excitement in discovery, and joy in accomplishment.[24] All these emotions shape how professors lecture, argue, discuss opposing views, conduct class discussions, and respond to student papers and exams. They motivate and partly comprise academic integrity.

In short, we need to augment Simon's principles of rationality with an appreciation of character. Whether manifested in morally committed argument, inspiration, expressions of moral caring, or emotional involvement, a professor's character invariably influences students' beliefs in ways that should be celebrated within very wide limits. Good teaching is *provocative*, thought-provoking in ways some students might find engaging and others find offensive. At the same time, good teaching maintains a healthy tension between advocacy and fairness to other viewpoints, and especially between advocacy and respect for student autonomy.[25]

Abuses occur when professors are so preoccupied with crusading for one position that they fail to provoke students to think independently, typically by failing to discuss strong arguments for views opposed to their own. Value advocacy does sometimes cross the blurry line between effective teaching and undue influence. Course evaluations by students who complain that a professor's teaching is biased must be weighed in light of particular contexts, for example, the level of courses and the preparation of students. Are we talking about an introductory course in which many students are unprepared to challenge a professor's forceful advocacy on particular issues, or a graduate seminar in which students are both well-prepared and eager to respond critically to a professor? Is there a case for confronting a strong bias shared by most students on a particular issue? Are the topics covered consistent with the catalog and syllabus? Does a professor find that a particular teaching style tends to constrict the direction of class discussion and essay writing rather than stimulate critical responses? All these questions are complicated, because very different styles of teaching can be equally valid and effective, depending on the professor.

Teaching Styles

Teaching styles are personal ways of interacting with students in pursuing educational goals. Teaching styles combine classroom strategies, individual manner, and selected emphases in adapting goals, applying methodologies, and pursuing topics within disciplines. As such, teaching styles vary greatly among professors and even within the same professor in different contexts.

I will distinguish three teaching styles regarding advocacy, none of which is obligatory and each of which has distinctive moral implications. Each has its own risks and benefits that need to be managed responsibly in meeting truth responsibilities and respect responsibilities. To provide a focus, I discuss introductory ethics courses that typically blend ethical theory with practical issues such as abortion, euthanasia, capital punishment, world hunger, animal welfare, environmental ethics, sexual ethics, and affirmative action.

Teach How, Not What, to Think

One approach is for professors to withhold their conclusions on controversial issues while presenting two or more opposing views, including arguments for the views as well as problems surrounding the views that students should grapple with. The benefit of this approach is that it encourages students to work out their own positions with minimal pressure to agree with the professor. This approach is captured in a familiar motto: Teach how to think, not what to think.

Unfortunately, the distinction between "how" and "what" is not clear-cut in studying ethics. To exercise moral autonomy is not merely to think as one pleases, nor simply to "opt" for one among several options presented by professors. Instead, it is to engage in cogent and sensitive moral reasoning. The primary point in teaching moral issues is to develop moral sensitivity and reasoning, to teach that sensitivity and reasoning have some moral content ("what to think"), and to teach procedures in reasoning ("how to think"). Furthermore, moral education (and autonomy) means developing and exercising rational thought on a foundation of moral understanding.[26] If that foundation were absent, as it is in sociopaths and nihilists, ethics courses would become "academic" in the worst sense of the word. In the main, however, it is possible to distinguish reasonable patterns of argument (how to think) from substantive moral conclusions (what to think) about practical moral issues.

Professors run risks in always withholding their views. For one thing, doing so may lead students to question a professor's integrity. Students expect professors to develop deep (and reasoned) convictions about issues of fundamental justice, and doesn't the courage of one's convictions sometimes require taking a stand? For another thing, students may suspect that professors who withhold their views are not being completely "up front" with them, that they have a hidden agenda of sneaking their views into class presentations rather than openly acknowledging them. By far the greatest risk, however, is that systematically refraining from advocacy might convey the disastrous attitude that any view is as good as another (perhaps as long as a student has some reasons for it), thereby inviting moral shallowness and cynicism.[27] These risks can be managed if professors find a way to convey their faith that reasonable answers can be found and to convey that they have have convictions which they withhold solely as a pedagogical strategy.

Defenders of this first teaching style see it as fostering honesty rather than shallowness and cynicism. Elias Baumgarten writes, "For a humanities teacher to present all available arguments but no definite conclusions is only to convey the disappointing truth, that we have no absolute certainty on most of the enduring questions that are worthy of discussion."[28] Baumgarten recommends generalizing Bertrand Russell's statement about philosophy to all the humanities: "Philosophy is to be studied, not for the sake of any definite answers to its questions, since no definite answers can, as a rule, be known to be true, but rather for the sake of the questions themselves."[29]

The phrase "definite answers" is ambiguous, however. Russell meant incontrovertible certainties, but the phrase can also mean reasonable answers that individuals, upon reflection, believe to be warranted. Usually there are answers in the latter sense, and professors need to convey a conviction that some answers are better than others. That is what makes moral issues worthy of serious attention as part of a search for meaningful life. It also justifies teaching about moral issues. Rather than being disheartening, discovering that reasonable persons differ about moral issues can help foster a liberating vision of moral pluralism, a vision quite compatible with sustaining personal moral commitments.

Teach as an Equal Participant

A second approach is to engage in vigorous, conscious, and strong advocacy on key issues, but to do so as an equal participant in moral conversations with students. Assuming it matches one's personality, this style has a greater chance of evoking students' moral engagement. Indeed, some have argued that this style is obligatory, at least when it promotes rather than closes discussion: "Faculty in the classroom need to model what they want students to learn in the class. Students should observe faculty demonstrating what it means to be ethically sensitive and ethically educated citizens and members of particular professions. . . . One cannot model decision-making skills involving ethical issues without taking positions on what should be done in particular circumstances."[30]

I agree only partly. Faculty should provide models of moral sensitivity and sound reasoning, but they can do so without always taking stands on practical issues. Effective teachers demonstrate sensitivity to the arguments on opposing sides of issues so as to reveal the complexity of the issues and to encourage tolerance for honest and reasonable differences. Moreover, this second style has its own limitations and risks. Is it realistic to think that most students will perceive their professors as genuinely equal participants? Typically, professors not only have far greater erudition in their subject matter, but they have the authority to grade. The equal-participant approach disguises how even the most well-intentioned professors can intimidate and alienate students who have not developed sufficient confidence to challenge them. It may reinforce the passivity of students who rely on professors to give them "the answers." And it can lead students to bend their thinking, or at least their statements in essays and class discussion and on exams, to please the professor in order to gain a higher grade. All these distortions undermine serious truth-seeking. Occurring within authority-governed relationships involving enormous grade pressures, they also fail to respect students' autonomy. In any case, the attempt to make this or any other teaching style obligatory neglects the importance of matching teaching styles to professors' personalities and talents.

Use Advocacy as a Teaching Tool

A third approach is a hybrid of the previous two: Engage in advocacy on some issues and selectively withhold one's views on other issues, indicating when (and why) one is doing so for pedagogical purposes. This approach has the virtue of flexibility combined with some benefits of the previous approaches. But it has risks as well. They include possible confusions when professors are not explicit about whether advocacy is taking place and, more worrisome, the possibility that students will suspect a hidden agenda when views are withheld.

Given my personality and the undergraduate context in which I teach, I find this approach best in navigating between the Scylla of moral skepticism and the Charybdis of undue influence. I tend to express my views in several areas. Certainly I express my attitudes in areas where I expect or hope to evoke a widely shared understanding. At the beginning of a course I remind students that we can engage in cogent moral dialogue because we all agree that rape and killing for mere fun are grossly immoral, and because nearly all of us agree that there is a presumption against dishonesty, unfairness, and ingratitude. Obviously this reminder would not work if I encountered an ethics class full of sociopaths, but then there would be no point in teaching such a class.

I also engage in advocacy on some theoretical issues that are especially complex or fundamental in providing a foundation for a course. I make it clear why a course on ethical reasoning cannot proceed far without opposing crass forms of relativism, including the view that moral reasoning is nothing more than venting one's feelings (ethical subjectivism), conforming to the dominant beliefs of a group (ethical relativism), or maximizing one's own private good (ethical egoism). These views are reductionistic—they reduce moral reasons to something they are not. They also constitute moral skepticism that precludes the serious study of reasons used by morally autonomous people. If ethical relativism were true, moral reasoning could be replaced by taking opinion polls. If ethical subjectivism were true, moral disagreement would be impossible. And if ethical egoism were true, we would lose the central imperative to respect all persons as having inherent moral significance.[31] In presenting major ethical theories, however, I avoid a narrowly partisan approach, concentrating instead on how all major ethical theories—including rights ethics, duty ethics, rule-utilitarianism, and virtue ethics—provide helpful contexts for approaching practical moral issues. What matters is the details in how they are spelled out, and each can be developed in many different directions.

In addition, I express my views on selected practical issues when withholding them would violate integrity. Integrity (which includes the courage of one's convictions) does not require expressing one's views on all moral issues, even where basic moral commitments are at stake.[32] Teachers can recognize "client autonomy" as a compelling reason for limiting their value advocacy, when doing so contributes to meeting their responsibilities to educate students to think for themselves. Nevertheless, at some point integrity is compromised when professors withhold advocacy on issues about basic respect for persons. Thus, I argue that there are no sound moral reasons for condemning homosexuality, and in doing so I explain why remaining neutral on this issue would be akin to tolerating racism and sexism.

Does a similar appeal to integrity justify homophobic professors in condemning homosexuals? Certainly not: It is immoral to degrade persons because of their sexual orientation. Not only are those professors in need of moral enlightenment; their advocacy constitutes a failure to respect their gay and lesbian students. To be sure, there are complications. Do not professors who on religious grounds believe homosexual acts are sinful have a right to express that view, assuming the context is appropriate—say, in a course on sexual religious ethics? The professors do have such a right, but they also have an obligation to find a way of engaging in advocacy that does not degrade homosexuals as persons, and that is not an easy task.

In teaching some topics I interweave advocacy and nonadvocacy. For example, I work hard at sympathetically presenting the main arguments on all sides of abortion (conservative, liberal, and moderate) regarding three issues: (i) What is the moral status or significance of the fetus? (ii) How should we balance that status against the woman's rights and other moral considerations? (iii) What laws and government policies concerning abortion are most defensible? Because the majority of my students happen to be liberals on abortion, I take special care to present the arguments of conservatives and moderates. Typically I withhold my own conclusions (which are moderate to liberal), especially on the first two issues. I do, however, advocate views at the "meta" level concerning the nature of the abortion disputes. I argue that abortion is controversial because fundamental moral values, specifically respect for human life and respect for individual autonomy, can be interpreted and balanced in different ways by equally intelligent and morally concerned individuals. I also advocate the pluralistic view that there are several morally reasonable views on issues as complex as abortion.

I am not suggesting that my approach to teaching abortion issues is best. I use the example to illustrate the interplay between advocating personal commitments and ideals, having an individual teaching style, and meeting professional responsibilities. Conservatives might object to my my advocacy of moral pluralism, and liberals might object to my withholding my views on an issue as important as abortion. As I see it, these criticisms reflect the critics' values and perhaps their style of teaching, but they do not establish that I lack academic integrity when I selectively engage in advocacy and nonadvocacy as a pedagogical tool.

Campus Wars

The advocacy issue was politicized during the culture wars, whose battles were fought on many fronts: abortion, sexual orientation, the family, affirmative action, censorship in the arts, and even the effectiveness of higher education (prompting the obsession with "assessment" of programs and schools to prove their claims of providing quality education). In a wave of best sellers, conservatives argued that education should teach Western values and prepare students to participate in a capitalist society.[33] They especially inveighed against professors of literary criticism, ethnic and multicultural studies, and feminist studies, who proselytize on behalf of leftist agendas. Liberals countercharged that conservatives are at fault for advocating patriarchal and ethnocentric values, especially in schools of business and economics. Often silenced in this debate were moderates who advocated that humane tolerance and responsible citizenship are more important than crusading for any narrow agenda.[34]

The campus and culture wars generated much confusion and dangerous hyperbole—dangerous because they eroded public trust in higher education. Yet the disputes also produced a rich literature concerning advocacy and the goals of higher education. Here I respond to one theme in that literature that poses an objection to my approach to the advocacy issue.

I framed the advocacy issue in terms of the tension between professors' dual responsibilities to pursue truth and to respect students' autonomy. But what if there is no objective truth, at least concerning values?[35] What if truth is wholly *perspectival:* Gender, race, class, and additional personal factors not only influence but dictate one's perspective on truth, rationality, reason-giving, justification, fairness, and moral autonomy? Shouldn't a postmodern, perspectival understanding of beliefs prompt us to abandon traditional responsibilities to seek truth and to respect autonomy?

In one version, yes; in another version, no. Adapting Laura Purdy's distinction, we can distinguish two very different groups that endorse perspectival positions: radicals and liberals.[36] *Radicals* dismiss traditional standards, in education and elsewhere, as irredeemably corrupted by racial, gender, and class bigotries. They reject all value rankings and claims to objectivity as symptoms of a patriarchal, racist, and hierarchical society that should be overthrown. They also criticize the Kantian idea of rational autonomy. Rather than respecting student's autonomy, they see their task to be attacking the false consciousness generated in their students by corrupt societies. In their view, the classroom is a political arena in which pressures are brought to bear to provoke students into self-transformation based on postmodernist views that objective truth does not exist.

The radicals' skepticism would indeed nullify an ethics of academic integrity of the sort I have outlined. Education could no longer be understood as a search for truth guided by respect for autonomy. The professional responsibilities of truth-seeking and respect for autonomy would be replaced by revolutionary power struggles in which nonrational techniques replace objective reasoning during attempts to transform students' attitudes.

Extreme skepticism does not, however, make my approach to the advocacy issue otiose. Although radical skepticism has its defenders, their numbers are too small to undermine the wide consensus about professional ethics needed to govern higher education. Moreover, in reducing values to assertions of power, radicals are vulnerable to the charge that their form of power is no more justified than any other. As professors, they remain accountable in terms of the standards and academic authority of institutions in which they participate.[37] I should add that such skepticism is rarely maintained consistently. Invariably it presupposes substantive moral claims about the responsibility to respect people, to avoid bigotry, and to help empower oppressed groups.

In contrast to radicals who reject academic standards, *liberals* accept the standards but insist that they be critically examined and applied equally in order to remove biases inherited from the past. Objective standards are possible, and the important educational aim is to ensure that standards are applied fairly in appreciating the achievements of women and people of color. Moreover, objective standards are not assumed to be identical with those used traditionally, and historical conceptions of objectivity and fairness need to be refined and expanded. In tune with my earlier critique of Simon, feminist liberals urge the importance of emotions and other personal dimensions of rationality and autonomy.[38] And, in general, liberals call for greater moral clarity and consistency about core traditional values, not for overthrowing them. Liberals allow that valid moral standards have an objective dimension that in practice becomes interwoven with variable social conventions.

My sympathy with liberal revisionists does not mean that I support advocacy of politically liberal agendas in ways that violate the truth and respect responsibilities. The argument I have presented provides grounds for criticizing professors who use the classroom as little more than a place to proselytize on behalf of liberal political agendas in disregard of standards of fairness, balance, and truth-seeking. It provides grounds for criticizing a professor who would never give an "A" to a student unsympathetic to feminism or who approaches education as primarily a way "to save students from their parents, their religion, and twelve years of state-mandated indoctrination."[39] My argument provides equal grounds for criticizing conservative professors who approach education with a hidden curriculum of patriarchal and ethnocentric values.

There will always be controversy about the precise meaning and application of standards for truth-seeking. The controversy is rooted in the same differences that generated the advocacy issue in the first place—differences about aims and means in education. Nevertheless, we can sustain a rough consensus about the principles of professional ethics that should govern educators, partly through making reasonable compromises that lead to general principles in codes of ethics and partly by engaging in continuing dialogue about good teaching. That dialogue should enter periodically into courses on ethics, beginning with the first-day orientation, and perspectival issues arise naturally in most courses on values.[40] In any case, there is every reason to believe that the fundamental values of academic integrity will survive scrutiny and, with some revision and flexibility, will continue to provide the foundation for professionalism in higher education. They will provide this foundation while allowing extensive freedom for professors and students alike to engage in advocacy in the classroom.

Finally, isn't something awry in framing the advocacy issue in terms of professionalism, authority relationships, and students as "clients"? Socrates would be appalled at this professionalizing of the pursuit of wisdom! In reply, Socrates was not a professional; he was an unpaid volunteer who served the public without salary and outside organizational authority relationships. In contrast, professors are professionals hired by organizations to offer services for paying clients, to exercise authority in the form of grading, and to heed organizational and professional standards. That does not mean professors should emulate the formality of judges or the clinical detachment suited to forensic pathologists. At least according to my personal ideal, caring about students remains professors' central commitment—and caring about them in far deeper and more sustained ways than is possible in most professional-client relationships. That commitment sustains both respect for students' autonomy and enthusiasm in participating with students in a Socratic dialogue aimed at increasing understanding.

PART III

Shared Responsibility and Authority

How rich this community is in meaning, in value, in membership, in significant organization, will depend upon the selves that enter into the community, and upon the ideals in terms of which they define themselves, their past, and their future.

—Josiah Royce, *The Problem of Christianity*

8

RESPECT FOR AUTHORITY

According to a traditional image, "true professionals" are independent agents who, unlike businesspersons, serve clients without having to submit to the authority of managers. This image once fit attorneys and country doctors, but it never applied to most engineers, teachers, military officers, and nurses. As a result, the latter were sometimes regarded as less than full-fledged professionals, especially when elitism and sexism reinforced the secondary status of female-dominated professions such as nursing and teaching. Things have changed. With the advent of managed health care and large legal offices, most physicians and attorneys now work within authority-structured corporations. Indeed, all issues in professional ethics, not only those surrounding personal commitments, increasingly concern interactions between professionals and their organizations, and also among members of different professions. Hence, we need a more integrated approach to professional ethics centered on sharing responsibility within authority-structured organizations.

I will discuss three aspects of shared responsibility. One is the interplay between professionals' authority as experts and managers' authority within organizations—especially managers who themselves have a professional identity. A second aspect is the possibility of corporations and professionals serving shared or widely overlapping goals. The third aspect is showing how respect for authority is compatible in principle with professional autonomy. These opportunities for sharing responsibility do not, however, remove all tensions between respect for authority and wider responsibilities, and in the last section I explore professionals' right of conscience that leave room for personal ideals within authority relationships. As in the next chapter, I focus on the profession of engineering, but the main points apply to all professions.

Shared Agency

Authority takes two forms, as indicated earlier.[1] *Executive authority*, also called organizational or institutional authority, is the legitimate power to make decisions and direct the conduct of others in pursuing an organization's goals. *Expertise authority*, by contrast, is mastery of a field of knowledge and practical skills. We tend to think of authority as unidirectional: Employees accept the right of their managers to make final decisions. Less often do we think of managers' reciprocal responsibility to respect the expertise authority of professionals they supervise. Yet, there is a dynamic interplay between the expertise authority of professionals and the executive authority of managers who themselves increasingly have professional identities, an interplay illustrated by the *Challenger* tragedy.

On January 28, 1986, the *Challenger* exploded before the horrified eyes of children watching classroom televisions to see school teacher Christa McAuliffe become the first civilian in space. The night before, senior engineers at Morton Thiokol, designer of the booster rockets for the space shuttle, recommended against the launch. The temperature at Kennedy Space Center was well below the tested range of safety for the temperature-sensitive O-rings (rubber gaskets) that helped seal the segments of the booster rockets. Led by O-ring specialist Roger Boisjoly, the engineers made their recommendation on the basis of years of concern about the erosion of the O-rings on previous flights. But the immediate worry was whether the cold temperatures would prevent the O-rings from forming a tight seal during the first fraction of a second at liftoff, a seal essential to prevent the escape of flammable gases.

Four top managers at Morton Thiokol rejected the engineers' recommendation: Senior Vice President Jerald Mason, Vice President for Space Projects Calvin Wiggins, Vice President for Booster Programs Joseph Kilminster, and Vice President for Engineering Robert Lund. Lund and Kilminster at first opposed the launch, but Lund changed his mind when Jerald Mason requested, "Take off your engineering hat and put on your management hat." Subsequently, the NASA officials at Marshall Flight Center, especially Director of the Solid Rocket Booster Project, Lawrence Mulloy, deliberately withheld the engineers' recommendation from other NASA officials who had final authority to approve the launch.

The usual emphasis on unidirectional, hierarchical executive authority narrows our attention to the fatal decision by top officials to launch *Challenger*. But this culminating exercise of executive authority was preceded by a long series of interactions involving both expertise and executive authority. While investigating the accident, the Rogers Commission identified several long-term pressures and organizational flaws that contributed to the launch decision, and these findings have subsequently been confirmed and expanded by numerous scholarly studies in management theory, communication theory, and political science.[2] The key factors included the pressures for NASA to appear successful in the eyes of Congress in order to retain funding during a time of severe economic cutbacks. Because of Congress's attunement to public attitudes, the pressures also included the mass media that highlighted every launch delay. Another factor was the tendency to erode safety practices, ever so gradually. And there were pressures closer to the launch decision, including public relations efforts to make the launch on Friday when the nation's school children would be watching during school hours, not to mention NASA's desire for President Reagan to allude to a successful launch in his State of the Union message to be given the evening following the launch. Finally, there were flawed communication channels that prevented top NASA officials from hearing the engineers' recommendation.

These pressures and organizational flaws should temper blame toward the individuals involved, but they do not eliminate questions about personal responsibility. What were the responsibilities of the managers and engineers, and how should those responsibilities have been coordinated in the months and years preceding the launch? Based on twenty-twenty hindsight, obviously the managers should never have approved the launch. But given what the managers' knew, did their moral responsibilities dictate the same answer at the time? And should the engineers have done more, not just on the night before the launch but far earlier? In general, regarding matters of safety, how should we conceive of the respective roles of professionals and the managers to whom they report?

Questions about professional obligations are usually discussed within separate professions—in engineering ethics, management ethics, government ethics, and so on. This compartmentalized approach emerges from the very structure of professions, each of which is defined by its special expertise in pursuing an aspect of the public good. It is further encouraged by the consensus paradigm, which reduces a profession's ethics to the shared standards applying to all members of a particular profession. Thus, there is a large literature about professional-client relationships but far less written about professional-professional interactions. [3]

I will set forth three normative models of the safety-related responsibilities of managers and the professionals they supervise. The models are "normative" in that they constitute perspectives on the morally desirable roles of managers and the professionals. Each model construes managers as professionals who possess both expertise and executive authority.

Employers' Agents

The first model limits engineers (and other experts) to providing expert advice about risks and options, together with carrying out managers' directives, and relegates judgments and decisions about safety and quality entirely to managers. Essentially, professionals are glorified technicians—hired guns—charged with identifying the probability of risk and measuring its severity. Risk is exposure to something harmful or otherwise unwanted, as measured by values handed to the engineer by managers. Managers make the judgments about safety, quality, and the acceptability of specific risks, specifying the standards for engineers who carry out their mandates.[4]

Joseph R. Herkert, an engineering professor, endorsed this model in discussing the *Challenger* disaster:

> In the case of the space shuttle program the task of measuring risk should have fallen upon the engineers and other technical experts. The task of judging acceptability of risk in the shuttle program ultimately falls upon the American public through their elected representatives who fund the space program. But for any given launch, judging the acceptability of risk was the responsibility of the NASA managers.[5]

Herkert explains the *Challenger* disaster as resulting primarily from Morton Thiokol managers' poor judgment about safety and partly from the failure of lower-level NASA management to convey the engineers' risk assessments to higher-level NASA officials. He also traces the disaster to outright dishonesty on the part of the managers who misrepresented their decisions about safety as being an "engineering assessment": "The managers . . . had absolutely no business putting on engineer hats in an attempt to justify questionable managerial decisions."[6]

Professions' Standardbearers

The second model expands the advising role of engineers (and other professionals) to include judgments about safety, quality, and the acceptability of risks embedded in products and services, based on the standards established as their professions' current consensus. On this model, the general standards of safety are set by the engineering profession as a whole, not by individual engineers. Samuel C. Florman, who expresses a version of the consensus paradigm, says that engineers should not engage in "filtering their everyday work through a sieve of ethical sensitivity" about safety, which would result in organizational chaos.[7] They should abide by the codes of their profession, the laws of their society, and the directives of their managers.

Florman praises the fourteen engineers at Morton Thiokol for making sound safety judgments, but he points out that the managers who rejected their advice were also engineers. They held engineering degrees and did not stop being engineers when they put on their hats as managers, any more than physicians stop being doctors when they enter into administrative positions. Most of the NASA administrators involved were also engineers, including Lawrence Mulloy. Florman regards the launch decision as an engineering decision: The engineer-managers' decision to recommend launch constituted "bad engineering as well as bad management."[8] Florman directly opposes Herkert, who objected to the launch decision as a management gamble disguised as an engineering judgment about safety. Ironically, Florman adds, it was only because the managers were technical experts that they had the hubris to approve the launch as based on sound engineering: "No sane politician or administrator would go ahead without solid professional support" of the fourteen engineers.[9]

Shared Agency

The third model regards professionals and managers as shared decision-makers in matters of safety, risk, and quality. There is a role differentiation between engineers and managers, but it is not all-or-nothing, and individual engineers have a more active role to play in making value judgments. The shared-agency model portrays engineers as *advocates* for safety, rather than as mere advisers, where advocacy includes personal participation in determining the appropriate safety standards applicable in particular situations.[10] This model takes fuller account of the personal and organizational dynamics that sometimes pressure professionals to sacrifice safety. It makes engineers responsible for resisting such pressures and for vigorously supporting safety in all aspects of their work. Professionals are not hired guns; nor are managers the sole decision makers, even though they have final executive authority. At the same time, this shared-agency model incorporates the elements of truth in the first two models: Engineers do have obligations of loyalty to their employers which imply recognizing the legitimate authority of managers, and engineers are also standardbearers for their profession in maintaining state-of-the-art excellence.

The shared-agency model best promotes public safety. Because technology is increasingly complex, the public must depend on competent and committed advocates for safety, and engineers are in the best position to be those advocates. Or are they? Are engineers—and perhaps most other professional groups today—so thoroughly dominated by management that they lack sufficient autonomy to render the shared-agency model realistic?

Of course, organizations differ greatly in their commitments to safety. Nevertheless, the shared-agency model is widely used in industry. Based on a series of sixty interviews with employees of ten companies, Michael Davis and his colleagues found that engineers actively participate in a process of seeking consensus on safety matters: "Instead of the rigid, hierarchical, and compartmentalized decision process . . . we found a highly fluid process depending heavily on meetings and less formal exchange of information across even departmental boundaries."[11] Whereas managers tend to emphasize wider organizational priorities, especially schedule, cost, and customer satisfaction, engineers tend to emphasize safety and technical quality. When engineers believe that their managers are not sufficiently responsive to matters of safety, they should and often do push harder. When much is at stake, they should be willing to "go to the mat."

The shared-agency model leaves open exactly what advocacy and going to the mat might require in particular situations. Certainly in most everyday situations, engineers will acknowledge managers as having final authority and responsibility for decisions about safety, although only after their safety concerns have been fully expressed and understood, including in some cases obtaining a ruling from higher management. What about the fourteen Morton Thiokol engineers? In their situation, did vigorous safety advocacy require blowing the whistle by contacting NASA officials directly? Unlike the first two models, the shared-agency model forces us to take seriously questions about whistleblowing, but it does not by itself answer them. As I argue in chapter 9, the engineers did have a prima facie obligation to whistleblow, but the public has no right to blame them for not doing so, given its own failure to pass laws protecting responsible whistleblowers from the often draconian penalties they suffer.[12]

Short of whistleblowing, should the fourteen engineers have pushed harder, perhaps communicating with stronger language such as: "This decision could kill seven people"?[13] On the night before the launch, the engineers probably did everything that can be required of safety advocates in their situation—given the absence of legal protection for whistleblowers. Should they, however, have done more earlier within their organization, before a crisis situation arose? In fact, they did vigorously advocate their views, in memos and personal conversations. Why did their managers fail to respond responsibly during the months and years before the launch? The answer is not that the managers were oblivious to safety concerns, but instead that a variety of organizational flaws and subtle dynamics among professionals resulted in something less than fully responsible judgments about safety.

Managers are well aware that engineers are trained to be advocates for safety. As a result, managers will tend to increase productivity and profit by chipping away at engineers' demands for large safety factors, that is, building extra safety into products in order to take account of unforeseen risks. William H. Starbuck and Frances J. Milliken draw attention to this dangerous "fine-tuning process."

> Although engineers may propose cost savings, their emphasis on quality and safety relegates cost to a subordinate priority. Managers, on the other hand, are expected to pursue cost reduction and capacity utilization, so it is managers who usually propose cuts in safety factors. Because managers expect engineers to err on the side of safety, they anticipate that no real risk will ensue from incremental cost reductions. . . .[14]

Starbuck and Milliken argue that this fine-tuning process gradually eroded safety during the development of the space shuttle. The process was compounded by the excessive optimism generated by the twenty-four previous shuttle missions that had taken place successfully. But whatever the psychological explanation, the managers lacked sufficient commitment to safety.

As counterbalancing the fine-tuning tendency—which also occurs in other professional settings, especially managed health care—two additions to the shared-agency model are needed. First, managers must themselves be safety advocates. While we expect engineers to manifest the highest degree of safety advocacy, we should also demand deep commitment to safety on the part of managers. All participants in technological development share the same general responsibilities not to cause harm and not to endanger lives unnecessarily, unreasonably, and without voluntary informed consent. In the case of the four Morton Thiokol managers, this meant heeding the safety judgment of the engineers with the greatest expertise authority. That is true whether the managers thought of themselves as professionals, employees, or simply as human beings with a duty not to cause a loss of life.

Second, with regard to engineers, safety advocacy must be balanced as well as vigorous. If safety advocacy becomes so vigorous that it eclipses other legitimate engineering and management goals, such as cost, schedule, and customer demands, then organizations could not function efficiently to produce useful products. Insensitivity to these wider considerations leads managers to discount engineers' safety judgments and to pursue fine tuning with a vengeance. In Lon Fuller's words, we need an "enlightened and tolerant partisanship" on the part of all advocates for particular needs within technological projects.[15] Let us refine the third model, then, to require vigorous but balanced safety advocacy that is responsive to both teamwork and managers' legitimate authority.

Shared Goals

The shared-agency model is plausible only when professions and the organizations in which they are embedded share the same or substantially overlapping goals. The "goals," of course, are aims actually pursued by organizations, not just the aims stated for purposes of public relations. In the context of free enterprise, economic efficiency implies profitability, but profit by iself is not the sole or even primary goal. Thus, the primary goal of engineering and of technological organizations ought to be the production of safe, useful, and economically efficient products or services. This does not mean that personal ideals are irrelevant, merely that they must be congruent with legitimate corporate and professional goals.

Thinking of corporations as purely profit oriented is not the only way to eclipse the compatibility of corporations and professions. Another way is to idealize professions as solely devoted to public goods, as if they had no essential link to economic goals of organizations and individuals. That idealization is present in Alasdair MacIntyre's distinction between social practices—which include professions—and institutions. A rethinking of MacIntyre's distinction, however, paves the way for highlighting the common goals of professions and corporations.

According to MacIntyre, professions are practices: complex forms of cooperative human activity that promote distinctive *internal goods* when they are pursued according to appropriate standards of excellence. Internal goods are valuable products and services that partly define and are partly defined by the practice itself. For example, health is the internal good of medicine (MacIntyre's example) and safe, useful, and efficiently produced technological products constitute the internal good of engineering. These are also "public goods" for an entire community. In addition, internal goods include the enjoyments and valuable ways of life made possible for individuals who pursue excellence within professions. In contrast, *external goods* are the valuable products obtainable (by individuals and organizations) through most practices, goods definable without reference to any specific practice. They include money, power, authority, and prestige. These are also "private goods" in that they belong to individuals or private organizations. Institutions are characteristically preoccupied with external goods, in ways that threaten the internal goods of practices: "The ideals and the creativity of the practice are always vulnerable to the acquisitiveness of the institution."[16]

I believe it is a mistake to equate internal with public goods, and external with private goods, but I will postpone that criticism until chapter 11. Here I want to challenge MacIntyre's dichotomy between professions as devoted to public goods and corporations as devoted to private goods.[17] This dichotomy unduly idealizes professions and unfairly denigrates corporations.

On the one hand, professions are not devoted exclusively to public goods. They are, after all, forms of work—relatively well-paid and prestigious work. We could not begin to understand them as actual social practices without mentioning the private goods of money and prestige. Without this reference, they would be distinctively different kinds of activities, perhaps philanthropic ones. As I emphasized in chapter 2, professionals pursue their work with mixed motives of compensation, craft, and moral concern. They promote public goods, but they also seek to make a living. Indeed, professionals are fully aware that they can continue their work only when it is productive and profitable. And professionals employed by nonprofit organizations, universities, and government agencies know that their jobs depend upon balancing their organizations' budgets.

On the other hand, turning to institutions, we can agree that corporations have a large potential to corrupt professional standards, as occurred in the *Challenger* disaster. But institutions should not be conceived as mere profit producers and power brokers, concerned solely with private goods. Corporations are communities of people who produce products and services that serve the public good by satisfying customers' desires, providing jobs, generating wealth, paying taxes, and sometimes even engaging in philanthropy.[18] Technological organizations, as much the professions embedded in them, should be committed to producing safe and useful products, as well as profitable ones. Organizations should also foster within their communities the basic virtues that enable them to meet their morally permissible and desirable goals. In this way, responsible organizations can themselves be called honest, just, and caring—caring about people and the public good.[19]

MacIntyre notes, in passing, that practices can survive only when they are sustained by institutions that are "bearers" of the practice. Had he developed this idea further, he might have balanced his one-sided emphasis on how organizations corrupt practices with how they contribute to practices. When organizations "bear"—embody, incorporate—professions, they enable professions to prosper. They do so by pursuing many of the same goals of the professions they bear. Indeed, institutions do not passively accept the goals of professions; instead, they help shape what those goals are.

Thus, law is a practice aimed at justice, but precisely what justice amounts to depends on how it is implemented into legal institutions. Education is a practice aimed at learning, but what that means concerns what is practicable within particular schools and universities. Medicine is a practice aimed at promoting health, but "health" is a value-laden term that is partly defined by how organizations understand the normal functioning of individuals.[20] And while engineering is a practice aimed at creating safe and useful products, the precise degree of safety depends in part on what is feasible within technological organizations. Safety is always a matter of degree and of trade-offs. We condemn the *Challenger* launch decision because of contextual factors indicating poor judgment in making trade-offs that eroded safety standards.

Safety is largely defined by state-of-the-art engineering practice, together with the preferences of customers, clients, and the general public (expressed through laws and regulations). Yet, to an important degree, safety is also understood through the insights of engineers like Roger Boisjoly who have the professional skills to identify the hazards of technology. Technological organizations must put together these sometimes conflicting standards of acceptability, thereby establishing operationalized definitions of safety with regard to particular products.

Needless to say, some corporations insincerely proclaim concern for the public, as do some professionals, in the absence of any genuine commitment. But most organizations are committed to the public they serve, both directly and because they know that in the long run ethics and successful business go together. Texas Instruments, to cite just one example, takes as its central commitment "to create, make, and market useful products and services that satisfy the needs of customers throughout the world."[21] Safety is understood as integral to quality. The company has created an elaborate ethics program, involving a corporate ethics director, ethics workshops for employees, brochures discussing specific ethical dilemmas, and a special phone line where any employee can discuss in confidence an ethical question with an ombudsperson.

Prior to the *Challenger* disaster, NASA also had an outstanding record of commitment to safety. NASA was known for hiring exceptional people, requiring them to work with painstaking attention to detail, fostering vigorous and open discussions of safety matters, and demanding that everything be tested and retested. During its first two decades of operation, it explored space without a single casualty in flight (although three astronauts were killed on the ground in 1967). Given the nature of the work, there was always enormous risk, but during NASA's golden era, as an Apollo program leader said, "We would never fly a manned vehicle if we knew something was wrong with it until we fixed it."[22] Safety had to be established before approving a launch.

Then began a gradual erosion of safety priorities, as economic, political, and bureaucratic pressures increased. Even before the 1969 landing of humans on the Moon, government funding was cut back. Pressure from the top, including from President Reagan, led to the 1982 declaration that the space shuttle program was "operational," encouraging the illusion that space shuttles were just space airplanes. NASA began to be more like a conventional bureaucracy, and management developed the attitude that a launch could be stopped only by proving a lack of safety, exactly the opposite attitude of establishing safety prior to approving launch. The *Challenger* explosion does not illustrate an organization that lacked a commitment to the "internal good" of safety. Instead, it illustrates how an organization betrayed its own commitment to that good.

Authority and Autonomy

Even when shared agency and shared goals are present, managers' executive authority places limits on professionals, even as it makes possible their work. Is respect for the legitimate executive authority of managers compatible with exercising professional autonomy in the pursuit of professional standards and personal ideals? There is a conceptual problem here, what I will call the *reason-compatibility paradox:* The types of reasons for acting in matters concerning the public good required of the morally responsible professional and the loyal employee appear incommensurable. It seems logically impossible to function simultaneously in the two roles. Professionalism demands exercising autonomy in forming and acting on an independent view of what promotes or threatens the public good. Fidelity to an employer seems to demand foregoing that autonomy by submitting to the directives of an employer, directives based on the employer's view of what the organization owes the public.

Why is there a need for authority relationships in the first place? The need arises in circumstances where the unrestrained individual discretion conflicts with a desired degree of social organization and order. Submitting to authority typically involves a willingness to accept some policies and directives that one finds less than optimal. Even to submit to the authority of a basketball referee requires playing by occasionally bad or even outrageous rulings. Similarly, employees who regard their employers as having legitimate authority over them acknowledge the obligation to adhere to at least some directives and regulations whose rationale they find lacking. Doing so voluntarily is part of being a faithful (loyal) trustee of the employer. Presumably this holds true for the many areas of business operations that affect the safety, health, and welfare of the general public. Yet, professionals are supposed to exercise their independent skilled judgment so as to avoid harm and promote the well-being of the public. Hence the reason-compatibility paradox: How can professionals both respect employers' authority and act on their independent judgment?

Consider two proposed responses to the reason-compatibility paradox: (i) Loyalty to employers and recognition of their authority requires accepting directives without any critical review of them in light of professional and moral considerations; (ii) professionals' moral obligations to the public require that all their work conform to their own direct calculations of their impact on the public good.

The first proposal implies that professionals cannot both respect authority (which requires suspending critical review of employers' directives) and exercise professional judgment with regard to the same actions. Instead, they must determine the areas of action in which they respect managers' authority and the areas in which they act autonomously, compartmentalizing their work accordingly. Herbert Simon endorsed this proposal in his influential treatise, *Administrative Behavior.*

According to Simon, a subordinate accepts the superior's authority when he or she "holds in abeyance his own critical faculties for choosing between alternatives and uses the formal criterion of the receipt of a command or signal as the basis for choice."[23] This means the subordinate abdicates choice based on personal reasoning. The superior's suggestions and orders are accepted "without any critical review or consideration."[24] At most, subordinates' reasoning is aimed at anticipating commands by asking how the superior would wish them to behave in the given circumstances.[25] Simon emphasizes that all employees—even the most submissive ones—place limits on the "zone of acceptance" in which they submit to management. But Simon portrays the loyal employee within that zone as "relaxing his own critical faculties" and permitting "his behavior to be guided by the decision of a superior, without independently examining the merits of that decision."[26] The justification for doing so lies in the benefits from securing coordinated group behavior. As backed by sanctions, it maximizes the responsibility of the employee to the employer and helps assure efficiency and productivity.[27] Here, at a micro level, we sense the legacy of Adam Smith's compartmentalization approach to thinking about marketplace values.

It is clear that salaried professionals cannot recognize employers as having authority in the way Simon specifies. Professionals are bound by ethical norms that guide all dealings with their employers. They cannot recognize zones of acceptance in which they altogether suspend critical scrutiny of their managers' directives in light of professional obligations. There must always be a moral ground outside the confines of business dealings on which they are willing to take a stand in assessing whether the directives are within the bounds of moral permissibility, if not desirability. Blind obedience is too high a price to pay for increased social organization.

The second proposal is that all of professionals' actions conform to their own direct calculation of what best promotes the public good. To be sure, professionals' decisions are informed by the wider consensus within the profession, but ultimately their decisions are grounded in their own personal assessment of how to benefit the public. This second view is equally mistaken in that it would make a mockery of employers' authority. Thereby, it would destroy the degree of coordination essential to the effective functioning of complex organizations.

Hence, both of the two extreme views are unacceptable. On the one hand, Simon's model of accepting authority is incompatible with being a professional or indeed with being a moral agent. On the other hand, acting solely on one's independent judgment of what best promotes the public good is incompatible with being a faithful employee within an efficiently operating authority-governed organization. The truth lies somewhere between these extremes.

Submitting to an employer's authority does not mean abandoning responsibilities, as a moral agent and as a professional, to assess the moral permissibility of an employer's orders. At the very least, professionals are responsible for forming (within their areas of competence) and expressing (within their organizations) their own independent views of how their projects impact the public good. Nevertheless, submitting to an employer's authority does involve giving special weight to the employer's directives, a weight that must be set against the professional's autonomous estimate of the independent merit of the act directed by the employer. Assuming that the organization meets minimum standards of justice, the contract between employers and employees creates a distinct moral obligation that prevents professionals from acting always and solely on an independent personal assessment of the public good. Although they must continuously exercise independent *judgment* about the consequences of their work, that judgment legitimately takes into account their responsibilities to employers. Professionals cannot in their *actions* disregard the organization's directives concerning the safety, health, and welfare of the public.

"Loyalty" does not mean foregoing all other professional opportunities for the sake of helping one's corporation. Such sacrifice may be admirable where corporations reciprocate, but the 1990s downsizing made clear that the requisite long-term reciprocation is absent more often than not. Loyalty does, however, mean serving the legitimate interests of the corporation out of concern for its well-being, which is largely the well-being of the community which it comprises. Such loyalty shapes the pursuit not only of personal ideals but also of other responsibilities incumbent on all members of a profession. For example, precisely what is required of professors in teaching their students is constrained by university resources and budgetary constraints that shape everything from class size and mandatory office hours to money for student-faculty colloquia and social events. Again, the duty to maintain strict confidentiality between physicians and patients has been drastically modified by the demands of modern hospitals where many individuals have legitimate access to patient records.

It follows that professional autonomy and respect for employers' authority are not incommensurable. Loyalty to an employer is itself a professional responsibility, rooted in employer-employee contracts but ultimately justified in terms of the public benefits from coordination and efficiency in production to which it contributes. Indeed, ties of loyalty sometimes humanize the employee-employer relationship in ways that elevate it beyond a purely money-based relationship. Each act of obedience need not be justified in terms of good consequences for the public. Within limits, the obligation of respect for authority can carry an importance that outweighs the results of a direct calculation of the public good.

These conclusions might readily be granted regarding the "public good." That term is notoriously vague and ambiguous. It has at least the following meanings: what the majority of people affected desire or want; what they would want if they were well informed; what is objectively good for them, whether they want it or not; what best satisfies the rights and legitimate claims of those affected. Moreover, the impact of engineering and other professional products and services on the public's welfare includes such things as aesthetic features, durability of products, energy efficiency, and impact on environment. But how about direct impacts on public health and safety?

First, is it ever permissible for engineers—qua professionals with obligations to the public good—to submit to employers' orders to undertake projects they believe too risky in terms of public health and safety? The two extreme views offer simple "yes" and "no" responses, but the answer is "Sometimes yes and sometimes no." Suppose an engineer is assigned to work on a new airport facility that has been approved on the basis of the same hard facts known by the engineer and by the vast majority of voters affected by the project. The engineer may disagree with the voters and feel that the health hazards that will arise from noise and air pollution are too great to warrant the project, but he or she need not be acting immorally in acceding to the employer's orders to work on the project.

Robert Baum points out that such cases are closely analogous to situations where a patient has the right to make the final decision about whether to undergo an operation. After all, a judgment of safety is a judgment of acceptable risk, and within limits the user of products has the right to make personal value judgments concerning the acceptability of risk probabilities (assuming he is capable of doing so).[28] Baum goes too far, however, when he concludes, "It is especially important to recognize that doing something that one believes is harmful is not morally wrong, if the parties most affected want it done."[29] That might justify atrocities on masochistic consenters and wholesale disruption of the professional's integrity. It is sometimes morally permissible for a doctor to perform an operation chosen by an informed patient even though the doctor views the operation as too risky. But there are limits: It is patently wrong for physicians to work in abortion clinics if they view most abortions as unjustified killing, even though the abortions are both legal and chosen by an informed patient. Similarly, it is at least prima facie wrong for engineers to participate in forms of military work that they believe are beyond the bounds of decency. Nevertheless, respect for autonomy is a fundamental value that often permits expressing one's view as advice and then acceding to the views of clients.

Second, is it ever morally permissible for engineers, qua professionals, to conduct projects in a manner that they believe goes against public health and safety? The tempting extreme views, with their comfortable simplicity and certainty, would have us answer with an unqualified "yes" or "no." But again, there are cases and cases. Professionals must always seek to work at least according to standards of accepted engineering practice. But what about instances where engineers' autonomous judgment suggests that those standards are not high enough to ensure what they believe is an adequate degree of public safety? Suppose, for example, that automotive engineers believe that the accepted safety standards for car bumpers are grossly inadequate. After expressing their views vigorously, the engineers are justified in following employers' design specifications, while doing what they can to upgrade the standards accepted by the profession, the employer, and the public.

The cases I have cited are special in that the expressed desires of the client, the majority of the public, and the group using and consenting to the use of the product are roughly the same. The moral violations that justly outrage us are those in which an employer orders an engineer to collaborate in withholding essential safety information from groups affected. An employer orders silence concerning known defects in the design of a passenger jet's cargo door,[30] the design of wheels of a fighter jet,[31] or the construction of a nuclear power plant.[32] No justification in terms of fidelity to the employer can be given for disregard of human life.

In many ways, the moral status of a professional who is a loyal employee parallels that of a moral agent who is a loyal citizen. Both are sometimes confronted with orders or regulations they do not view as best for the public's good. Both are obligated (a) to identify such regulations by regularly forming an independently reasoned view concerning the public good, (b) to express their views freely either within the general limits of responsible speech or the organization's limits, (c) to seek to promote free expression of responsibly formed views by creating an atmosphere of tolerance and liberal channels of communication within organizations, and (d) to be willing to refuse to participate in projects that create extreme danger to the public.[33]

Rights of Conscience

What should occur when an individual's conscience is at odds with the directives of corporate employers and when the applicable professional code is silent, too vague to be helpful, or even misleading? In such cases, is there such a thing as a professional's right of conscience, that is, a right to pursue one's moral convictions inside the corporation? (This problem is akin to the Kevorkian issue, discussed in chapter 3, but now arising with regard to employers' authority.)

The notion of a right of conscience is not a philosophers' invention. Historically its initial natural habitat was in political and religious controversies, but it has since entered into the forum of employer-employee relations. Consider the following remarks made by two speakers at one of the earliest conferences devoted to engineering ethics.

> H. B. Koning: "I think that one item that should be in the code of ethics [of engineering societies] is that engineers have the right at all times to exercise the dictates of their own consciences. For example, they need not apply their knowledge, skill and energy to scientific or technical business actions or plans which they feel will violate or lead to the violation of their personal or professional ethical standards. Those engineers, who feel that they, through the interaction within large corporations, cannot participate in particular projects should be protected. They should have a right to follow their consciences."

> N. Balabanian: "Few engineers are self-employed. The vast majority work for others. What is desperately needed for engineer employees is to have a right of conscience. It isn't so much a matter of forcing engineers to conduct themselves ethically but to give them room—room for action— to carry out their own personal ethical convictions without threats of retribution."[34]

Notice that the two engineers are not merely urging that engineers in corporations be allowed to do what everyone agrees is their moral obligation. They are in addition claiming a right to pursue *personal* ethical standards and convictions, even though those convictions may not be officially endorsed by the majority voice expressed in codes of ethics.

Notice, too, that the engineers are claiming a moral right that places corresponding obligations on others, in particular on employers, not to fire or otherwise penalize them for pursuing the right. Ronald Dworkin is mistaken in suggesting that rights of conscience merely mean that it is morally permissible to pursue one's moral convictions, even though it may also be permissible for others to block that pursuit. According to Dworkin, when we ascribe a right of conscience to someone, "We mean that he does no wrong to proceed on his honest convictions, even though we disagree with these convictions, and even though, for policy or other reasons, we must force him to act contrary to them."[35] But clearly the engineers have in mind a stronger notion of rights, one which places some obligations on others not to interfere with the exercise of these rights. A right of conscience refers to a moral right to form and to act upon one's own sense of what is morally obligatory or good without being penalized for doing so.

So far I have discussed the meaning of rights of conscience, but do such rights exist? If so, what is their justified extent and limits inside corporations? I believe there are rights of conscience to pursue reasonable interpretations of professional responsibilities, even though it is difficult to delineate the extent of these rights with any precision. I proceed by distinguishing several kinds of situations.

One type of situation lies within the area of widely shared agreement about professional responsibilities. A classical example is a mechanical engineer in charge of supervising the welding at nuclear power plants under construction who detects numerous defective welds. Wrong materials and improper procedures are being used, including in the water pipes carrying coolants to the core of the reactor. The defects could eventually lead to a serious nuclear accident if the pipes ruptured, causing the core to overheat. Upon reporting these hazards to his supervisor, he is told to be quiet and take no further action, and he is threatened with dismissal if he refuses to obey. [36]

Conscientious engineers might appeal to rights of conscience in such cases, whether as a basis for refusing to participate in the projects or to be allowed to make an appeal to higher management, a professional group, or government. But probably they would instead appeal to the shared understanding within their profession as stated in their code of ethics. In this instance, codes of ethics are enormously helpful, as the consensus paradigm emphasizes, in providing support for responsible professionals.

Next consider some cases showing that the right of conscience is clearly limited and is wrongly invoked to justify conduct. The project engineer for a new clock radio thinks it is in the consumers' best interests to create a product that will last ten years, but her employer directs that a less expensive model be developed having a built-in obsolescence that limits its average lifespan to only five years. The engineer goes beyond vigorous protest and threatens to take her case to the local newspapers, appealing to her right of conscience in fulfilling her responsibilities to the public. Or a biochemist undergoes a radical change in her views and comes to regard continued participation in the development of chemical weapons as immoral. She initiates a campaign within the company to convince her colleagues that they are engaged in immoral work, and in the name of conscience she boycotts her present job assignments.

These cases remind us of the obvious: Rights of conscience at the workplace are not absolute in the sense of having no limits. As employees, professionals have obligations to their employers, colleagues, and stockholders to serve the good of the company, and these obligations place strong restrictions on the pursuit at the workplace of one's own view of the public good. Hence we must reject Koning's provocative claim: "Engineers have the right at all times to exercise the dictates of their consciences. For example, they need not apply their knowledge, skill and energy to scientific or technical business actions or plans which they feel will violate or lead to the violation of their personal or professional ethical standards." At most these statements apply to responsible engineers acting on reasonable interpretations of their responsibilities, but even then the rights of conscience must be limited by the legitimate interests of corporations and the rights of others affected. When an individual's conscience clashes fundamentally with a corporation's basic aims, then it is time to seek a new job more compatible with personal conviction.

The ground is now prepared for attending to contexts where the right of conscience is most often appealed to: contexts where responsible professionals disagree over an important moral issue. Here are three illustrations. First, a senior information scientist is hired to work on a project adding a new computer system to an established on-line system. The system is the computerized police car dispatching system for a large city, and the new addition will be the processing of law enforcement records. The scientist has serious reservations about the safety of making the addition, fearing that it might extend the emergency response time of police vehicles by precious seconds. Her supervisor disagrees with her and tells her to drop the matter. Against his expressed directives, she expresses her views in confidence to the public safety committee overseeing the project, informing her supervisor beforehand that she plans to do so.

Second, a chemist believes that the level of pollutants emitted from her plant poses a serious threat to the water supply of the local community, but only a few of her colleagues share her fears. Management insists that, since standard practice is being followed, there is no need for new studies to be conducted. The chemist persists, however, and during her lunch hours begins conducting some informal tests of her own. Before long her superiors learn about the tests and threaten to demote her if she does not let the matter drop.

Third, an expanding electronics company wins a large contract for the first time from the army to develop a highly specialized circuit that will be used in the computer system of a classified weapon being developed. A physicist assigned to the project requests to be reassigned to a different project unrelated to the military contract. He explains that he is a pacifist who came to work for the company because of its nonmilitary orientation, and that he cannot in good conscience participate in the military work that he regards as adding to the already terrifying dangers confronting human life. The reassignment would cause temporary inconvenience to the company but no major harm.

Each of these examples involves several features that make rights of conscience applicable. (a) At stake is something having great moral importance, such as the protection of human life. (b) No substantial harm is done to others, including to the company, in acting on conscience. (c) The individuals are acting in responsible ways and continue in good faith to be concerned to meet their responsibilities to their companies and to the wider public. Of course, there are many other cases where it is unclear or debatable whether some of these features are present. But uncertainty about the precise extent of rights of conscience does not negate their importance. All basic rights are somewhat vague, including rights to life and liberty.

How can we justify a right of conscience, that is, show that it exists? We might locate it within a general ethical theory such as rights ethics—for example, try to derive it from a more basic right to pursue one's legitimate interests. But here I suggest two appeals that cut across abstract ethical theories.

One appeal is to respect for professionals' moral integrity, understood as the unity of character around a core of justified moral values, a core that precludes irresponsible conduct while leaving room for differences among reasonable moral agents. Each of us is accountable for maintaining our integrity, and our integrity is unjustifiably threatened by others who place us into dilemmas where it becomes exceptionally difficult to act responsibly. Ordering engineers to implement policies that they believe are seriously dangerous constitutes disrespect for their integrity and thereby disrespect for them as persons. Refusing them even a fair hearing in voicing their objections denies the importance of their moral commitments. And denying them opportunities to work on alternative projects, at the cost of minor inconvenience, shows disrespect for their status as moral agents.

The second appeal is to the shared responsibilities of professionals, the ones highlighted in the consensus paradigm. As we have seen, these responsibilities leave room for interpretation in terms of personal commitments. Codified professional obligations cannot be fully explicit, precise, or straightforwardly applicable to every conceivable situation. Precisely how the obligations to protect public safety, to support colleagues, to loyally serve employers, and so on, are to be implemented calls for responsible personal judgment. Insofar as professionals have any responsibilities at all, they have a right to pursue those responsibilities responsibly—a "right to behave responsibly."[37] It would be a mockery to demand that professionals accept and live up to their professional obligations while refusing to acknowledge their right to pursue those obligations. In particular, it would be inconsistent and inhumane to demand that engineers protect the public safety and then to endorse employers' authority to fire them at will whenever they speak vigorously about safety hazards.

To conclude, the right of professional conscience is not absolute: Like all rights it has limits and must be balanced with the rights of employers and other relevant parties. Yet at the very least it implies a right to speak one's views as conscience dictates, without intimidation or fear of reprisals. And where one's convictions are that a project is simply too dangerous, professionals have a right to alternative assignments available without extraordinary disruption to the corporation. On a more positive note, it is a mistake to construe employers' authority as entirely restrictive, either of personal commitments or shared professional responsibilities. The pursuit of personal and professional commitments is, for the most part, furthered by the authority-structured organizations in which professionals work and where they interact with members of other professions, including managers who affirm professional identities. Within the realm of possibilities given by economic pressures, corporations make possible the pursuit of the public goods aimed at by professions.

9

WHISTLEBLOWING

L ife and death issues in the professions are riveting because of dangers to innocent clients, customers, and bystanders, but also because of the agonizing decisions professionals must make in light of their fundamental moral commitments. For example, medicine presents us with questions about whether to remove life-support systems or to assist in the suicide of patients with very low quality of life. Law disturbs us with the need for attorneys to defend clients they know are morally guilty of murder and who may engage in further violent crimes if released. And engineering confronts us with wrenching decisions about whether to whistleblow in order to warn the public of hazards.

To be sure, whistleblowing is an issue in all professions with regard to an array of topics. Thus, some of the most dramatic cases of whistleblowing in recent years have occurred in the tobacco and managed health care industries where lucrative profits eclipsed even minimal standards of honesty. What I say is relevant to all whistleblowing. Nevertheless, there is good reason for focusing on safety issues in engineering, where whistleblowing has been something of a preoccupation. Engineers work on projects affecting the safety of large numbers of people. As professionals, they live by codes of ethics that ascribe to them a paramount obligation to protect the safety, health, and welfare of the public, an obligation that frequently implies whistleblowing. Yet, as employees of corporations, their obligation is to respect the authority of managers who sometimes give insufficient attention to safety and who also severely punish whistleblowers for their alleged disloyalty and damage to the corporation. The upshot is a clash of professional obligations to employers and to the public, as well as conflicts between codified professional duties, personal ideals, and personal well-being.

The voluminous literature on whistleblowing has neglected the relevance of personal commitments to professional responsibilities. I will concentrate on these issues: personal rights and responsibilities in deciding how to meet professional obligations; increased personal burdens when others involved in collective endeavors fail to meet their responsibilities; the role of virtues, especially personal integrity and self-respect, as they bear on "living with oneself"; and personal commitments to moral ideals beyond minimum requirements.

Concept and Cases

By "whistleblowing" I refer to the actions of employees (or former employees) who identify what they believe to be a significant moral problem concerning their corporation (or corporations they deal with), who convey information about the problem outside approved organizational channels or against strong pressure from supervisors or colleagues not to do so, with the intention of notifying persons in a position to take action to remedy the problem (regardless of whatever further motives they may have beyond this intention).[1] Examples of significant moral problems include fraud, grand larceny, misuse of public funds, immoral treatment of clients or employees (such as sexual harassment), deception and—my emphasis here—producing technological products or services that are unacceptably dangerous to the public.

Whistleblowing takes various forms. *External* whistleblowing occurs when information is passed outside the corporation (for example, to government officials, the press, or professional societies). *Internal* whistleblowing occurs when information is passed to higher management against corporate policy or against one's supervisor's directives or desires. *Open* whistleblowing means identifying oneself, as occurs in the cases I discuss. *Anonymous* whistleblowing, withholding one's identity, is a legitimate option in some situations, but usually acknowledging one's identity and credentials for commenting on a problem is necessary in order to be taken seriously.[2] In any case, corporations have ample resources to hunt down "leaks" in order to identify whistleblowers, and individuals who attempt to remain anonymous are often reluctantly forced to acknowledge their identity.

Let us bring to mind three classic cases, beginning with the *Challenger* disaster discussed in the chapter 8.

(i) Recall that Roger Boisjoly and other senior engineers at Morton Thiokol firmly recommended that *Challenger* not be launched.[3] The temperature at the launch site was substantially below the known safety range for the O-ring seals in the joints of the solid rocket boosters. Top management overrode the recommendation. Early in the launch the booster rockets exploded, killing the seven crew members. A month later Boisjoly was called to testify before the Rogers Commission, which was charged to investigate the tragedy. Against the wishes of management, he engaged in whistleblowing when he offered documents to support his interpretation of the events leading to the disaster—and to rebut the interpretation given by his boss. Over the next months Boisjoly was made to feel increasingly alienated from his coworkers until finally he had to take an extended sick leave. Later, when he tried to find a new job, he found himself confronted by companies unwilling to take a chance on a known whistleblower.

(ii) In 1972 Dan Applegate wrote a memo to his supervisor, the vice president of Convair Corporation, telling him in no uncertain terms that the cargo door for the DC-10 airplane was unsafe, making it "inevitable that, in the twenty years ahead of us, DC-10 cargo doors will come open and I would expect this to usually result in the loss of the airplane."[4] As a subcontractor for McDonnell Douglas, Convair had designed the cargo door and the DC-10 fuselage. Applegate was Director of Product Engineering at Convair and the senior engineer in charge of the design. His supervisor did not challenge his technical judgment in the matter. The supervisor did, however, tell him that nothing could be done because of the likely huge costs to Convair in admitting responsibility for a design error that would need to be fixed by grounding DC-10s. Applegate did not blow the whistle, although doing so would almost certainly have forced the Federal Aviation Adminstration (FAA) to take corrective action. Two years later the cargo door on a Turkish DC-10 flying near Paris opened in flight, decompressurizing the cargo area so as to collapse the passenger floor—along which run the controls for the aircraft. All 346 people on board died, which at the time was a record casualty figure for a single-plane crash. Tens of millions of dollars were paid out in civil suits, but no one was charged with criminal or even unprofessional conduct.

(iii) Frank Camps was a principal design engineer for the Pinto automobile.[5] Under pressure from management, he participated in coaxing the Pinto windshield through government tests by reporting only the rare successful tests and by using a Band-Aid-fix design that resulted in increased hazard to the gas tank. In 1973, undergoing a crisis of conscience in response to reports of exploding gas tanks, he engaged in internal whistleblowing, writing the first of many memos to top management stating his view that Ford was violating federal safety standards. It took six years before his recommendations for redesign were finally incorporated into the 1979 model Pinto, after nearly a million Pintos with unsafe windshields and gas tanks were put on the road. Shortly after writing his memos he was given lowered performance evaluations, then demoted several times. He resigned in 1978 when it became clear his prospects for advancement at Ford were nil. He filed a law suit based in part on age discrimination, in part on trying to prevent Ford from making him a scapegoat for problems with the Pinto, and in part on trying to draw further attention to the dangers.

As the first two cases suggest, there are double horrors surrounding whistleblowing: the public horror of lost lives, and the personal horror of responsible whistleblowers who lose their jobs and even careers. Most whistleblowers undergo serious penalties for what one whistleblower called "committing the truth." Some studies suggest that two out of three whistleblowers suffer harsh criticism, lowered performance evaluations, demotions, punitive transfers, loss of jobs, or blacklisting that can effectively end a career.[6] Sad and tragic stories about whistleblowers are not the exception; they are the rule.

Traditional Approaches

The literature on whistleblowing is vast and still growing, but three approaches merit special attention. One approach is to condemn whistleblowers as disloyal troublemakers who betray their companies and undermine teamwork within the hierarchy of corporate authority. Admittedly, whistleblowers' views about safety concerns are sometimes correct, but final decisions about safety belong to management, not engineers. At least when it comes to whistleblowing issues, engineers (and other professionals) are hired guns whose sole responsibility is to obey their employers. When management errs, the corporation will eventually pick up the costs in law suits and adverse publicity. Members of the public are part of the technological enterprise which both benefits them and exposes them to risk. When things go wrong they, or their surviving family, can always sue.

I once dismissed this approach as callous corporate egoism disguised by perversely inflating corporate loyalty as a moral absolute, as having more importance than protecting human life. However, if—and it is a big "if"—the public accepts this approach, as revealed by how it expresses its will through legitimate political and legal processes, then so be it. Terrible wrong is done to individual victims of corporate malfeasance when professionals fail to blow the whistle because the public fails to protect them. Whether that wrong is an injustice needs to be assessed partly within the framework of political systems that specify the responsibilities and rights of citizens. If the public refuses to protect whistleblowers, it tacitly accepts the added risks from being denied important safety information. As citizens, each of us shares responsibility for providing more than the present hit-or-miss protections for whistleblowers, and each of us must share responsibility for the harm caused by failing to support responsible whistleblowers, a point to which I return later.

A second approach, insightfully defended by Michael Davis,[7] regards whistleblowing as a tragedy to be avoided. On occasion, whistleblowing may be a necessary evil or even admirable, but it is bad news all around. It is proof of organizational trouble and management failure. It threatens the careers of managers on whom the whistle is blown. It disrupts collegiality by making colleagues feel resentment toward the whistleblower. It damages the important informal network of friends at the workplace. It shows that the whistleblower lost faith in the organization and its authority and, hence, suggests that he or she is more likely to be a troublemaker in the future. And it almost always brings severe penalties to whistleblowers who are viewed by employers and colleagues as unfit employees.

In reply, I wholeheartedly support efforts to avoid the need for whistle-blowing. Many things can be done to improve organizations in ways that make whistleblowing unnecessary. Top management can—and must—set a moral tone and then implement policies that encourage free communication about safety concerns (and unpleasant news in general). Specifically, managers should keep doors open, allowing engineers to convey their concerns without retribution. When feasible, corporations should have in-house ombudspersons and appeal boards, and even a vice president for corporate ethics—as dozens of large corporations now have. For their part, professionals should learn to be more assertive and effective in making their safety concerns known, learning how to build support from their colleagues. (Could Dan Applegate have pushed harder than he did, or did he just write a memo and drop the matter?) Professional societies should explore the possibility of creating confidential appeal groups where engineers can have their claims heard.

Nevertheless, this second approach is not enough. There will always be corporations and managers willing to cut corners on safety in the pursuit of short-term profit, and there will always be a need for justified whistleblowing. Even when corporations adopt the most enlightened open-door policies, some supervisors will pressure their subordinates to keep their mouths shut (which is why I took care to include this kind of situation in my definition of whistleblowing). Labelling whistleblowing as a tragedy to be avoided should not deflect attention from pressing issues about justified whistleblowing and protection for responsible whistleblowers.

We need to remind ourselves that responsible whistleblowing is *not* bad news all around. It is very good news for the public protected by it. The good news is both episodic and systemic. The episodic benefits are that lives are directly saved when professionals speak out rather than being forced to maintain silence in order to keep their jobs. The systemic benefits are that lives are saved indirectly by sending a strong message to industry that legally protected whistleblowing is always available as a last resort, thereby adding an additional motive for managers not to override safety concerns in the pursuit of short-term profits. It is noteworthy that in all three cases—the *Challenger,* the Pinto, and the DC-10—management made shortsighted decisions that resulted in enormous costs in law suits and damaged company reputations.

In this day of (sometimes justified) outcry over excessive government regulation, we should not forget the symbolic importance of clear, effective, and enforced laws as a way for society to express its collective vision of a good society.[8] Laws protecting responsible whistleblowing express the wider community's resolve to support professionals who act responsibly in protecting public safety. Those laws are also required if the public is to meet its responsibilities in the creation of safe technological products.

A third approach to whistleblowing is to affirm unequivocally the obligation of engineers and other professionals to whistleblow in certain circumstances, and to treat this obligation as paramount—as overriding all other considerations, whatever the sacrifice involved in meeting it. Richard T. De George set forth the classical statement of this view.[9] External whistleblowing, he argued, is oligatory when five very strong conditions are met (by an engineer or other corporate employee):

(1) "Serious and considerable harm to the public" is involved;
(2) one reports the harm and expresses moral concern to one's immediate superior;
(3) one exhausts other channels within the corporation;
(4) one has available "documented evidence that would convince a reasonable, impartial observer that one's view of the situation is correct"; and
(5) one has "good reasons to believe that by going public the necessary changes will be brought about" to prevent the harm.

De George says that whistleblowing is morally *permissible* when conditions (1)–(3) are met; it is morally *obligatory* only when 1–5 are met.

As critics have pointed out, conditions (4) and (5) are too strong. Where serious safety matters are at stake, there is some obligation to whistleblow even when there are only grounds for hope, short of certainty, that whistleblowing will significantly improve matters, and even when one's documentation is substantial but less than convincing to every rational person.[10] Indeed, often whistleblowing is intended to prompt authorities to garner otherwise-unavailable evidence through official investigations.

Moreover, having a reasonable degree of documentation is a requirement even for permissible whistleblowing. Otherwise, there is a risk of making insupportable allegations that unjustifiably harm the reputations of individuals and corporations. Permissible whistleblowing also requires having a reasonable hope for success, lest one waste everyone's time and energy.[11] Hence, De George's sharp separation of requirements for permissibility and obligation begins to collapse. There might be an obligation to whistleblow when conditions (1)–(3) are met and a professional has a reasonable degree of documentation as well as a reasonable hope for success in bringing about necessary changes.

My main criticism of this third approach, however, is more fundamental. I question the entire attempt to offer a general rule that tells us when whistleblowing is mandatory, *tout court*. Final judgments about obligations to whistleblow must be made contextually, not as a matter of general rule. And they must take into account the burdens imposed on whistleblowers and their families.[12] Granted, in routine situations, individuals are simply required to do what their professional responsibilities specify. But whistleblowing situations are not routine. Here, professionals' personal responsibilities to their families and to themselves acquire added significance.

Personal Life

In my view, there is a strong prima facie obligation to whistleblow when individuals have good reason to believe that there is a serious moral problem, and when they exhaust normal organizational channels (when appropriate, and except in emergencies when time precludes doing so), have available a reasonable amount of documentation, and have reasonable hope of solving the problem by blowing the whistle. Nevertheless, however strong, the obligation is only prima facie: It can have justified exceptions when it conflicts with other important moral considerations in the situation. Moreover, the considerations which need to be weighed include not only prima facie obligations to one's employer but also considerations about one's personal life. Before they make all-things-considered judgments about whether to whistleblow, professionals may and should consider their responsibilities to their family, other personal obligations that require having an income, and even their rights to pursue their careers and the personal commitments that enliven those careers.

Engineers are people as well as professionals. They have personal obligations to their families as well as sundry other obligations in personal life which can be met only if they have an income. They also have personal rights to pursue their careers. These personal obligations and rights are moral ones, and they legitimately interact with professional obligations in ways that sometimes make it permissible for professionals not to whistleblow, even when they have a prima facie obligation to do so. Precisely how these considerations should be weighed depends on the particular situation. And here, as elsewhere, we must allow room for morally reasonable people to weigh moral factors differently.

In adopting this contextual approach to balancing personal and professional obligations, I am being heretical. Few discussions of whistleblowing take personal considerations seriously, as being morally significant rather than mere matters of prudence and self-interest. But responsibilities to family and to others outside the workplace, as well as the right to pursue one's career, are moral considerations, not merely self-interested ones. Hence, further argument is needed to dismiss them as irrelevant or automatically overridden. I will consider three such arguments.

(i) The *Prevent-Harm Argument* says that morality requires us to prevent harm and, in doing so, to treat others' interests equally and impartially with our own. This assumption is often associated with utilitarianism, the view that we should always produce the most good for the most people. Strictly, the Prevent-Harm Argument relies on "negative utilitarianism," which enjoins constant effort to minimize total harm, treating everyone's interests as equally important with our own. The idea is that even though professionals and their families must suffer, their suffering is outweighed by the lives saved through whistleblowing. Without committing himself to utilitarianism (in discussing this topic), De George uses a variation of the impartiality requirement to defend his criteria for obligatory whistleblowing: "It is not implausible to claim both that we are morally obliged to prevent harm to others at relatively little expense to ourselves, and that we are morally obliged to prevent great harm to a great many others, even at considerable expense to ourselves."[13]

The demand for strict impartiality in moral decision making has been under sustained criticism by some leading ethicists during recent decades.[14] Those criticisms block any straightforward move from impartiality to absolute (exceptionless) whistleblowing obligations, thereby undermining the Prevent-Harm Argument. One argument is that a universal requirement of strict impartiality, as opposed to a limited requirement restricted to certain contexts, is self-demeaning. It undermines our ability to give our lives meaning through special projects, careers, and relationships that require the resources which we would have to give away if we were guided by strict impartiality. The general moral right to autonomy—the right to pursue our lives in a search for meaning and happiness—implies a right to give considerable emphasis to our personal needs and to those of our family.

As an analogy, consider the life-and-death issues surrounding both world hunger and scarce medical resources. It can be argued that all of us share a general responsibility of mutual aid to alleviate the tragedy of tens of thousands of people dying each day from malnutrition and lack of medical care. As citizens paying taxes that can be used toward this end, and also as philanthropists who voluntarily recognize a responsibility to give to humanitarian organizations, each of us has a prima facie obligation to help. But there are limits. Right now, you and I could dramatically lower our lifestyles in order to help save lives by making greater sacrifices. We could even donate one of our kidneys to save a life. Yet we have a right not to do that, a right to give ourselves and our families considerable priority in how we use our resources.[15] Similarly, engineers' rights to pursue their life-sustaining and meaning-giving careers, as well as to pursue the projects and relationships made possible by those careers, have relevance in understanding the degree of sacrifice required by a prima facie whistleblowing obligation.

(ii) The *Avoid-Harm Argument* proceeds from the obligation not to cause harm to others, noting that engineers are in a position to cause or avoid harm on a large scale. As a result, according to Kenneth Alpern, the ordinary moral obligation of due care in avoiding harm to others implies that engineers must "be ready to make greater personal sacrifices than can normally be demanded of other individuals."[16] More generally, according to Gene James, whistleblowing is required when it falls under the obligation to "prevent unnecessary harm to others" and "to not cause avoidable harm to others," where "harm" means violating their rights.[17]

In reply, of course there is a general obligation not to cause harm. That obligation, however, is so abstract that it tells us little about exactly how much effort and sacrifice is required of us, especially where many people share responsibility for avoiding harm. I have an obligation not to harm others by polluting the environment, but it does not follow that I must stop driving my car at the cost of my job and the opportunities it makes possible for my family. That would be an unreasonable and unfair burden. These abstract difficulties multiply as we turn to the context of engineering practice which involves collective responsibility for technological products.

Engineers work as members of authority-structured teams which sometimes involve hundreds of other professionals who share responsibility for inherently risky technological projects.[18] Engineers are not the only team members who have responsibilities to create safe products. Their managers have exactly the same general responsibilities. In fact, they have greater accountability insofar as they are charged with the authority to make final decisions about projects. True, engineers have greater expertise in safety matters and hence have greater responsibilities to identify dangers and convey that information to management. But whatever justifications can be given for engineers to zealously protect public safety also apply to managers. In making the decision to launch the *Challenger*, Jerald Mason, Senior Vice President for Morton Thiokol, reportedly told Robert Lund, "Take off your engineering hat and put on your management hat." As noted in chapter 8, this change in headgear did not alter his moral responsibilities for safety.

Dan Applegate and Roger Boisjoly acted responsibly in making unequivocal and trenchant safety recommendations; their managers failed to act responsibly in response to those recommendations. Hence, their moral dilemmas about whether to whistleblow arose because of unjustified decisions by their superiors. Now, it is reasonable and fair to ask engineers to pick up the moral slack for managers' irresponsible decisions—as long as we afford them legal protection to prevent their being harassed, fired, and blacklisted. Otherwise, we impose an unfair burden. Government and the general public share responsibility for safety in engineering. They set the rules that business plays by. It is hypocrisy for us to insist that engineers have an obligation to whistleblow to protect us—and then to fail to protect them when they act on the obligation.

(iii) The *Professional-Status Argument* asserts that engineers have special responsibilities as professionals, specified in their codes of ethics, which go beyond the general responsibilities incumbent on everyone to prevent and avoid harm and which override all personal considerations. This argument is an application of the consensus paradigm, which equates professional responsibilities with codified duties. Most engineering codes hint at a whistleblowing obligation with wording similar to that of the code of the National Society of Professional Engineers (NSPE):

> Engineers shall at all times recognize that their primary obligation is to protect the safety, health, property and welfare of the public. If their professional judgment is over-ruled under circumstances where the safety, health, property or welfare of the public are endangered, they shall notify their employer or client and such other authority as may be appropriate.[19]

The phrase "as may be appropriate" is ambiguous. Does it mean "when morally justified," in which case the question of whistleblowing is left open? Or does it mean "whenever necessary in order to protect the public safety, health, and welfare"? The latter interpretation is the most common one, and it clearly implies the need for whistleblowing in some situations, no matter what the personal cost. In general, professional codes never hint that personal considerations can be relevant to professional decisions, and codified professional responsibilities are widely assumed to automatically override all personal considerations.

The obligation to protect public safety is a fundamental professional obligation that deserves constant emphasis in engineers' work, as well as in the work of other professionals. It is not clear, however, that it is intended to be paramount in the technical philosophical sense of overriding all other professional obligations in all situations. In any case, I reject the general assumption that codified professional duties are the only morally important considerations in making whistleblowing decisions. That is the view implied by the consensus paradigm, which reduces the duties of professionals in their work to what their professional codes specify. As I have granted, professional considerations do require setting aside personal interests in most situations. But personal commitments have some legitimate role in making decisions about how far to go in sacrificing one's family and career in pursuing professional ideals.

I would even suggest that spouses have a right to participate in professional decisions involving whistleblowing, at least within healthy and viable marriages.[20] In most situations, professionals should consult their families before deciding to engage in acts of whistleblowing that will seriously affect them. And critics who condemn engineers for failing to whistleblow without knowing anything about their family situation risk overlooking morally relevant considerations.[21]

Where does all this leave us? It is clear that there is a minimum standard which engineers and other professionals must meet. They have strong obligations not to break the law and not to approve projects which are immoral according to standards of due care in pursuing their profession. They also have a prima facie obligation to whistleblow in certain situations. Just how strong the whistleblowing responsibility is, all things considered, remains unclear until we closely examine particular contexts. Certainly this unclarity remains as long as there are draconian penalties and inadequate legal protections for even the most responsible whistleblowers.

The upshot is that whistleblowing responsibilities must be understood contextually, weighed against personal rights and responsibilities, and assessed in light of the public's responsibilities to protect whistleblowers. We must look at each situation. Sometimes the penalties for whistleblowing may not be as severe as expected, perhaps because protective laws have been passed and are enforced; and sometimes family responsibilities and rights to pursue a career may not be seriously affected. But our all-things-considered judgments about whistleblowing situations cannot be formulated as absolute general principles that automatically override every other consideration.

Yes, the public has a right to be warned by whistleblowers of dangers— assuming that the public is willing to bear its responsibility for passing laws protecting whistleblowers. In order to play their role in respecting the public's right, engineers should have a legally backed right of conscience to take responsible action in safety matters beyond the corporate walls.[22] As legal protections are increased, a trend underway in some contexts,[23] then the relative moral weight of personal life to professional duty changes. Professionals will then be able to whistleblow more often without the kind of suffering to which they have been exposed, and thus the prima facie obligation to whistleblow will be less frequently overridden by personal responsibilities.

Conscience and Character

The general tendency for self-interest to overshadow moral considerations already discourages whistleblowing. Will abandoning the search for absolute, all-things-considered, principles for whistleblowers further discourage whistleblowing, to the detriment of the public good? Until adequate legal protection is secured, won't my contextual approach result in fewer whistleblowers who act from a sense of responsibility in seeking to protect innocent lives? Perhaps, but I suspect not.

If all-things-considered judgments about whistleblowing are not a matter of general rule, they are still a matter of personal conscience and good moral judgment. Good judgment takes into account whatever rules provide helpful guidance, but essentially it is an expression of good character. Good character, as defined by the virtues, is a further area in which personal aspects of morality bear on ethics in engineering and other professions.

Virtues are those desirable traits that reveal themselves in all aspects of personality—in attitudes, emotions, desires, and conduct. They are not private merit badges, and to view them as such is the egoistic distortion of self-righteousness.[24] Virtues are desirable ways of relating to other people, to communities, to social practices such as engineering, and to oneself. Which virtues are most important for engineers to cultivate?

Here are some of the virtues most significant in engineering and the professions in general, sorted into three general categories.[25]

(i) *Virtues of self-direction* are those which enable us to guide our lives. They include the *intellectual virtues* which characterize technical expertise: a sense of excellence in one's craft, mastery of one's discipline, ability to communicate, skills in reasoning, imagination, ability to discern dangers, a disposition to minimize risk, and humility, understood as a reasonable perspective on one's abilities together with the absence of arrogance toward others. They also include *integrity virtues* which promote coherence among one's attitudes, commitments, and conduct based on a core of moral concern. They include honesty, courage, conscientiousness, self-respect, and fidelity to promises and commitments—both those in personal and professional life. And wisdom is practical good judgment in making responsible decisions. This good moral judgment, grounded in the experience of concerned and accountable engineers, is essential in balancing the aspirations embedded in the next two sets of virtues.

(ii) *Teamwork virtues* include (a) loyalty: concern for the good of the organization for which one works; (b) collegiality: respect for one's colleagues and a commitment to work with them in shared projects; and (c) cooperativeness: the willingness to make reasonable compromises. Reasonable compromises can be integrity preserving in that they enable us to meet our responsibilities to maintain relationships in circumstances involving moral complexity, disagreements, factual uncertainty, and the need to maintain ongoing cooperative activities—exactly the circumstances of engineering practice.[26] Unreasonable compromises are compromising in the pejorative sense: They betray moral principles and violate integrity. Only good judgment, not general rules, enables engineers to draw a reasonable line between these two types of compromise.

The teamwork and self-direction virtues, along with contractual duties of service to employers, need to be taken seriously in thinking about whistleblowing. Whistleblowing can cause great and unwarranted harm to employers when it is rooted in vengeance and poor judgment. At the same time, responsible whistleblowing frequently has an eye on the long-term good of organizations, and is not automatically incompatible with teamplay virtues. The next category of virtues, however, is salient in responsible whistleblowing.

(iii) *Public-spirited virtues* are those aimed at the good of others, both clients (as a group) and the wider public affected by one's work. *Justice virtues* concern fair play. One fundamental virtue of justice is respect for persons: the disposition to respect people's rights and autonomy, in particular, the right not to be harmed in ways one does not consent to. *Community virtues* center around enlightened cherishing of community and a loyalty to sustaining and improving valuable practices (such as professions) and institutions. Important, too, is simple compassion for the actual or potential suffering of members of the community, in particular those individuals affected by one's work.

The public-spirited virtues illuminate the sense of responsibility that often motivates whistleblowers. Under the influence of the consensus paradigm, professional ethics has neglected personal moral ideals, just as it has ignored the moral relevance of personal life to professional responsibilities. Many personal ideals evoke higher aspirations than the minimum responsibilities incumbent on all professionals.[27] These ideals are important to understanding both the conduct and character of morally concerned whistleblowers.

Depth of commitment to the public good is a recurring theme in whistleblowers' accounts of their ordeals. The depth is manifested in how they connect their self-respect and personal integrity to their commitments to the good of others. Roger Boisjoly, for example, has said that if he had to do it all over again he would make the same decisions, because otherwise he "couldn't live with any self respect."[28] Similarly, Frank Camps says he acted from a sense of personal integrity.[29]

Boisjoly, Camps, and whistleblowers such as these two also report that they acted from a sense of responsibility. In my view, they probably acted beyond the minimum standard that all engineers are required to meet, given the absence of protective laws and the severity of the personal suffering they had to undergo. Does it follow that they are simply confused about how much was required of them?

As discussed in chapter 4, there is such a thing as voluntarily assuming a responsibility and doing so because of commitments to (justified) ideals, to a degree beyond what is required of everyone. Sometimes the commitment is shown in career choice and guided by religious ideals: Witness Albert Schweitzer or Mother Teresa of Calcutta. At other times it is shown in professional life in an unusual degree of pro bono publico work. And at still other times it is shown in whistleblowing decisions.

According to this line of thought, whistleblowing engaged in at enormous personal cost, motivated by moral concern for the public good, and exercising good moral judgment is both (a) supererogatory—beyond the general call of duty incumbent on everyone, and (b) appropriately motivated by a sense of responsibility in light of one's personal ideals. Such whistleblowers act from a sense that they must do what they are doing.[30] Failure to act would constitute a betrayal of the ideals to which they are committed and also a betrayal of their integrity as persons committed to those ideals.

To conclude, I have identified a further way in which personal life is relevant to professionals' decisions about whistleblowing. Earlier I drew attention to the importance of personal rights and responsibilities as well as to the unfair burdens when others involved in collective enterprises fail to meet their responsibilities. Equally important is the need to appreciate the role of personal integrity grounded in supererogatory commitments to ideals. The idea of being able to live with oneself should not be dismissed as a vagary of individual psychology. It is a matter of the virtue of self-respect, of duties owed to oneself, rather than of self-esteem (feeling good about oneself). Being able to live with oneself morally concerns the ideals to which we commit ourselves, beyond the minimum standard incumbent on everyone. This appreciation of personal integrity and commitment to ideals is entirely compatible with a primary emphasis on laws that make it possible for professionals to serve the public good without having to make heroic self-sacrifices.

10

RELIGION ETHICS

At a time when all professions are under intense public scrutiny, mentioning religion and professional ethics together might bring to mind a series of well-publicized scandals. In particular, televangelist Jim Bakker, head of the PTL (Praise the Lord) Television Network, was sent to jail for tax evasion after bilking $100 million from his followers. The event took a comic twist when Jimmy Swaggart, Bakker's rival who blew the whistle on him, was himself exposed as having a voyeuristic obsession with watching prostitutes perform sex acts. Far more sinister are reports of sexual harassment, molestation, and pedophilia by priests, rabbis, and ministers. Such gross abuses of religious authority are widely condemned by the religious communities affected as well as by the general public.[1] In contrast, the issues taken up here concern controversies in which most members of a religious community believe their religious leaders are exercising legitimate religious authority.

What is the proper role of religious commitments by individuals and groups in providing professional or profession-like services, especially within authority relationships? The answer is complex. Outside of religions, professional detachment often requires distancing one's professional work from one's religious beliefs, and there are strong limits regarding the treatment of children and other vulnerable populations. In dealing with consenting adults, however, religions and the professionals they employ have considerable freedom to establish guidelines that depart somewhat from usual professional norms. After surveying some representative issues in the opening section, I discuss in some detail Margaret P. Battin's *Ethics in the Sanctuary*. One might think that religious professions would be the one place where personal commitments would be fully appreciated. Yet, while Battin deserves much credit for establishing this new branch of applied ethics, her book manifests the same tendency to underappreciate personal commitments in professional life.

Faith, Consent, and Decency

A few distinctions will be helpful at the outset. "Religion ethics," as I call it, is the branch of applied ethics that studies the moral implications of religious organizations, including organizations' general practices and the ideals and conduct of their members. In contrast, "religious ethics" refers to the moral beliefs and practices grounded in religious perspectives; in a related sense, it refers to the study of these beliefs and practices.[2] Like other branches of applied ethics, religion ethics is an interdisciplinary enterprise. Some ethicists will approach it with religious-ethics perspectives and others with secular perspectives.

Religion ethics includes moral studies of professional clergy, lay clergy, and non-clergy religious professionals. *Professional-clergy* include all ministers, rabbis, imam, and other service-oriented religious providers who have a professional identity in a sense comparable to that of physicians, lawyers, teachers, and other professionals. Typically, they have advanced education, provide services requiring complex skills, and proceed according to special ethical guidelines. *Lay-clergy*, by contrast, are providers of religious services who do not affirm a professional identity. And *non-clergy religious professionals* are counselors, health professionals, attorneys, and other non-clergy professionals who serve in official capacities within religions or are in other ways religious-oriented in the services they provide.

I am especially interested in communities of faith grounded in *religious authority*, that is, the executive authority exercised by people holding positions within religious organizations. This is a human authority, distinct from the *divine authority* that God is claimed to have.[3] Of course, many theists believe that God delegates divine authority to humans as the basis for their religious authority, perhaps to persons holding positions of executive authority within religious organizations or through inspiring other church members. We can also distinguish two senses of religious authority, de facto and justified. *De facto religious authority* is the institutional power or rights granted to individuals by members of faith communities rooted in a common religious belief, practice, and (usually) sacred texts claimed to express divine authority. *Justified religious authority*, in a strong sense, requires the truth of religious beliefs, for example, the existence of a deity who grants special power and rights to religious officials. I will concentrate on de facto religious authority, cognizant that believers regard it as justified—despite their disagreements about exactly when religious officials have divine authority and are speaking with divine inspiration.

To begin with non-clergy religious professionals, let us consider some of the many positive connections between religious faith and professionalism. Religious faith is a potent source of moral motivation in choosing careers and selecting jobs, as I emphasized earlier in discussing David Hilfiker, Albert Schweitzer, and Katie Cannon. Religious faith guides interactions with clients in many additional ways.

For example, Deborah Fernhoff is a psychotherapist who, as a practicing Orthodox Jew and a feminist, derives special satisfaction from working with women and Jewish clientele. She acknowledges the importance of shared standards governing the work of all psychotherapists, including those requiring a certain detachment and avoidance of paternalism. Nevertheless, she rejects the idea that mental health, which is the primary goal of psychotherapy, is or should be understood in exactly the same way by all therapists and patients. In her view, defining mental health entirely in terms of self-esteem and personal autonomy neglects its interpersonal dimension, manifested in meaningful human relationships. There are some "situations where the problem lies within a patient's search for a meaningful life," involving "emotional conditions which have their roots in issues of meaning."[4] Many of her clients seek her help with problems that combine anxiety conflicts and spiritual crises. Thus, one couple came to her because of their religious disagreements which arose because only one spouse was attracted to Jewish Orthodoxy. The disagreements had escalated to the point where they threatened their marriage.

To cite a different profession, architect Larry Sones at mid-career refocused his career on church structures, primarily Baptist but also Methodist and Presbyterian. Doing most of his work in the Bible-Belt region around Missisippi, he moved away from modernist architecture and toward more traditional forms with arches and steeples. He reports that his work is a spiritual endeavor and that "Every meeting I attend is usually opened and closed with prayer."[5] The prayer is aimed at invoking divine guidance for the shared effort of clients and professsionals in achieving religiously inspiring structures. The influence on his work was a deepened sense of community and caring.

The cases of Fernhoff and Sones remind us that religious faith can be a morally valuable influence, capable of strengthening and deepening professional commitments. The religious influence is morally unobjectionable, as regards clients, for two reasons. First, the participation of clients is voluntary. The clients agree to, indeed desire, that the professionals not set aside their religious beliefs in providing their services, as would otherwise normally be required by professional distance. Nor did government or other legal authority preclude the contractual arrangements involved. Second, the modifications of professional roles are within the realm of moral decency, as defined by widely shared humane values. There are no violations of principles of justice such as those forbidding coercion, exploitation, and unwarranted forms of paternalism.[6]

Most of the difficult issues in religion ethics arise when these two conditions—consent and decency—are not met, or at least when there are serious questions about whether they are met. I will consider several contexts in which religious authority comes into conflict with the authority of law within democracies: science, medicine, and government service.

Science and Religion

In 1991 John Peloza was reprimanded by the Capistrano Valley School District in Orange County, California, for teaching creationism and for refusing to teach evolutionary theory according to the state-mandated educational curriculum for high school biology classes. According to reported complaints from students and parents, Peloza would on occasion preach to his students and even allude to the danger of hell for those who refused to believe in Jesus.[7] He did so at school, both in the classroom and after classes. Peloza was a born-again Christian who regarded evolution as a "mere theory" and a false one at that. He believed that he had the right to introduce creationism as a competing theory based on the religious authority of a literal reading of the Bible. Eventually the school district reassigned Peloza to teach physical education classes, for which they judged him better qualified, given that he held bachelor's and master's degrees in physical education and only an undergraduate minor in biology.

Following the reprimand and related conflicts with school administrators, Peloza filed a $5 million lawsuit against the school district, the student newspaper, and a number of individuals, claiming violation of his free speech. His suit became a cause celebre supported and funded by Christian fundamentalists. Eventually the Ninth Circuit Court of Appeals judges rejected as frivolous the claim that free speech permitted a high school biology teacher not to teach evolutionary theory as prescribed in the state-mandated curriculum, and the Supreme Court refused to hear the remaining claim that free speech permitted teaching creationism. Defense costs to the school district ran into the hundreds of thousands of dollars, money urgently needed for other educational purposes, but Peloza viewed his efforts as justified by his religious commitments.

Unlike the cases of Deborah Fernhoff and Larry Sones, the Peloza case involved clients—both students and their parents—who did not endorse Peloza's particular faith-oriented approach to his profession. More generally, the case pitted government and scientific authority against de facto religious authority. Peloza was backed by a large religious community that thought government authority is abused when it sides with science at the expense of their faith. The case illustrates that sometimes there are forced alternatives, genuine either-or's that cannot be resolved by compromise, and that legal authority must be invoked as the final appeal in democratic societies. Of course, not everyone must agree with how legal authority is exercised in each case in order for that authority to be valid. Yet legal authority can sustain wide support only if it is kept within the limits recognized as reasonable by most citizens within a democracy. Also of interest, the case involves government authority affirming the expertise-authority of the scientific community. Hence, the issues concern the profession of science itself as well as the teaching of science.

Medicine and Religion

Questions about consent frequently arise in situations where science-based medicine clashes with faith-based healing. Sissela Bok cites the 1976 case of Anneliese Michel, a twenty-two-year-old student in Germany who had a history of epileptic seizures and anorexia nervosa.[8] The local parish priest interpreted her seizures as evidence of possession by devils, and he consulted with Germany's leading specialists in satanology. For ten months the religious experts conducted an exorcism in which Anneliese willingly participated. During that time she ate very little and her health eroded. Shortly after the exorcism was declared a success, Anneliese was found dead. The priests and parents believed that they were acting from a genuine concern for Anneliese, and during the time of the exorcism they did not consult medical authorities because they feared doing so would threaten Anneliese's physical and spiritual healing. Government authorities saw things quite differently. They convicted the priests and parents of negligent homicide and sentenced them to six months in jail.

Anneliese was an adult, but her disturbed mental state rendered it questionable whether she had the capacity to give informed consent to the exorcism proceedings. The next case involves children who are clearly unable to give informed consent.

Christian Scientists, that is, members of the church founded by Mary Baker Eddy in the nineteenth century, believe that illness is caused by inappropriate mental states rather than by physical factors per se. Following Eddy, they allow that some afflictions of the body are "merely mechanical," as when a bone is broken or a limb severed, and those afflictions are legitimately subject to the remedies of physicians. However, Christian Scientists believe that mental and spiritual failures explain a great many problems that medicine instead understands as physically caused illnesses treatable by physicians. Moreover, they believe that young children suffer illnesses caused by their parents' failures to maintain genuine faith. These beliefs have sometimes resulted in tragedy.

Larry May discusses two examples. A highly publicized case occurred in 1986, when two-year-old Robyn Twitchell suddenly became unable to keep food down and felt intense abdominal pain over several days. His parents called a Christian Science practitioner and later a Christian Science nurse, but the parents did not consult a physician. Within a week Robyn was dead from a bowel obstruction that could have been corrected with a simple and nonrisky surgery. The parents were convicted of involuntary manslaughter, although the conviction was overturned seven years later by the Massachusetts Supreme Court.

In a less-publicized case in Delaware during 1990, three-year-old Colin Newmark suddenly became severely ill. His parents rushed him to the hospital where his intestinal blockage was diagnosed. The parents consented to simple surgery to remedy the "mechanical" problem. Postoperative tests revealed that Colin had cancer, and the consensus of six physicians was that chemotherapy and radiation could have given him a 40 percent chance of recovery. The parents refused to consent to the procedures, which even if successful could have side effects ranging from hair loss to sterility, increased risk of infection, and need for repeated blood transfusions. The hospital attempted to gain temporary custody of Colin in order to provide the treatment against the parents' will. The Delaware Supreme Court refused the hospital's request, ruling that the parents had the right to make the decision. Colin was placed in the care of a Christian Science practitioner and later died.

According to May, these cases turn on opposing claims to authority by Christian Scientists and the medical community. He proposes that these groups need to work out a compromise along the following lines: "Medical science should be more attuned to the whole person who is the patient, especially in non-life-threatening situations, and hence should be open to nonstandard approaches to health. Christian Science should be more open to the diagnostic services of medical science [in particular, in diagnosing 'mechanical' problems], so that it can be ascertained what type of spiritual healing is needed, and so that informed decisions can be made about when to consider medical help, especially in life-threatening situations."[9] Such a compromise would encourage Christian Scientists to have sufficient trust to obtain the medical diagnoses which would enable them to identify mechanical problems, thereby preventing tragedies such as Robyn Twitchell's death. It would also enable the medical community to have greater tolerance for reasonable differences in judgment about how cases such as that of Colin Newmark should be handled.

May is surely right to call for greater sensitivity to opposing viewpoints, and he proposes insightful compromises. Nevertheless, I believe he does not fully confront the most troubling question: Within democracies, who has the authority to interpret and protect the moral and legal rights of children?

Although the medical community provides relevant information and services, ultimately it is not in competition with Christian Scientists about decision-making authority, as May suggests. Instead, the competing group is society as a whole, through the legal safeguards it provides for children. In tune with its human rights tradition, the United States has reached the reasonable view that competent adults have the right to refuse medical treatment for themselves but not an unlimited right to make similar refusals for their children. What is needed is not so much a compromise between physicians and Christian Scientists but a judicial balancing between parents' and childrens' rights—"judicial" in the double sense of legal and wise.

In my view, Robyn Twitchell's parents were guilty of moral and legal negligence. It is doubtful, however, that Colin Newmark's parents were negligent. The doubt arises for a reason independent of their religious beliefs: It is uncertain whether any parents who made a similiar decision in their situation would be acting within the broad range of loving and reasonable decision-making. The important point is that no compromise can preclude the need for such cases to be adjudicated, either by a judge or by a legally authorized ethics committee. No compromise should permit religious commitments to remove democratic protections for children, its most vulnerable citizens.

Government Service and Religion

If legal authority must be invoked to resolve clashes involving religions, the question arises whether religious beliefs should be allowed, within pluralistic democracies, to enter into decision making by judges and legislators themselves. I believe the answer is generally no, but with a few caveats.

Democratic liberties, including the liberty of moral and religious conscience, are preserved when public officials use commonly shared forms of argument as the basis for their reasoning about public policy and law. As John Rawls reminds us, allowing public officials to use religious appeals would subvert the separation of church and state in ways that inevitably violate the liberties of minorities. Rawls reminds us of a long history of religious intolerance by citing St. Thomas Aquinas's view that heretics deserve the death penalty for destroying the soul by corrupting the true faith, as determined by ecclesiastical authority.[10] The example is extreme, but it highlights the importance of preventing religious views from setting policies within pluralistic democracies whose goal is to keep basic liberties paramount.

Kent Greenawalt agrees with Rawls that legislators, judges, and other public officials should not be permitted to appeal directly to their religious beliefs as a basis for public policy or legal rulings. Nevertheless, he argues that public officials should be allowed in limited and indirect respects to be guided by their religious views, although they should rarely allow their religious faith to go against a wide majority of their constituents' or citizens' views. An example of an indirect influence is allowing their religious understanding to illuminate what is at stake in certain religious practices: "For example, whether creches in public parks constitute a forbidden establishment of religion has been thought to rest partly on whether people understand the creche in that context in a religious way, and therefore view the creche as amounting to state sponsorship of religion. Thus, the religious convictions of the public could figure in this narrow domain to a limited extent."[11]

This is an interesting example, but note that it concerns judges' understanding of religious practices, not acting on their own religious convictions. Presumably an atheist could have the pertinent understanding and draw on it in precisely the same way as a Christian judge without either using it as a basis for a ruling. Moreover, Greenawalt gives excessive power to the majority views of constituencies and pays insufficient attention to the constitutionally defined rights of minorities. At the very least, if creches are to be permitted in public parks, then comparable religious expressions by minority groups should be permitted.

Greenawalt's most troubling claim is that when laws and statutes fail to provide adequate precedence for deciding cases, and hence that judges must make independent judgments, their religious views may permissibly influence them. "Let us suppose, for example, that the judge is interpreting an environmental statute and the statutory language is unilluminating for the problem at hand. Resolution of the issue seems finally to turn on how much respect is owed by humans to the natural world, with no clear guidance from the statute itself or legislative history. I see no escape from the proposition that the judge, like the legislator, may in such settings find it necessary to rely on his religiously informed answers to what is right. . . ."[12] But to the contrary, as Kenneth I. Winston argues, the charge to public officials is to search for modes of argument that keep alive the search for truth rather than closing it off. In the context of making and enforcing laws, appeals to private religious beliefs threaten to close the search for truth. Whether the topic is environmentalism, abortion, or homosexuality, public officials are expected to act impartially, "to act with detachment, to take into account the interests of all relevant parties, and to make judgments in accordance with standards appropriate to the enterprise they are engaged in."[13]

An important caveat pertains to laws giving judges discretion. Here legislators, representing the general public, intend judges to have greater latitude in exercising their moral judgment, and I agree with Greenawalt that such judgment is often interwoven with religious beliefs in ways that render it impossible to pry apart. Thus, as I suggested in chapter 6, judges' personal moral ideals, which are interwoven with their religious beliefs, permissibly play some role in shaping their general approach in sentencing convicted criminals. Even there, however, judges are expected to exercise fair and balanced judgment, which implies not allowing their religious views to bias their rulings.

Another caveat concerns legislators. I agree with Greenawalt that there may be more room for public officials' decisions to be linked to their religious beliefs when doing so is part of their representative function and when they remain within the bounds of the separation of religion and state. It may be annoying that some religiously conservative states make it difficult to purchase wine and liquor by forbidding its sale in grocery and drug stores. Yet the tradition seems to be within the bounds of acceptable influence of predominant local religions on legislators, especially given that there are also secular reasons for regulating alcohol as a dangerous drug.

Membership Consent

In the remainder of this chapter, I focus on clergy and proceed by responding to Margaret P. Battin's provocative and groundbreaking book, *Ethics in the Sanctuary*.[14] Battin lays the foundation for "ecclesioethics," which she describes as a new branch of professional ethics focused on religions. I interpret her book, however, as exploring the wider field I call religion ethics. Secular ethics has always engaged in moral criticism of particular religious practices, not to mention wholesale Nietzschian and Marxist assaults on religions, just as religions have criticized secular practices, each other, and opposing factions within themselves.[15] What is new in Battin's book is the systematic application of principles from contemporary professional ethics in thinking about religious practices.[16]

I am sympathetic with Battin's project in that I think it sheds new light on the interplay of morality and religious practices. Nevertheless, I will identify wider areas of freedom than she allows for clergy and adult members of religious organizations to pursue their personal commitments. The discussion is organized as three challenges to her methodology. First, we need to distinguish more sharply than Battin does between professional and nonprofessional religious practitioners as well as between professions and religions. Second, and most important, we need to bear in mind the moral relevance of voluntary membership in religious organizations, especially where individuals voluntarily submit to religious authorities on the basis of commitments. Third, we should reject Battin's way of delineating the proper realm of inquiry by applied ethicists.

The first criticism is that rather than sharpening the distinction between professional-clergy and lay-clergy, Battin blurs it.[17] She uses interchangeably the terms "religious professional" and "religious practitioner," where the latter term encompasses both professionals and nonprofessionals holding positions of authority in religious groups (8). In portraying ecclesio-ethics as a new branch of professional ethics, she greatly expands and ultimately distorts the concept of professionals to include essentially anyone holding a position of authority in a religion.

For example, only part of the opening chapter on confidentiality deals with professionals, specifically with Catholic priests. Much of the chapter is devoted to the practices of Mormon bishops who are neither educated, paid, regulated by law, nor regarded by themselves and others as professionals. In their religious roles, they are laypersons (although of course they may in other roles have professional identities as dentists, doctors, and so forth.). They are nonprofessional volunteers. Unlike Catholic priests, they receive none of the advanced education in preparing for their work that characterizes professionals (7–8). The same is true of Mormon missionaries, Protestant lay ministers, Jehovah's Witnesses, faith healers, college students who proselytize for Campus Crusade for Christ, and other nonprofessional practitioners that Battin discusses in subsequent chapters.

Why does Battin think the distinction between professional- and lay-clergy is unimportant for her purposes? I believe she has two reasons, neither of which is adequate. On the one hand, her primary interest is to apply (secular) principles from professional ethics to religious practices, rather than to religious professionals per se. As she writes, "To employ a principle adopted from professional ethics to examine organized religion is not to presuppose that religious functionaries are all professionals in the fullest sense. Clergy of the mainstream denominations have traditionally been regarded in this way, though cult leaders, evangelists, faith healers, gurus, and the like have not" (117). As illustrations, Battin applies the principle of confidentiality to the practice of religious confession, the principle of informed consent to high-risk religious practices (such as going to a Christian Scientist rather than to a physician for medical care), and the principle of paternalism to proselytizing practices. In many additional ways, she repeatedly applies professional principles to all religious practitioners.

What can be gained from applying ethical principles for professions and professionals to nonprofessional religious practices and practitioners? Battin promises increased clarity, and she keeps this promise by providing illuminating comments on how nonprofessional religious practitioners depart from the ethical standards applicable to professionals. Sometimes Battin is happy with clarity alone and even cautions against expecting applied ethicists to provide solutions to difficult moral problems (252), but at other times she develops strong criticisms that certain religious practices involve "the violation of basic moral rules" (57) or at least "appear to be clear moral abuses" (263). Many of these criticisms come from applying principles of professional ethics to nonprofessionals, such as Mormon bishops, thereby charging *non*professionals with *un*professional conduct. As I see it, this charge disregards the rights of religious groups to decide whether they want their clergy to have a professional identity. It also disregards their rights to modify secular professional standards—within limits of basic decency and informed consent—to serve religious ends.

To be sure, some of Battin's specific criticisms of religious practices are difficult to pin down. Almost imperceptibly, she shifts from carefully formulated professional standards to less carefully formulated ordinary (nonprofessional) moral standards. She does so deliberatively, adopting a two-pronged or "pincer approach" in studying religious practices: (i) Begin by applying principles of professional ethics, and (ii) when it becomes clear that we are dealing with nonprofessionals, shift to ordinary moral principles applicable to everyone, not just to professionals (10–12). Now, at the point where Battin holds nonprofessional religious practitioners to ordinary moral standards, she is engaged in a traditional critique of religion rather than embarking on a new branch of professional ethics. It is important to emphasize this continuity with traditional critiques lest it appear that nonprofessionals are being criticized for failing to meet professional standards which neither the religion nor society imposes on them.

Some passages even blur the distinction between professions and religions: "What is of interest is not so much whether organized religion *is* a profession—though it has traditionally been regarded that way—but what specific institutional structures and professional roles it shares with some or all of the secular professions" (7).[18] Yet it is of great importance to bear in mind that religions are *not* professions, not even those religions which employ professional-clergy. Organized religions, at least in contemporary democratic societies, are voluntary organizations that provide services primarily to their members, rather than (as professions do) to the public at large.

In this same connection, Battin says that religions have a monopoly of services to their members, comparable to the monopolies held by other professional groups (9). Yet surely the two kinds of monopolies are strikingly different. There is nothing like the detailed public overseeing (moral and legal) of religions that occurs with the professions. Physicians and attorneys, for example, are required by the public to establish high standards of competence in providing services, but such government involvements in religion are inappropriate. The specific justification for this difference resides in rights of religious freedom, but also pertinent are the wider rights of autonomy of individuals to associate together voluntarily for purposes of their choosing.[19]

This brings us to a second criticism. We need to bear in mind the moral relevance of voluntary submission to religious authority. Organized religions are voluntary associations whose adult active members typically consent to membership based on their religious faith. Adults are free to join or leave although, of course, children are often raised as nonvoluntary members. In my view, *membership-consent* is a central moral concept in religion ethics, perhaps *the* central concept, unlike professional ethics. Yet membership-consent is not discussed by Battin at all. To be sure, she carefully analyzes consent in connection with members' specific decisions concerning whether and when to engage in particular practices, especially high-risk ones. But she provides no comparable analysis of membership-consent in choosing to join and participate in a religious group, even when that analysis bears directly on consent to specific religious practices.

What are the moral implications of voluntary submission to the religious authority of church officials as part of membership-consent? Religious authority, which plays a key role in most of the religions that Battin discusses, is a form of executive authority that contrasts sharply with the expertise authority of professionals' theory-based technical know-how. There is a striking dissimilarity between (a) professionals who have duties not to exert their religious perspectives on nonconsenting clients, and (b) religious practitioners who have membership authorization to exert pressure in influencing the values and conduct of church members.

To illustrate the moral significance of membership-consent, as well as to illustrate the importance of distinguishing professional and nonprofessional religious practitioners, consider Battin's discussion of confidentiality in the Mormon religion. She cites the case of Clair Harward who admitted to his bishop that he had AIDS (21). Using that information, the bishop convened a disciplinary hearing which led to excommunicating Harward. According to church policy, the bishop could not divulge the information learned during Harward's confession, but he could and did pressure Harward to divulge the information to the disciplinary group. The Mormon Church authorizes the bishop to "urge" and "attempt to persuade" the member to release information to other church authorities and even to "emphasize" that refusing to divulge information suggests a lack of repentance which has implications during the disciplinary proceedings (32). Church authorities also pressured Harward's roommate to confess and then excommunicated him.

Like Battin, I find the church's actions morally repugnant, but our reasons differ. As I see it, the church's actions were morally objectionable on grounds having nothing to do with professional misconduct in matters of confidentiality. The central issue is homophobia, manifested in the effort by church authorities to remove sexually active gays from church membership. I object to the church's actions on the grounds of ordinary moral considerations about tolerance, decency, compassion, and respect for persons. In this instance, Battin's "pincer" approach leads us to overlook fundamental concerns about bigotry by narrowing our attention to confidentiality norms, initially professional norms and then everyday norms about confidentiality.

In order to refocus on the confidentiality issue, then, let us modify the example. Keeping all the details about confidentiality the same, change Harward's "sin" to polygamy. Regardless of our view of polygamy, I suspect that we would not be deeply troubled by the bishop's and the church's actions in following their confidentiality conventions in order to excommunicate polygamists, especially given the church's concern not to be identified any longer with the polygamy it once practiced but abandoned in the nineteenth century. We would strongly object, however, to professionals using similarly loose confidentiality conventions.

Why the difference? In the religious context we focus on the particular case, on the specific policies of the religion as well as the particular type of harm done by divulging information. In contrast, in the context of secular professions, we insist that much stricter standards of confidentiality be met, so strict that sometimes only legally sanctioned exceptions are permitted (such as to report child abuse or to protect third parties from extreme harm). I suggest that the difference turns on the moral relevance of membership-consent to church practices involving confidentiality. By participating in religions, and especially by submitting to religious authorities, individuals subject themselves to suffering, guilt feelings, fears, peer pressures, and influence by religious authorities—in addition to possibly gaining an array of psychological, social, moral, and spiritual benefits. There is no professional principle forbidding individuals from submitting themselves to these burdens. In the revised Harward example, some burdens were linked to the relatively free flow of information within religious communities about their members, including negative information, a degree of free flow that would be entirely unacceptable in professional contexts.

Because lay-clergy are involved, there is no professional principle of confidentiality that applies in the revised Harward case. Shifting to the other prong of Battin's pincer, is there some ordinary moral principle precluding this freer flow of information within religions?[20] I know of none. Ordinary moral principles about confidentiality are too vague and flexible to preclude religious groups from adopting special customs in matters of information flow among themselves, much less forbidding them from putting pressures on each other to conform to their church's teachings. Admittedly, the Mormon Church could do a better job of informing their membership about what is involved in church practices of confession to a bishop and discipline of members, but the present issue concerns the practices themselves, not information about the practices (33).

To return to our revised case of Harward, the bishop was a Mormon who had role-responsibilities to the church and to church members who submit to church authority. These responsibilities of the lay-clergy contrast sharply with professionals' responsibilities to society at large to follow the standards of their profession. Harward was himself a member, presumably not just an "on-the-books member" (a so-called "Jack Mormon"), but instead an affirming participant. Participating adult Mormons voluntarily subject themselves to religious authority. Their membership-consent opens them to church discipline and pressures and ultimately to discipline for violating church policies.

Am I tacitly condoning what was done to (the real) Harward, since he was a consenting member of the church? No, for I already said that he was a victim of bigotry that is as objectionable within religious organizations as elsewhere. Am I saying that voluntary membership in the Mormon religion implies endorsement of all its practices? No, and perhaps most members of churches see some room for improvement within their organizations. Nevertheless, membership-consent renders participants vulnerable to official church procedures being applied to them. The moral relevance of membership-consent calls into question all of Battin's specific charges against Mormon bishops and their practices, including charges of immoral forms of deceiving, breaking promises, and coercing (56–57). There are no promises of strict confidentiality, no refusals to use pressure in encouraging people to meet church standards, and even no assurances of complete openness about all details of church policy and procedures.[21] The bishop's conduct would be unethical in the professions, but we are dealing with voluntary submission to the religious authority of lay-clergy.

As an additional example, let me shift from confidentiality to risk taking, a topic to which Battin devotes a lengthy chapter. Membership-consent, I will again urge, complicates moral issues surrounding risk taking, for example, in connection with the practices of Christian Scientists (a version of faith healing), Jehovah's Witnesses (refusing blood transfusions), and poisonous snake-handling in some Holiness Churches.

The lynchpin in Battin's argument against religious practitioners who encourage undue risk taking is the fiduciary principle: "In religious contexts, the fiduciary principle asserts that the developed practices, doctrines, methods, and teachings employed by religious professionals or their religious organizations must meet (secular) ethical criteria wherever the individual participates in these practices to advance his or her self-interests" (122, italics deleted). It is clear that by "self-interest" Battin means *secular* self-interest, self-interest conceived in secular terms, as opposed to salvation or other religiously defined concepts of self-interest. Thus, she says the fiduciary principle does not apply when Christian Scientists go to their practitioners to strengthen their faith. However, when they seek medical help from their practitioners in order to get well, the fiduciary principle applies because of the self-interested issue of health. There, the fiduciary principle assures "the same freedom from coercion, from impairment [of their judgment], and to the same adequate information to which an ordinary medical patient would be entitled in seeking to get well" (122). In particular, Christian Scientist practitioners are at fault in failing to provide impartially the hard scientific data about the rates of cure using their services as compared with those of modern medicine.

Now, I agree that the fiduciary principle applies *if* the practitioner claims professional status and is so regarded by society. There is a clear moral and legal mandate for the public through its government to regulate all health professionals. But in most states the public (society at large) refuses to count Christian Scientists as health professionals, and for good reason. Christian Scientists—practitioners and ordinary members alike—reject scientifically based standards for health professionals. As they see it, their self-interest in matters of health lies in having faith in church authority and in church practices—precisely those practices which reject the fiduciary principle. For them, physical health is not an entirely secular concept, or solely a matter of secular self-interest, precisely because of their religious interpretation of healing as a divinely directed process in response to religious faith.

Moving to the other jaw of the pincer, does ordinary morality require that all religious authorities heed the fiduciary principle? That would be to impose a principle of secular ethics concerned with secular well-being on religions which reject the principle where spiritual interests are at stake. What is the justification for that imposition? Battin argues that the fiduciary principle, as applied to religions, is essential for ensuring trust by members that church authorities are concerned for their well-being (117). But Christian Scientists, both practitioners and the members they serve, believe that they are maintaining that trust, based on mutual loyalty and caring. Trust, like self-interest, must be understood in light of membership-consent.

The "must" in the fiduciary principle is a secular "must," based on replacing Christian Science beliefs with the beliefs of secular medicine. Accordingly, the principle is nonapplicable to the Christian Science practitioners, at least if we are willing to tolerate their view of health as transcending secular self-interest. Alternatively, the principle is false because it overgeneralizes from secular professional-client relationships to voluntary religious organizations whose membership-consent implies renouncing the principle. Whether we see the principle as irrelevant or false, membership-consent enters into our understanding of what counts as trust, self-interest, and coercive pressures in matters of risk taking.

Let me add a large caveat. I have focused on the relevance of membership-consent in understanding the rights of church members not to model their religious activities on the professions. Yet we should distinguish between (a) their rights, (b) what is all right (morally permissible), and (c) what is morally ideal. Certainly (a) bears on (b), as I have suggested. Nevertheless, other moral considerations are also relevant, such as sensitivity to the suffering caused in the cases Battin discusses. Moreover, once we realize that respect for members' autonomy prohibits us from condemning many of their acts and customs as immoral, we can still make suggestions about morally preferable or ideal procedures. These suggestions, when backed by good reasons—and combined with public pressure expressed through the mass media—may encourage religions to rethink their positions.

In a subsequent rejoinder to my criticisms, Battin concedes that voluntary membership should become a central concept in religion ethics, but she finds the notion "thoroughly problematic." She suggests that membership is not fully voluntary where "it is a defining characteristic of one's life" and where religious groups "form and reform one's most basic attitudes towards the universe, towards human relationships, towards oneself, and towards whatever is conceived of as God."[22] Now, I grant that it is sometimes difficult to identify when membership-consent is fully voluntary, especially within religions that rely on authority to shape members' beliefs from childhood on. Nevertheless, surely much of adult members' consent is substantially voluntary, and it is this to which my critique applies. It would be implausible and patronizing to charge, as do Marxists, that religions are wholly a product of "false consciousness" or brainwashing. Moreover, there is a moral presumption that adults should try to achieve a high degree of voluntariness in their decisions about the religious groups in which they participate, given how much is at stake. Religions have enormous power to shape us, as do innumerable other social practices and organizations, including marriage, participation in service organizations, and indeed professions. As adults, with normal capacities, we choose to sustain these involvements. Voluntariness implies the absence of coercion but not the absence of strong influences to which we choose to submit.

Scope of Religion Ethics

Battin believes that some religious beliefs and practices are directly vulnerable to secular critique, but others are out of bounds to the applied ethicist (43–47, 59). The out-of-bounds—O-level—doctrines are fundamental beliefs, such as beliefs that God exists. Applied ethicists should be methodologically agnostic with regard to O-level doctrines, neither embracing nor rejecting them. Ecclesioethics should focus on *first-order* principles that put O-level principles into practice, for example, principles specifying particular ways of engaging in confession or taking risks on behalf of the church. It should also focus on *second-order* principles that concern problems arising from the previous order principles. Another focus should include *third-order* principles used to excuse failures and deal with discomforts arising from first- and second-order principles.

As a final two-part criticism, I will challenge the workability of Battin's typology and reject the attempt to make O-level doctrines immune to scrutiny by applied ethicists.

(1) Battin grapples with the identification problem: How do we identify the O-level principles that are substantially off base to the applied ethicist? She thinks that careful historical and scriptural studies enable us to identify the fundamental doctrines. I believe that sometimes they do but often not. A religion will usually have an official view of what is basic; various members will have other views; and scholars will have their versions. This disagreement greatly complicates Battin's approach, as she is aware, but there is a deeper problem connected with religious authority that she fails to address.

A fairly common O-level religious principle is that some authorities in the organization's hierarchy have special dealings with God; specifically, top church leaders are divinely inspired in their formulations of first-, second-, and third-level principles. Thus, Mormons believe in ongoing revelation to the church's president, and Catholics believe in the Pope's infallibility in interpreting eternal truths. Of course, there are questions about exactly when the leader is speaking with divine inspiration rather than as a fallible human being. Nevertheless, the point remains: The O-level doctrine about ongoing revelation carries over to doctrines at the other levels, essentially collapsing the levels together in ways that the applied ethicist cannot disentangle by looking at scripture or historical developments within the religion.[23] Hence, to challenge a higher-level doctrine accepted by the membership as a direct revelation from God is implicitly to challenge the O-level doctrine of ongoing revelation, thereby violating Battin's procedural agnosticism.

Consider confidentiality again, this time within the Catholic Church and regarding priests who are professionals. Battin challenges the seal of confession, that is, the promise (based on God's law) that priests have an absolute obligation not to divulge what is confessed. She cites the case of Jürgen Bartsch who confessed a murder to his priest. The priest tried unsuccessfully to convince Bartsch to turn himself in to the police. Subsequently, Bartsch sexually tortured and killed three other eleven-year-old boys and attempted to murder many other victims. The question is whether the priest was morally required to prevent these horrors by violating the seal of confession.

Battin claims to present and assess the arguments pro and con in terms of secular ethics. As she sees it, the particular form of confession is a first-level matter open to scrutiny by the methodologically agnostic professional ethicist. Ultimately, she rejects the Church's practice as objectionable in extreme situations such as the Bartsch case. I agree with that conclusion, but here is the rub. Regardless of in what level we place the seal-of-confession doctrine, the Catholic Church will claim that particular practices concerning confession are matters of revelation. Hence, O-level faith in the Pope's access to revelation carries over to first-level ways of implementing the revelation. In this way, any higher-level tenet believed by the faithful to have been revealed to the top church authorities could acquire O-level status, thereby becoming immune to scrutiny by the applied ethicist. Hence, the faith in ongoing revelation to church authorities collapses the levels and breaks the boundaries Battin tried to establish, thereby closing off large areas of inquiry to the applied ethicist.

(2) This brings us to the last difficulty, fortunately one whose resolution will regain and expand territory for the applied ethicist by rejecting procedural agnosticism about O-level doctrines. Why does Battin insist on setting fundamental, O-level, doctrines largely out of bounds to the applied ethicist? Her rationale is that to challenge a tradition's fundamental doctrines "would be to question the religious tradition altogether, not to address the systemic moral problems it generates" (46). It is "premature," she says, in that it is analogous to beginning legal ethics by challenging the entire advocacy system as immoral or beginning business ethics by denouncing capitalism.

I disagree, both with the analogies and with the entire effort to shackle applied ethicists. Let applied ethicists roam freely, in religion ethics as in professional ethics, trusting that their critiques of foundational beliefs can be more nuanced than wholesale dismissals of valuable human endeavors. Part of their work in professional and business ethics should be devoted to foundational issues and, if there are parts of the foundations that are rotten, they should be rooted out. Even in the early stages of religion ethics, criticisms of O-level doctrines need not be premature nor imply dismissing religious traditions altogether.

The important point is that O-level doctrines typically comprise a cluster of doctrines. We can challenge one or two fundamental doctrines without challenging all, hence without completely rejecting the entire religious tradition. In fact, piecemeal criticism limited to selected basic doctrines and practices regularly occurs among the faithful members of religions. For example, suppose an O-level doctrine of a religion is that only males are permitted by God to hold the priesthood or to become bishops. This belief is an O-level doctrine that is deeply entrenched in the traditions and scriptures of Mormons and Catholics as well as it is linked to other basic beliefs about God being male. If the doctrine were to change, these churches would take on a fundamentally—though not completely—different character. Surely feminist applied ethicists can legitimately raise moral objections on this score, both feminists who are Mormons and Catholics as well as feminists who are neither.

In this regard, there are loyal Mormons and Catholics today who are trying to convince their churches to rethink what is most fundamental to their faith. They seek to overthrow institutionalized sexism as inconsistent with a proper understanding of a morally perfect deity and with the real mission of their churches. As an analogy, in the 1970s the Mormons abandoned a very basic doctrine that throughout their tradition had denied the priesthood to African-American males. They did so believing that God had revealed a new doctrine to the Church's president. This piecemeal change fundamentally altered Mormonism—for the better—but it did not overthrow it.

We should distinguish two senses in which a religious doctrine is "fundamental." In both senses, the word "fundamental" implies that the doctrine is deeply entrenched in the religion's historical tradition and central practices, and hence is important in defining what the religion is, vis-à-vis other religions, secular society, and its own past. In the first sense, a doctrine is fundamental if it is deeply entrenched and has great importance from a moral point of view. That was true, for example, of the previous Mormon ban on black males holding the priesthood and of the current restrictions on women holding it, not to mention its views about homosexuality.

In the second sense, a doctrine is fundamental if its denial would amount to rejecting the religion as a whole or at least to renouncing its claim to provide a justified worldview and way of life. The denial of the priesthood to African-American males was not fundamental in this sense. In contrast, presumably for Mormons the belief in the existence of God is fundamental in this second sense. Even here, however, we need to be careful. There is a difference between a few individual members rejecting a fundamental doctrine and an entire religious community doing so. An individual might reject belief in God and yet remain a participant in the Mormon community. A noteworthy example is Sterling M. McMurrin, arguably the most distinguished of all twentieth-century Mormon philosophers, who vigorously affirmed his Mormon identity even though he apparently abandoned belief in a supernatural deity and embraced a metaphysics of "naturalistic humanism."[24]

Views will differ concerning what is fundamental in both senses, but the disagreements should not preclude direct moral criticism of practices that are fundamental in the first sense. When an O-level doctrine is flagrantly inconsistent with justified basic principles of ordinary morality, the doctrine is open to direct challenge by applied ethicists. That includes very basic claims such as that God is male.

Where does all this leave us? Battin establishes that clergy ethics deserves greater scrutiny from applied ethicists. She also gives us a set of new tools and approaches in pursuing religion ethics. The tools yield greater clarity in seeing how religions depart from standards of professional ethics. There are doubts, however, about how often the tools from professional ethics will yield decisive criticisms of nonprofessional religious practitioners. And before concluding that religions violate ordinary moral principles, we must carefully take into account the moral import of membership-consent.

To conclude, are we limited to familiar perspectival moral judgments: From the perspective of secular ethics, X is the case; from the perspective of a particular religious ethics, Y is the case; and so on? Can we never drop the perspectival "from" and make all-things-considered claims? Of course we can make all-things-considered claims insofar as we believe our perspective is correct, but our perspective will always be in the background, especially in applying "ordinary" secular moral standards. We seem stuck, then, with our disagreements about moral perspectives as applied to religious practices. However, moral dialogue need not end when perspectives clash, and moral progress is possible by engaging in dialogue across moral and religious perspectives.

PART IV

Threats to Integrity

However great may be the force of the external pressures on
people, we still need to understand the way in which those
people respond to the pressures. . . . [To] approach evil merely
by noting its outside causes is to trivialize it. Unless we are
willing to grasp imaginatively how it works in the human heart,
and particularly in our own hearts, we cannot understand it.
            —Mary Midgley, *Wickedness*

11

EXPLAINING WRONGDOING

Just as personal commitments shape the character of professionals, failures of personal commitment and character enter into understanding their wrongdoing. We can distinguish two types of explanations of wrongdoing. *Character explanations* appeal to features of persons, either general flaws or specific failings manifested in immoral acts.[1] *Social explanations*, in contrast, appeal to outside structures and pressures that contribute to misconduct, including influences within professions, corporations, and the wider society. Social explanations dominate the thinking of scholars in the social sciences, criminal justice, organizational consulting, and even much applied philosophy devoted to the professions.[2] Usually it is taken for granted that sound explanations focus exclusively on the structures and pressures within social institutions, disregarding failures of personal commitment. Character explanations are dismissed as naive, superficial, subjective, and even incompatible with scientifically rigorous social explanations.

I agree that for many purposes, especially the improvement of social structures and policies, social explanations deserve priority. Nevertheless, character explanations contribute to our understanding of wrongdoing. They do so "from the inside," in terms of the meaning that agents discern in light of their various commitments to craft, compensation, and moral concern. I seek to renew an appreciation of character explanations, distinguish some of their main varieties, and show how they complement rather than compete with social explanations. Professionals are not merely hapless victims of external forces (although occasionally they are). They are responsible moral agents who make choices in response to outside influences.

The opening section clarifies how character explanations carry explanatory meaning and why their reference to values does not render them suspect. The next section illustrates how character and social explanations are complementary. The concluding section integrates the two types of explanations within a virtue-ethics framework for understanding mixed motives in response to multiple social influences. Once again I draw upon and recast Alasdair MacIntyre's distinctions between internal and external goods and between public and private goods.

Explanation and Evaluation

Character explanations can be global or situational. *Global* character explanations identify general character traits of the agent—dispositions to wrongdoing, vices, and the absence of virtues. For example, they might portray fraudulent acts at the workplace by citing the tendencies to ambition, greed, envy, or moral apathy of the individuals involved. In contrast, *situational* character explanations are act oriented and context sensitive. Rather than citing general patterns of character, they locate a specific instance of wrongdoing within one or more character-defined categories. Thus, a single theft by an employee might be identified as an act of vengeance, weakness of will, or greed. These features may or may not be general traits, typical of the employee's usual ways of behaving. In what follows I will highlight situational explanations, both because of their precision and because they overthrow the stereotype of character explanations as simplistic blaming of "bad apples."

In contrast to both types of character explanations, social explanations attempt to identify the structures and influences within professions, organizations, and the wider community that contribute to wrongdoing. Social explanations are group-typical: They characterize how average professionals are likely to act or be tempted to act when confronted with specific pressures and temptations. For example, social explanations might explain a professional's uncharacteristic incompetence as the result of burnout from long hours of unrewarding work. Social explanations ignore character differences among individuals by assuming a general psychological and moral (character) profile of people in general or of members of a particular society.

Somewhat in parallel to character explanations, however, we might distinguish between situational and global character explanations. Situational social explanations pinpoint influences within specific organizations and professions. Global social explanations refer to wider cultural, social, and economic structures and forces. For example, a situational social explanation of employee theft might understand it as a response to a particular company's abusive management policies. A global social explanation might explain an increase in employee shoplifting in terms of a downturn in the economy or an upsurge of envy among workers.

A host of prejudices against character explanations contributes to the hegemony of social explanations. The most damaging prejudice is that character explanations fail to explain anything. Thus, to portray an action as manifesting weakness of will or malicious intent is to evaluate the action and the agent but not to explain the action. Explanation is one thing, evaluation is altogether different. To explain is to identify causes; to evaluate is to apply standards of moral assessment, usually in terms of blaming and praising.

In reply, it is true that character explanations involve value judgments and also true that explaining and evaluating are distinct activities. Nevertheless, the two activities occur together in character explanations, in tandem rather than in opposition. The unity is possible because character explanations employ or imply the language of reasons for conduct. Moreover, evaluation should not be reduced to blame and praise.

Reasons for acting are Janus-faced, combining motivation with attempts at justification. As motives, reasons function as causes of actions and thereby as explanations of why actions occur. Motives are typically specified in terms of desires (to do something) and beliefs (about how to do it): The manager sexually harassed the secretary because of a sexual-aggressive desire as well as both his conscious belief that the secretary was interested in him and his less conscious belief that she was vulnerable. In turn, directly or indirectly, motives and cognitions make reference to the values of individuals, to their commitments, ideals, standards, attitudes, preferences, interests, caring, and moral beliefs—or lack thereof. The manager valued his eroticized power more than the rights and well-being of the secretary.

As justifications, reasons provide the rationale for actions, whether or not the rationale is fully sound or entirely superficial. Reasons are fundamental in thinking about actions. By definition, voluntary and intentional actions are done for reasons, in contrast with mere events over which we have no control.[3] These reasons can be put forth as attempts to justify the action or at least to indicate why the agent thought the action was justified. They are also open to critical assessment as good or bad, reasonable or unreasonable, reasons.

It is no accident that the motivational and justification roles of reasons are merged in "folk psychology," that is, the ways of thinking about human psychology embedded in everyday language. As humans, we are valuing creatures. Nothing is more central to our identity than our tendency to reflect upon and assess the reasons why we do and why we should act. Hence any complete explanation of wrongdoing, including the most sophisticated social explanations, must ultimately make contact with folk psychology. Invariably, social explanations simply assume as a background that humans value certain kinds of things. Too often those assumptions are simplistic and reductionistic, most notably when psychological egoism is assumed (discussed in chapter 2). Character explanations often succeed better in capturing the complexity of human conduct.

To be sure, everyday character explanations are frequently too blunt, resting content with general terms such as "good" and "evil." Yet, character explanations, especially situational ones, are open to considerable refinement, to fine-tuned expressions that convey more specific types of character flaws.

As illustrations of a few major categories of wrongdoing, each of which has many subcategories, I will consider bad preferences, lack of rational self-control, and moral indifference.[4] Locating an act of wrongdoing within these categories simultaneously evaluates and explains it. The categories, which are overlapping, focus on normative understandings of conduct and mental states, not on blame. The normative understandings are often used as the basis for blaming, but evaluating and blaming are distinct. Blame is an angry or hostile attitude in response to (perceived) wrongdoing, and acts of blaming are verbal or behavioral expressions of that attitude. Blame may be entirely reasonable or extremely inappropriate. Certainly there are other responses to instances of wrongdoing: excusing, forgiving, future-oriented calling for change, being indifferent, and so forth. Excessive eagerness to engage in vicious forms of blaming is itself a moral failing of self-righteousness and perhaps cruelty. In any case, the question of when blame is reasonable, and how much of it is appropriate, must not be confused with the use of character explanations in understanding wrongdoing.

(1) *Bad preferences* are having harmful desires or undesirable values. One subcategory is *perverse immorality:* having bad moral principles that one mistakenly believes are morally permissible or even obligatory. Extreme examples are the anti-Semitic doctors, attorneys, accountants, and other professionals who participated with conviction in the Holocaust.[5] Another subcategory is *preferential immorality:* knowing that an action is wrong but preferring it over what is right. Examples include professionals employed by tobacco companies who for decades knew that deceiving the public about the hazards of their product was wrong but who preferred to maintain their lucrative salaries.

Placing an action in the category of bad preferences evaluates the act and the agent, but it also explains the act by referring to the distorted values that prompted it. In perverse immorality, a person affirms as right (obligatory or otherwise desirable) or as all right (permissible) what in fact is immoral. In preferential immorality, a person knows what is right but values it less than something else. With regard to both perverse and preferential immorality, character explanations might cite episodic greed, hubris, or cruelty. In addition, explanations of preferential immorality might also identify preferences for money, power, fame, or revenge over heeding professional standards. In all these instances, evaluation and explanation are combined in the characterization of an agent's reasons for committing a wrong.

(2) *Lack of rational self-control* refers to the absence of sufficiently strong moral motivation or rational self-guidance to meet one's responsibilities. *Moral weakness* is one subcategory: knowing what is right but lacking sufficient motivation to do it. The lack of moral motivation may be accompanied by, and itself defined by, opposing passions, fear, fatigue, low self-respect, internal conflicts, or simple lack of effort. A familiar type of case is knowing that one should not obey a patently unethical directive from a supervisor, but nevertheless obeying it from fear of losing one's job. With preferential immorality, the agent prefers wrongdoing more than right conduct; in con-

trast, with moral weakness the agent prefers the right act, in the sense of judging it to be better, but lacks the willpower to do it.

Moral negligence is a second subcategory of lacking rational self-control. It consists in allowing desires, emotions, or other influences to distort judgment so that one mistakenly believes an act is permissible. The distortion may occur inadvertently, through impulsiveness (thoughtlessness) or carelessness (paying some attention but not due regard to all morally important factors). Or the distortion may occur willfully, through recklessness (deliberate or wanton disregard for morally important factors), rationalization (biased reasoning), or self-deception (refusing to acknowledge to oneself truths important in one's situation).

Identifying how an act results from lack of rational self-control explains it by pinpointing a flawed basic component of intentional action, but the flaw takes different forms in moral weakness and moral negligence. In moral weakness, the flaw centers on motivation, on the absence of sufficiently strong desires, emotions, and value commitments to act as professionalism demands. In moral negligence, the flaw centers on cognition, on the absence of sufficient knowledge, good judgment, and sound reasoning to act professionally (although the inadequacy may ultimately be due to distortions caused by desires). The categories are not mutually exclusive, however. Much wrongdoing by professionals and others is caused by a combination of weakness and negligence. The ultimate explanation of moral negligence is frequently moral weakness in failing to try harder to meet professional responsibilities, and weakness can lead to negligence.

(3) *Moral indifference* is a lack of sufficient concern for the well-being of other people or for oneself. In a wide sense, virtually all forms of wrongdoing manifest insufficient moral concern, but here two specific forms of indifference are intended: amorality and moral detachment.

Amorality is failing or refusing to accept moral principles applicable to the act being explained.[6] An extreme case is the sociopath who engages in terrible cruelty, including murder, without feeling remorse. No doubt a few sociopaths manage to enter the professions, but they cause only a small fraction of the overall harm. At the same time, sociopathy need not be all or nothing. As with other character flaws, it comes in various degrees and levels of severity. And, fortunately, most sociopaths are not violent.

Moral detachment is the more common type of indifference: knowing but not caring that one's moral principles show a particular action to be immoral. Moral detachment constitutes a limited and situational absence of appropriate caring, in contrast to the more extensive indifference characteristic of sociopaths. Like all of us, professionals are prone to moments, interludes, and specific areas of moral indifference. They are vulnerable to more pronounced indifference when they become burned out, disillusioned, and deeply resentful. In most cases, assigning an act of wrongdoing to the category of moral indifference explains the act by identifying a diminishment of a professional's normal degree of caring.

As all these categories of wrongdoing illustrate, character explanations carry explanatory force by identifying the bad preferences, lack of rational self-control, or moral indifference that lead to wrongdoing. In categorizing actions, they allude to psychological elements that cause actions. References to moral values and moral reasons merge into, rather than exclude, causal explanation. That is because identifying reasons for acting represents an entirely legitimate level of causal explanation, indeed, the most fundamental and common-sense level.

If we now grant that character explanations explain as well as evaluate, it may still seem that they are suspect—precisely because of their evaluative dimension. According to this new objection, value judgments are too subjective, controversial, and unverifiable to be of much use in understanding wrongdoing. Social explanations, in contrast, are scientific in the sense of being rigorous, universal, and empirically verifiable independent of value assumptions.

This objection to character explanations is rooted in positivism, a worldview that establishes a sharp dichotomy between objective facts and subjective values. Positivism eclipses the objective dimension of moral judgments. It overlooks how moral judgments can be justified or unjustified, depending on whether they are supported by good moral reasons. It also tends to reduce moral reasoning to blame and praising rather than, say, identifying objective harms and benefits to humanity. As such, positivism is a sophisticated version of the skepticism about moral reasoning that permeates so much of our culture. Accordingly, perhaps the strongest way to counter this criticism of character explanations is to identify how even social explanations refer to values. They do so in two important ways, each of which presupposes that value judgments can be supported by good reasons.

First, social explanations refer to moral values in that they explain wrongdoing! Wrongdoing is immorality, not merely mistakes, regrettable choices, or unforseeable accidents. Parents may painfully regret loaning their car to their teenager daughter who is tragically killed by a drunk driver, through no fault of her own. But the parents did nothing wrong. Even though their feelings of guilt are natural and understandable, they are unwarranted. Wrongdoing means an action is morally objectionable and, unless there are excusing circumstances, culpable and blameworthy. Thus, when we seek to explain wrongdoing in the professions, we are presupposing a moral perspective that identifies professionals as having moral responsibilities which they fail to meet. Social explanations, just as much as character explanations, presuppose that reasons can be given establishing that professional responsibilities exist and have been violated.

Second, social explanations are inevitably selective in ways guided by values. Human actions are usually the product of multiple influences. Typically, explanations single out some of these influences against a background of more routine factors. The selection process reflects both the value perspective and the pragmatic interests of the explainer in recommending particular reforms and types of social change. For example, the actions of 117 Navy officers who sexually harassed and assaulted women at their 1991 Tailhook Convention resulted from an array of influences: drunkenness, a particular tradition at such conventions, lax military discipline, a male-dominated military climate, a wider patriarchal society, male predatory instincts, and so on. In singling out one of these influences as "the" cause of the wrongdoing, a value judgment is made or implied about what is most important, frequently most important from a moral point of view. Thus, military experts might highlight lax supervision by senior officers, feminists might highlight the patriarchal structure permeating the military, and prohibitionists might see alcohol and drug abuse as the main problem. These explanations can be more or less insightful, but all will be guided by value perspectives and practical interests in making improvements to prevent similar events from recurring.

A further objection to character explanations concerns this pragmatic dimension of explanations. Social influences appear easier to change than human character. Business and the professions are concerned with large numbers of individuals. On average, the character of humanity is unchangeable, whereas the prospects for altering structural influences through social engineering are more promising.

In reply, we should reject the pessimism that regards average character as unchangeable, especially character in specific types of situations. If individuals can change, so can large numbers of individuals. Re-creating human nature is not the (impossible) goal; rather, the goal is to selectively change the attitudes of members of corporate cultures to make conduct more responsible within the professions. Faith in this possibility underlies the thousands of courses in applied ethics taught in universities, as well the many workshops on ethics within corporations and continuing education programs for professionals. Moreover, social engineering, to be effective, ultimately engages attitudes, reasoning, and character. This engagement reflects the connections between character and social explanations to which I turn next.

Flawed Apples in Flawed Barrels

Yet another prejudice against character explanations is the belief that they are incompatible with social explanations.[7] According to this objection, character explanations portray some professionals as "bad apples" whose thoroughgoing corruption explains their immoral acts. In contrast, social explanations explain how a typical professional is likely to act or be tempted to act in a given situation. The explanations seem to be competing, with the "real" explanation pointing to either an occasional uncommonly bad character or the common influences affecting everyone. Moreover, this appearance of incompatibility reinforces the belief that character explanations are simplistic because they disregard the complexity of modern organizations and professions.

I agree that bad-apple explanations are usually—though not always—simplistic, especially when they center on general dispositions or character traits. Usually it will not do, for example, to say that selfishness (that is, excessive self-seeking) explains wrongdoing, and leave it at that. We need social explanations that help us understand why selfishness tends to wreak havoc in some contexts rather than in others. But we also need a more nuanced and contextual understanding of character. As I have emphasized, character explanations are not limited to citing general dispositions. There are also situational explanations which locate acts within particular categories of wrongdoing. Thus, an isolated act of moral indifference characterizes the agent as lacking moral concern on one occasion, not as being habitually callous in the way suggested by the "bad apple" metaphor.

Moreover, even global explanations that identify general character flaws need not portray wrongdoers as entirely bad. Character is not a seamless web. No one instantiates all virtues, and even individual virtues are not all or nothing.[8] Individuals might manifest a virtuous disposition in some areas of their lives, for example, kindness toward their family members, but not in others, for example, callousness in professional life. Indeed, even in one area of life they might sometimes act responsibly and sometimes not.

The main point, however, is that character and social explanations are compatible in principle. Confusion generates this false dilemma: either global character faults or social problems within professions and organizations; either rotten apples or rotten barrels. The dichotomy omits the possibility that character explanations can be nuanced and can refer to specific flaws rather than to wholly bad character. It also overlooks the possibility that character and social explanations might amplify, enrich, and interweave with each other.

Character explanations complement rather than compete with social explanations. Character explanations examine conduct from within, in light of human personalities. Social explanations look at conduct from outside, in light of social settings and structures. There need be no conflict or inconsistency in the two perspectives. Social explanations abstract from individuals in that they assume a general psychological and moral profile of human beings. They attempt to identify how a typical professional might be tempted to act in particular situations, thereby ignoring differences among individuals. Nevertheless, they identify influences to which individuals respond when they engage in wrongdoing. Character explanations begin at this point. They characterize actions in terms of the faults involved in allowing social influences to either distort judgment or motivation or engage immoral preferences.

To illustrate the compatibility of character and social explanations, consider Joan C. Callahan's explanation of professional malpractice, using fraud in science as her primary illustration. Why, asks Callahan, do talented and otherwise decent scientists misuse grant money, forge data, lie about their credentials, or fail to give proper recognition to their sources? Advocates for the scientific community contend that scientific misconduct results from a few bad apples, from a minority of scientists who have corrupt character or severe mental problems. Thus, Philip Handler, then president of the National Academy of Sciences, testified before Congress in 1981 that fraud in science is "a relatively small matter": "One can only judge the rare acts that have come to light as psychopathic behavior originating in minds that made bad judgments—ethics aside—minds which in at least this one regard may be considered deranged."[9] Callahan rejects this bad-apple explanation as implausible and seeks to replace it with (what I call) a social explanation.

According to Callahan's social explanation, wrongdoing in science is so extensive that it must be understood in terms of profession-wide pressures to publish or perish, to obtain grants, and in other ways to be economically productive. Applying a feminist perspective, she traces these pressures to a patriarchal society dominated by men's preoccupation with "extreme individualism, productivity, and competition among persons rather than an emphasis on community, nurturing, and connectedness among persons" which are characteristic of women.[10] She calls for reforming the structures in the professions that pose moral risks for basically good people.

Callahan's feminist explanation is clearly value laden, but that is no reason for denying its explanatory power. As I emphasized, all explanations select some factors as more important than others, and the selection process inevitably involves values. If a feminist analysis is rejected, it should not be because it is value laden but instead because of its specific recommendations. I am sympathetic to much of Callahan's perspective, but rather than defending it further I will continue to remain focused on the interplay of character and social explanations.

At first glance, Callahan seems to endorse the dichotomy I am criticizing: Either wrongdoing is produced by corrupt character or by corrupt institutions, but not both. Rejecting (what I call) global character explanations, she recommends instead a social explanation in terms of harmful pressures generated by patriarchal systems. Yet there is a third possibility, namely, that most scientific malpractice results from a combination of flawed character and flawed social structures—imperfect apples in imperfect barrels. Regardless of how institutional influences are analyzed, the question remains why relatively few individuals succumb to those influences and most scientists do not. An answer in terms of character explanations complements rather than competes with social explanations.

In fact, a closer look reveals that Callahan does leave room for character explanations.[11] Using the example of false and misleading statements in science, she distinguishes blameless errors from culpable statements. She then sorts out culpable statements using a character-oriented typology: (a) believing one's statement is true but being blameworthy for not knowing it is actually false (bias, negligence); (b) knowing one's statement is false (deliberate fraud, self-deception); (c) cases lying between (a) and (b) (subtle forms of plagiarism and manipulations of data). Having set forth this character-oriented typology, however, Callahan fails to develop its implication: Wrongdoing by professionals is a product of imperfect character (of both women and men) interacting with imperfect institutions, rather than entirely the product of patriarchal structures. Yet, on balance, she can be interpreted as sharing my approach: not rejecting character explanations, but instead seeing them as complementing social explanations.

Michael Davis's essay, "Explaining Wrongdoing," is a more telling illustration of establishing a false opposition between social and character explanations. Davis argues that much, perhaps most, wrongdoing in the professions arises from ordinary modes of reasoning that professionals and managers are conditioned to use (a social explanation), not from moral faults (character explanations). Wrongdoing is "the result of normal processes" of reasoning rather than "a moral failing in the wrongdoer."[12] Specifically, Davis argues that wrongdoing can be explained by ordinary socialization into corporate roles. This socialization produces distinctive types of professional and managerial "rationality" (modes of reasoning) that embody "microscopic vision": enhancing the role-promoting information and downplaying role-impeding information.

Davis illustrates microscopic vision with corrupt practices such as price-fixing and insider trading, but he devotes most attention to Robert Lund's role in the explosion of space shuttle *Challenger*. As I discussed in chapters 8 and 9, Lund was Vice President for Engineering at Morton Thiokol Corporation, the NASA subcontractor which developed the booster rockets for launching the shuttle. His engineering staff, led by Roger Boisjoly, argued strongly against making the launch because temperatures at the launch site were lower than the O-ring joints for the booster rockets had been tested for. Lund initially agreed with the engineers' recommendation against launch, but he reversed his position when asked by his boss, who was under pressure from NASA officials to approve the launch, to "Take off your engineering hat and put on your management hat." His reversal was "rational from a particular perspective, that of an ordinary manager," and hence "the *Challenger* explosion was the natural outcome of ordinary management." The difficulty is that "Lund was not an ordinary manager; he was supposed to be an engineer among managers," and hence he should never have used a manager's microscopic vision that regards safety as only one of many pertinent factors.

In my terms, Davis offers a social explanation that identifies the influences within Morton Thiokol and NASA that led Lund to think like a manager. I find the explanation partly illuminating, but only partly. True, Lund should not have taken off his engineering hat in the sense of ignoring what he knew as an engineer. But equally true, Lund was a manager who should have weighed safety against many other factors (as all engineers must do at some level). The hat change was not a major factor, but reflected instead the power dynamics and Lund's personal response to them, as manifested in his response to the hat-change remark. Moreover, we need to ask: What character faults are manifested in allowing microscopic vision to operate in a situation, such as the *Challenger* launch decision, where responsibilities of professionals and managers require wider moral vision?

Davis goes to great lengths to exclude character explanations, arguing that Lund was not "careless, ignorant, incompetent, evil-willed, weak-willed, morally immature, or self-deceiving." His arguments are implausible, and I believe he was led to them because he mistakenly assumed that social explanations are incompatible with character explanations. Thus, he thought that in order to establish his social explanation he had to refute character explanations.

For example, Davis contends that the cognitive distortion generated by microscopic vision did not manifest excessive self-seeking. Lund's decision to take off his engineering hat went against his self-interest: "Had he refused to appprove the launch, he would *at worst* have been eased out of his position to make way for someone less risk averse. He would have had no disaster on his record and a good chance for another good job either within Thiokol or outside." Here Davis has in mind enlightened or long-term self-interest, but what matters in explaining Lund's decision were his actual desires and his perception of self-interest at the time, inaccurate though these may have been. Surely we can assume that Lund had a strong preference not to be demoted or otherwise penalized for failing to be a "team player," and this preference contributed to his failure to act responsibly.

Again, Davis remarks that "Lund did, of course, give in to pressure. But to say that is not to explain his decision, only to describe it on the model of a physical process (for example, the collapse of a beer can when we stamp on it)." I disagree. In speaking of the pressure Lund was under, we allude to the reasons he wanted to keep his job. It would not be pressure without his desire to survive and prosper at Morton Thiokol. If saying that Lund gave in to pressure does not by itself fully explain his action, it is only because the appeal does not suffice to explain why Lund failed to act responsibly when other people might have. To cite the pressure Lund was under alludes to factors that enter into understanding his intentions and character so as to round out a character explanation. Buckling under pressure does not refer to can-collapsing forces of compression. Instead, it raises questions about negligence, lack of courage, weakness of will, and self-deception.

Davis briefly discusses some of the latter questions, but only in order to dismiss them. He says, for example, that self-deception could not be involved, because it involves an "abnormal process" and a "conscious flight from reality," whereas Lund's decision fits the pattern of normal managerial thinking. But self-deception takes many forms, including some less conscious and more commonplace than he allows (as I discuss in chapter 12).[13] Lund might very well have failed to be perfectly honest with himself about allowing his short-term self-interest to affect his thinking. He might easily have failed to acknowledge to himself that he was paying less attention to safety than was required by his professional responsibilities. At least, we have no a priori reasons to rule out this possibility. Furthermore, Davis says that Lund was not careless, because "Too much time went into the decision." But instead of thoughtlessness, carelessness can mean moral negligence in failing to give due consideration to all morally relevant considerations.

In my view, negligence was involved. The explosion resulted, in part, from poor and morally negligent managerial decisions by Lund and others, not from "ordinary" or "rational" management. Their negligence constitutes a "moral failing in the wrongdoer," whether or not it involved microscopic vision, self-seeking, weakness of will, self-deception, or all of these. Routine socialization within organizations helps explain the wrongdoing, but it does not rule out character explanations. On the contrary, it prompts us to ask why Lund gave into organizational pressures, in contrast to Roger Boisjoly and other courageous individuals who tried to prevent the launch. And, turning the question around, it prompts us to inquire into the virtues needed to avoid wrongdoing.

Mixed Motives and the Virtues

Character explanations not only complement but mesh with social explanations. The primary point of integration is motivation, specifically mixed motives in response to multiple influences. Professions and corporations influence individuals through many avenues—incentives, supports, pressures, temptations—only a few of which are highlighted in social explanations. Individuals respond to these influences on the basis of an already complex set of reasons for action rooted in human needs and personal interests. As I have suggested, most professionals are motivated by a combination of craft motives (desires to exercise expertise and achieve excellence), moral caring (desires to help people and enter into caring relationships), integrity motives (desires to act ethically and maintain self-respect), and compensation motives (desires for social rewards such as money, authority, and prestige). The virtues play a key role in reconciling and integrating these and other motives in morally desirable ways.

To provide a framework for integrating character and social explanations along these lines, I will invoke Alasdair MacIntyre's virtue-oriented theory in *After Virtue*. As noted in chapter 8, MacIntyre develops a conception of social practices as complex cooperative human activities that, when pursued according to their standards of excellence, yield goods internal to the practice. His examples of social practices include architecture, science, and medicine, and it is clear that his definition fits all professions. Like other social practices, professions are embedded in and supported by moral communities which, in turn, are sustained by moral traditions. Key virtues—especially justice, courage, wisdom, and integrity—promote the internal goods of practices, sustain moral traditions, and support individuals' efforts to pursue good lives. Without the virtues, professions and professionals fall prey to the "corrupting power of institutions" preoccupied with the competition for external goods such as money, power, and status.[14]

The distinction between internal and external goods is useful in explaining corruption, but it is less central than MacIntyre thinks. What exactly is this distinction? Internal goods are practice specific in that they are defined and recognized in terms of particular practices. With regard to the professions, internal goods include (a) distinctive professional services and products (e.g., health care, legal justice, education), (b) the activities of providing those services and products, (c) the pleasures and satisfactions obtained by professionals engaging in that process, and (d) the distinctive kinds of meaningful lives made possible for professionals who engage in those activities and derive those satisfactions.[15] For example, the internal goods of science include scientific understanding, scientific technology, the enjoyments of doing science, and meaningful work within fields of science. In contrast, external goods are practice generic in that they can be obtained through any profession. They include money, prestige, and power, together with their accompanying pleasures. Corruption occurs when preoccupation with external goods overrides a commitment to a profession's internal goods.

MacIntyre fails to notice, however, that whether a good is internal or external depends on the level of generality at which it is specified. Suppose that a professional is concerned to win specific forms of recognition, fame, prestige, and status through a particular profession. For example, a physicist seeks not fame per se, but fame, prestige, and recognition *as* a physicist and *for* achievements in physics. These rewards are internal goods because they are practice specific; they are defined in terms of a particular practice and can only be gained by participating in that practice. Conversely, internal goods such as medical care, law enforcement, and scientific creativity become external goods, found in many different professions, when they are abstractly described as, respectively, helping people, promoting social order, and creativity. In short, the distinction between internal and external goods turns on the language used to describe intentions and goals as much as on the world external to human subjectivity.

This criticism is not a verbal quibble, resolvable by providing more detailed specifications of goods. Instead, it forces us to rethink what is essential in explaining corruption. The crux of MacIntyre's explanation is the more familiar distinction between private and public goods, not the technical distinction between external and internal goods. Private goods are goods possessed by individuals and institutions. Public goods are those shared within practices, communities, and community-minded organizations. The central theme in *After Virtue* is that practices, communities, and meaningful lives erode when narrow self-seeking for private goods, whether by individuals or institutions, overwhelms a shared appreciation of the public goods essential to community. This theme of private goods overwhelming public goods, rather than the internal-external distinction, is the crux of his explanation of wrongdoing. And traditional though it may be, his explanation is insightful.

Why, then, does MacIntyre make the internal-external distinction more prominent than the public-private distinction in explaining corruption? Quite simply, he confuses the two distinctions, conflating internal goods with public goods, and external goods with private goods. For example, in one passage he writes that the achievement of internal goods "is a good for the whole community who participate in the practice"; in contrast, external goods "are always some individual's [or organization's] property and possession."[16] Notice, however, that an individual's fame as a scientist is an internal (practice-specific) good that is a private possession rather than a community good (although a community's shared pride in the individual's recognition is a public good). Conversely, vast wealth is an external (practice-generic) good that is also a public good for an entire community when properly administered for public purposes by government or a non-profit organization.

I am not suggesting that we abandon the distinction between internal and external goods, as originally defined. Indeed, the distinction can usefully be reapplied to explain wrongdoing in more nuanced terms than as simply external goods undermining internal goods. For example, embezzlement and fraud typically involve excessive concern for some external goods (money) over internal goods (a particular high-quality service for customers), but they also show a disregard for other external goods (the corporation's good reputation). Or, when a scientist (or an institution such as a science lab) falsifies data in order to win fame in science, concern for one internal good (recognition in science) distorts another internal good (scientific truth).

I am suggesting, however, that we rethink MacIntyre's characterization of the goods defining professions and institutions. Professions and professionals aim at both private and public goods; so do morally responsible institutions. Explanations of wrongdoing must take these dual aims into account in understanding mixed motives and multiple influences.

On the one hand, returning to a point made in chapter 8, MacIntyre misleadingly stereotypes all institutions as devoted primarily to wealth, power, and reputation.[17] Many institutions have a primary focus on the same internal goods as of the practices they support. Thus, the primary goal of a not-for-profit hospital is to provide medical care for its community, and the primary aim of professional organizations is to serve the same goals as their respective professions. Even for-profit corporations tend to prosper in the long run by remaining focused on quality products and customer service. Many corporations conscientiously make organizational standards compatible with professional standards, both in policies, statements of business codes of ethics, institutional structure, and top-down governance.[18]

Of course, some organizations pose nightmares for committed professionals. In *Moral Mazes*, Robert Jackall describes an accountant who identified numerous corrupt practices, such as a double record-keeping scheme designed to misuse pension funds to stabilize fluctuating cost and profit reports.[19] His professional responsibility was clear: Reveal the truth to the company's chief executive officer, even against the orders of his immediate supervisor. Before doing so, he discovered that the CEO not only sanctioned but instigated the scheme, and the accountant's efforts to reform the company led to his being fired. Disillusioned, he concluded, "What is right in the corporation is what the guy above you wants from you."

Jackall studied only a few exceptionally bad corporations, in particular chemical and textile industries that at the time (the 1980s) were known for putting profits before environmental and worker safety. Most organizations, however, combine the pursuit of profit with a genuine concern for relevant professional standards, ideals of service, and community loyalties. Morally admirable organizations seek profit through a paramount commitment to quality and safety. Most wrongdoing in organizations, as in individuals, derives not from amorality but instead from allowing self-seeking (at the individual and corporate level) to distort a commitment to the public good.

On the other hand, we should not idealize professions as exclusively aimed at public goods, thereby dismissing money and power as somehow "external" to their essential nature.[20] Professions are relatively well paid and prestigious types of work that yield power and authority. Were they not, they would be very different kinds of social practices, for example philanthropic ones. Here, then, is the proper framework for understanding wrongdoing: Professions simultaneously serve public and private goods. So do most individual professionals who are typically motivated by mixed motives in pursuing their profession: concern for private goods (income, power, reputation) and concern for public goods (public service, caring about clients, excellence of craft). Most corruption occurs when concern for private goods overshadows concern for public goods.

The potential for corruption lies within professions themselves, as both Callahan and Davis remind us. I conclude by noting two fundamental dangers inherent in modern professions that threaten public goods.

First, professions combine the dual tasks of advising about services and providing them.[21] Professionals diagnose problems and give expert advice about the pros and cons of available options. Because of the complexity of the issues, clients must rely on that advice in making their decisions. After providing advice about needed services, professionals then provide or offer to provide the services. The upshot is a built-in conflict of interest that can result in a variety of ills: unnecessary services, withholding necessary services, overcharging, or shoddy work designed to increase profit.

In particular, one conflict of interest is inherent in traditional fee-for-services work. Professionals are tempted to advise more extensive or costly services in order to then provide the services in order to earn more money (for themselves and their corporations). Thus, attorneys prolong litigation to earn higher fees; corporate consultants suggest the need for extensive outside supervision of institutional changes they would be happy to oversee;

professors are tempted to advise students to study in their graduate programs in order to keep their funding secure; and so on.

Economic incentives create dilemmas in the opposite direction as well, resulting in impoverishing care. Contemporary managed health care organizations offer strong incentives to their salaried physicians not to provide costly services, thereby threatening proper health care. Especially egregious are organizations that offer direct financial incentives to decrease services, either in the form of bonuses or profit sharing. Whether quality control and peer review mechanisms will prove sufficiently strong to counter this built-in tendency in managed health care remains to be seen.[22]

Second, professionals are often "agents" of their clients in the sense that they are authorized by them, on a basis of trust, to perform acts on behalf of and in place of the clients' physical actions. For example, a lawyer has a "power of attorney" to sign documents and make decisions that count as the client's own actions, even though the client is not present and may even fail to grasp the precise nature of the act. This makes it tempting to think that the attorney performs an act ascribable only to the client. Indeed, according to the American Bar Association, attorneys are not personally responsible for the ends they pursue for clients, as long as the ends are legal.

More generally, when managers serve as the agents of stockholders, physicians act as the agents of patients, government officials act as agents of the government, and soldiers act as the agents of the armed forces, they easily feel excused from personal responsibility for the direction of services. The upshot is a systematic blurring of exactly what professionals are morally accountable for. In general, professions and organizations are replete with narrow roles that encourage professionals to view themselves as unaccountable hired guns for clients or employers. As Elizabeth Wolgast writes, our society has developed "a schizophrenic posture, for on the one hand we insist on knowing who did a misdeed; yet at the same time we obscure the determination of who did it."[23]

In conclusion, just as character explanations help us understand how social influences impact individual professionals, social explanations often pinpoint moral ambiguities inherent in professions that are relevant to character explanations and assessments. Sometimes the information provided in social explanations provides legitimate excuses that mitigate blame for wrongdoing or overthrow allegations of wrongdoing.[24] At other times it does not, because we reasonably expect professionals to deal responsibly with moral uncertainty and opacity. Either way, social and character explanations interact, as well as complement each other, in helping us to understand wrongdoing in professions.

12

SELF-BETRAYAL

I deals expressed in our work usually become central to our self-identity and self-respect. That is partly because of the enormous investments of time, energy, and commitment required by professions, and partly because work is a primary source of self-expression and social recognition. As a result, to betray personal ideals is to betray ourselves. Self-betrayal might be a single self-destructive act, perhaps a white-collar crime, that is easily describable in a case-study vignette of the sort familiar in professional ethics. More often, it is a gradual process of erosion of ideals involving both personal and professional life, an erosion whose full delineation would require the narrative skills and psychological insight of a gifted novelist such as George Eliot.

Eliot's *Middlemarch* is a novel about integrating work and love, vocation and marriage. The opening section of this chapter discusses failures of realism in pursuing high ideals, shown in different ways by Tertius Lydgate and Dorothea Brooke. The next section discusses corruption of ideals through combinations of egotism and purposeful self-deception manifested by Edward Casaubon and Nicholas Bulstrode. The last section explores the regrets, shame, and guilt experienced as the characters become aware of their self-betrayal. Throughout, I seek to elucidate and expand Eliot's moral psychology as it helps us understand how egotism and illusions undermine vocations and threaten self-respect.

More broadly, I seek to illustrate the important role fiction has in exploring personal commitments in professional ethics, as does biography, autobiography, and film. Works in the humanities constitute more extended "case studies" that permit us to reflect on the interplay over time between personal and professional values. Any number of other works might have been explored in this regard, including Charles Dickens' *Hard Times*, F. Scott Fitzgerald's *The Great Gatsby*, George Gissing's *New Grub Street*, Sinclair Lewis's *Babbitt*, Herman Melville's *Bartleby*, Arthur Miller's *Death of a Salesman*,

Peter Shaffer's *Amadeus*, and Leo Tolstoy's *Death of Ivan Ilyich*. Yet, the choice of *Middlemarch* is not arbitrary. The novel explores such a rich variety of themes and professions that it has aptly been called *the* novel of vocation.[1]

Realism and Aspiration

According to a familiar stereotype, ideals are inherently unrealistic and hence prone to tragic overreaching, personal frustration, and harm to others. Eliot has Mr. Brooke voice this objection more than once, for example when Brooke cautions that we should never go "too far" in thinking, feeling, or doing, but only up to a certain point (17).[2] Yet, she also portrays Mr. Brooke as a kindly buffoon—kindly, if we set aside his overt conventional sexism—who at age sixty has never seriously committed himself to anything beyond heeding Adam Smith's advice to look to his personal finances. Eliot celebrates humanitarian ideals, as enbedded in both work and in personal relationships. She is equally engaged by the need for realism—realism as practical wisdom in pursuing ideals, as opposed to realism as cynical renunciation of ideals. Oxymorons best capture her vision: Eliot is a practical idealist, an idealistic realist.

Realism in pursuing ideals has three dimensions: (i) moral caring, in particular the positive emotional attachment to justified moral ideals, (ii) caution, in the form of prudence and practical wisdom in acquiring available facts essential in pursuing the ideals, and (iii) commitment, shown in self-control, perseverance, and abandonment or modification of desires incompatible with the ideals. Each of the main characters is flawed in all three dimensions, but there is a striking division between the characters. Lydgate and Dorothea care deeply about their respective moral ideals; Casaubon and Bulstrode do not.

In a famous passage, the narrator, whom we may roughly equate with Eliot, complains about novelists' obsession with love to the neglect of vocation. Vocation is the other great human passion which, like love, "must be wooed with industrious thought and patient renunciation of small desires" (144). Vocations, too, can lead to either happy or unhappy weddings between desire and duty, feeling and commitment, preference and public role. Marriages and vocations interact within "webs" that support and sustain, but also constrain and ensnare. Eliot uses a medley of examples. Happy marriages and vocations are achieved by Will Ladislaw (politician), Fred Vincy (farmer), Caleb Garth (property manager), and Dorothea Brooke in her second marriage to Ladislaw (construing her philanthropy as a vocation). Troubled marriages and frustrated vocations result for Tertius Lydgate (physician), Edward Casaubon (religious scholar), Dorothea Brooke in her first marriage to Casaubon, and Nicholas Bulstrode (banker) after his social disgrace. Indeed, all the self-betrayals must be understood in terms of the interplay of work and marriage.

Why speak of self-betrayal, rather than simple failure, bad luck, or change of mind? For one thing, the commitments to ideals profoundly shape the individuals' sense of personal identity and worth. For another thing, the individuals corrupt or undermine ideals to which they continue to be committed. Equally important, the ideals are justified and value bestowing, such that self-betrayal suggests disloyalty to a higher or better self. The betrayal is a slow, subtle, and sad process of disloyalty to the individuals' own values, in which they abandon a higher self to a lower self, "till one day their earlier self walked like a ghost in its old home" (145). To be sure, Eliot carefully delineates how circumstances limit possibilities and pose temptations in the form of private goods such as money, status, and comfort. Yet she consistently portrays her characters as responsible for how they respond to constraints and temptations.[3] All the main characters manifest a combination of egotism and self-deception for which they are responsible.

Egotism and self-deception take different forms. Three distinctions will help sort them out. First, we can distinguish between egotism, self-respect, and self-esteem. *Egotism* is the habit of excessively and selfishly valuing things by reference to personal interest, without giving due attention to the good of others. In this sense, "egotism" is a pejorative term referring to the vice of excess and to inappropriate grounds in making appraisals and acting on them. *Self-respect* is the stable tendency to value oneself appropriately, in desirable ways and for sound reasons, both in attitude and action. Thus, "self-respect" is an honorific term that identifies a fundamental moral virtue. In contrast, "self-esteem" is a descriptive or value-neutral word that refers to emotions and attitudes of positive self-worth that may be excessive or deficient, justified or not. Egotism is an immoral distortion of self-esteem. In contrast, self-respect is a moral standard requiring appropriate self-esteem.

Second, self-respect takes two forms, according to its specific objects and justification.[4] *Dignity self-respect* is the proper recognition owed to ourselves as moral beings with inherent moral worth and dignity. *Character self-respect* is self-respect grounded in our morally desirable features, including our moral ideals and commitments. This distinction parallels two senses of respecting others (noted in chapter 5): dignity self-respect is the self-directed version of the recognition respect owed to each person because of his or her inherent dignity; character self-respect is the self-directed appraisal respect owed to people who manifest virtues. The two forms of self-respect are closely related, however. After all, a sense of one's moral dignity is itself a desirable character trait. As a virtue, the sense of one's moral dignity implies a concern to maintain self-control, honest reflection, taking care of our health, developing our talents, and other prerequisites for exercising moral agency. Failure to do so provides grounds for shame or even contempt, in our own eyes and in the eyes of others.

Third, we can distinguish between two combinations of egotism and illusion. Egotism takes innumerable forms, as Eliot reminds us: "Our vanities differ as our noses do: all conceit is not the same conceit, but varies in correspondence with the minutiae of mental make in which one of us differs from another" (149). Tacitly, Eliot marks a distinction between two general categories of conceit, according to whether the conceit involves intentional self-deception or nonintentional illusion. *Inner hypocrisy* is the willful, purposeful, and devious self-deceit manifested by Bulstrode and Casaubon and explored in the next section.[5] *Motivated illusion* is non-intentional but still motivated forms of rashness, negligence, or naiveté. Here a person's desires generate false beliefs which serve a vital purpose without the purpose consciously being embraced as a goal or purpose, as with Tertius Lydgate and Dorothea Brooke.

Of all the characters, Dr. Lydgate has the greatest promise to be creative in his profession. He is gifted with intelligence and ambition, confidence, and compassion. At age ten he developed a deep fascination with human anatomy that later led him to seek out the best medical education. By his mid-twenties he formed a life plan to pursue a dual ideal: serve as a healer while conducting scientific research on the human body. When he moves to the town of Middlemarch, he makes a promising beginning on both fronts. As a healer, he challenges the rampant quackery of his peers who casually prescribe unproven drugs. As a scientist, he sets out to discover a unified understanding of the human body.

Then he meets Rosamond Vincy, an enchanting woman who unfortunately has no interest in his career except for the money and prestige it promises. Lydgate's attraction to Rosamond is neither an accident nor a compulsion for which he lacks responsibility. In a way, he prepared himself for the attraction by nurturing a view of women as mere comforts and ornaments (94). After they marry, he finds the ornament is more expensive than he imagined, though he cannot blame Rosamond for unilaterally causing their financial difficulties. Lydgate is very much a coparticipant in living beyond their means. He takes for granted that a person of his stature should have fine furniture and all other desirable things in life. Unsupervised, his debts mount, bringing with them a suffocating preoccupation with finances. Eventually he seeks a large loan from Bulstrode, thereby ending the independence needed to pursue his research.

In addition to his misconceptions about women, Lydgate has another great illusion: confidence that he is incorruptible. Up to a point, his self-confidence is admirable in providing hope and a sense of meaning as he pursues medical reform and scientific discovery.[6] And his self-confidence has some foundation. He had made considerable sacrifice to attain the qualifications needed to pursue the plans, and he had deliberately moved to Middlemarch in order to escape the temptations he discerned in big-city medicine. But his self-assuredness is overblown. It leads him to take for granted that he is beyond temptation. Too casually, he ignores the need to avoid even the appearance of conflict of interest. He becomes easy prey to Bulstrode's financial control and even to Middlemarch's established society that early on "counted on swallowing Lydgate and assimilating him very comfortably" (154).

His illusions about women and about his incorruptibility are motivated by egotism: "Lydgate's conceit was of the arrogant sort . . . massive in its claims" (149). The complacent assumption that he is destined for comfort and control leads him to avoid seeing his life in its entirety. He has "two selves" that he fails to integrate—the passionate intellectual and the pleasure seeker (150, 152). Egotism motivates the failed integration, although he is not purposely self-deceiving. He simply fails to understand his life in its main respects. As Eliot wryly comments, the "distinction of mind which belonged to his intellectual ardour, did not penetrate his feeling and judgment about furniture, or women, or the desirability of its being known (without his telling) that he was better born than other country surgeons" (150).

Eliot's language of two selves is an apt metaphor. Lydgate does not merely have two simple desires that happen to clash but, instead, fundamentally opposed aspects of his personality. We might speak of different subselves, or, if such talk seems paradoxical, we can characterize Lydgate in terms of two conflicting patterns of desires-emotions-values-beliefs. The patterns are conflicting in that his commitment to medical research requires disciplining his expensive tastes in furniture, food, and entertaining. Ultimately, in his circumstances, it also requires a wife quite different from Rosamond, as the Reverend Farebrother advises him (174, 456). Lydgate saw the need for prudence in others, carefully adjusting his prescriptions for the poor to fit their means, yet he failed to exercise prudence himself. As Eliot observes, it is commonplace how people "have numerous strands of experience lying side by side and never compare them with each other" (589).

Motivated (but nonintentional) illusions are also the source of Dorothea Brooke's difficulties, although her dominant motive is altruism rather than arrogance. Her benevolence is so extraordinary that it might seem wrong to speak of self-betrayal in her case. She is introduced in the "Prelude" as having a "spiritual grandeur" on the scale of Saint Theresa (3). We are told several times that her failure to have a comparable historical impact is due to circumstances, in particular to the constraints on women that prevent them from gaining education and entering professions. We are also told of her blindness in certain matters of common sense, but the blindness constitutes imprudence rather than imperfect moral concern. We recognize her authenticity when she affirms this credo: "That by desiring what is perfectly good, even when we don't quite know what it is and cannot do what we would, we are part of the divine power against evil" (392).

Is there perhaps an element of egoism mixed with her altruism, specifically in her need to be the one who does the helping and in her inclination to paternalism in helping (361)?[7] Perhaps, but certainly egoism is not a major motive behind her illusions about changing the world or about Casaubon's character. If anything, we worry that she fails to care sufficiently about herself. As feminists point out, her ideal of selfless service needs to be tempered by a proper degree of self-respect, of regard for her own well-being. It is that failure, ironically, that prevents her from accomplishing as much good as she desires. Morality includes a recognition of our moral worth that is perhaps greater than Eliot allows in describing Dorothea as "trying to get light as to the best way of spending money so as not to injure one's neighbours, or—what comes to the same thing—so as to do them the most good" (805). Doing our neighbors the most good could imply giving away all our resources, leaving us destitute.

Does Dorothea betray her ideals of service? Yes, by marrying Casaubon. She envisions marriage as based on unqualified giving, combined with the opportunity to learn from Casaubon's seeming wisdom about how best to help others. Self-betrayal is involved, because she shares responsibility for allowing her illusions to lead her into the disastrous marriage. Even the trauma of being married to the self-absorbed Casaubon does not sufficiently prompt her to affirm her own needs. She comes alarmingly close to making a deathbed promise to Casaubon to carry on his massive writing project that she knew by then to be worthless. Given her puritanical conscience, she would have felt bound to keep such a promise, even with disastrous consequences to herself. Only later, in responding to her love for Will Ladislaw, is she liberated by the truth in his view: "The best piety is to enjoy—when you can. You are doing the most then to save the earth's character as an agreeable planet. And enjoyment radiates" (219).[8]

Tertius Lydgate and especially Dorothea Brooke engage us because their moral ideals are both genuine and valuable in their situation. Each shares some responsibility for their failures in pursuing those ideals. Yet, their errors take the form of blindness, combined with self-denial (Dorothea) or arrogance (Lydgate), rather than self-deceitful corruption. In this regard they stand in sharp contrast with Bulstrode and Casaubon, to whom I turn next.

Recognition and Self-Deception

Within broad limits, the drive for professional recognition is natural, healthy, and socially desirable. It increases energy in pursuing one's craft with excellence and in helping others, and it also contributes to character self-respect. The problem is that recognition motives are meshed with the wider desire for self-esteem—perhaps the strongest desire other than basic biological drives, and sometimes even stronger than self-preservation. Whether in the form of seeking power, prestige, fame, or money, the drive for recognition easily grows to excess and exceeds all bounds of reasonableness.[9]

A familiar symptom of lacking healthy self-respect is the anxious and insatiable preoccupation with recognition. For example, in his study on adult life cycles, Daniel J. Levinson describes an exceptionally accomplished and distinguished biologist whose unbounded desire for recognition nearly destroyed his life. Nothing short of a Nobel Prize would satisfy him. In fact, his research was Nobel-Prize quality, and he missed winning the Prize only because another scientist made the same discovery two weeks earlier. Although his accomplishments brought him international fame and membership in the National Academy of Science, "in his mind, he was a failure."[10]

The desire for professional recognition is tailor made to invite such excess. Professions encourage judging oneself and others according to high standards of excellence and also social success. They encourage strong competitiveness, not only to meet high standards but to outshine other professionals, especially one's colleagues. They promise great rewards of money and fame, and they create pressures in the form of personal and societal expectations of success. In this regard Eliot's portrayal of Bulstrode's and Casaubon's self-deceiving obsessions with professional recognition has contemporary interest.

Unlike motivated illusion, the idea of purposeful, conniving, and willfully executed self-deception generates considerable puzzlement. Jean-Paul Sartre identified two main paradoxes.[11] The first is cognitive: Forming an intention to lie to oneself seems to require knowing what one intends to conceal. If the intention succeeds, a person would then believe and yet not believe the same thing. The second paradox is volitional: An intention to deceive oneself seems to imply a conscious and willful effort to use what one knows in getting oneself not to believe it. Such an effort is incoherent, because the very consciousness of the truth would preclude getting oneself to believe the opposite falsehood.

Philosophers and psychologists have made numerous attempts to solve these and related paradoxes. Some invoke Freud's idea of unconscious beliefs and intentions. Others invoke various automatic reflexes (to unpleasant realities) that fall short of full-blown intentions. Still others reject the possibility of intentional self-deception altogether. Although Eliot does not state Sartre's paradoxes, her phenomenology of self-deception suggests a solution in terms of quite ordinary conscious and semiconscious activities. In fact, her solution is not dissimilar to the one set forth by Sartre, a sketch of which follows.

Regarding the cognitive paradox, contradictory beliefs need not be involved at all. Suspicions and fears, rather than full-blown belief or knowledge, suffice as the basis for turning away, not reflecting, or choosing not to explore unpleasant topics or truths. Regarding the volition paradox, self-deceiving intentions need not be described in paradoxical language. They include the quite ordinary intentions to avoid reflecting on disturbing topics, to avoid confessing and repenting of wrongdoing, and to avoid revealing certain facts to others. The complex pattern of evasion is plausibly understood as a purposeful activity aimed at evading painful truths and topics. But the purpose need never be explicitly formulated consciously, and if the individual momentarily becomes aware of it, the intention is quickly disregarded and the suspected truth rationalized away.[12]

Eliot explicitly distinguishes self-deceit from routine hypocrisy in which persons are fully aware of the deceptions they try to foist on others. "There may be coarse hypocrites, who consciously affect beliefs and emotions for the sake of gulling the world, but Bulstrode was not one of them" (619). Bulstrode's ideal was to become "an eminent Christian," initially as a minister but later as a businessperson (526). Apparently he had some genuine religious desires, but they were modest compared to his "immense need of being something important and predominating" (620). To reconcile these clashing desires, Bulstrode engages in monstrous self-deception.

Eliot's description of Bulstrode's self-deception has three parts: forming, implementing, and protecting illusions. First, self-deception is possible because there are large areas of indeterminacy and vagueness concerning the values that we use in appraising ourselves. In particular, there are no authoritative judges or social standards that prevent us from adopting moral values, religious faiths, and beliefs in our abilities that fit comfortably with our needs and wishes. It is easy and commonplace to adopt master illusions that permeate and dominate an entire life. Bulstrode is only one of innumerable persons who "believed without effort in the peculiar work of grace within him, and in the signs that God intended him for special instrumentality" (616). As long as he made some gestures of philanthropy, he could easily confuse Christian dogma with genuine sympathy for others. It was equally straightforward to believe that "he did everything for God's sake, being indifferent to it for his own" (617).

Second, once embraced, our illusions are applied and elaborated to maintain at least a rough consistency of outlook. Like Lydgate, Bulstrode has two selves, two strongly opposed strands of experience, but unlike Lydgate he purposefully distorts each to fit the other: "Bulstrode found himself carrying on two distinct lives; his religious activity could not be incompatible with his business as soon as he had argued himself into not feeling it incompatible" (617). Construing the Protestant work ethic to his own advantage, he interprets each new profit as sign that God wants him to be steward of the profit he takes from spendthrift sinners.

Bulstrode began his career as an accountant for a pawnbroker business that, although legal, became profitable by trading in stolen goods. Throughout his career he followed a similar path, heeding the letter of the law while maximizing profits. Before he married his first wife, he helped locate her runaway daughter. But he refused to convey this information to his future wife, thereby assuring that her wealth would go to him rather than to the daughter. He justified withholding the information through "little sequences, each justified as it came by reasonings which seemed to prove it righteous" (618). For example, convinced by his master illusion that he was God's chosen steward, he kept salient in his thoughts the greater good he could accomplish with the money, and he discerned virtue in preventing the irresponsible daughter from wasting the money.

Bulstrode uses the same self-righteous reasoning to conceal from himself his contribution to the death of Raffles, his former associate who returns to Middlemarch to bribe him and expose his past. Raffles, he tells himself, is an evil man to whom he owes nothing, not even medical attention. Thus he sees no great sin in failing to convey to his housekeeper, whom he asks to stay the night with Raffles, Dr. Lydgate's instructions concerning withholding alcohol and ministering only small doses of morphine.

Third, the entire set of rationalizations is protected by further maneuvers. On the one hand, our acquaintances must be prevented from saying things that would overthrow the self-deceit. This social dimension of self-deception requires deceiving others, but only about certain troublesome facts and circumstances, not by way of conscious lies about the self-deception. Bulstrode's conscience prevents him from engaging in outright lies, but he deliberately withholds pertinent information from other citizens whom he knows would interpret the facts differently.

On the other hand, we must prevent our own reason from overthrowing the rationalizations. Bulstrode experiences moments of self-doubt about his character, but he manages those through "mental exercises" of self-blame followed by resolve to carry on God's work (as steward of the money) with some contributions to philanthropy (618), keeping safely abstract the "doctrinal conviction" that he (like all humans) lacks merit, while avoiding genuine remorse for his wrongdoing and attempts at reform (521). Also, as time passes, he simply avoids thinking about the unsavory aspects of his past. Both with regard to others and to himself, Bulstrode was steeped in long habits of soothing his conscience in "the enfolding wing of secrecy" (711).

Bulstrode's self-righteousness is only one of countless varieties of self-deception in moral matters. Eliot cautions that "there is no general doctrine which is not capable of eating out our morality if unchecked by the deep-seated habit of direct fellow-feeling with individual fellow-men" (619). Casaubon, Eliot's second main example, also engages in religious self-deception, but his illusions primarily concern his intellectual creativity and accomplishments as a scholar.

Unlike Bulstrode's greed, the Reverend Casaubon's intellectual aspirations yield little vitality: "His soul was sensitive without being enthusiastic: it was too languid to thrill out of self-consciousness into passionate delight" (279). At the same time, Casaubon's self-deceit is far more ambitious than Bulstrode's. His aim is to discover and write the "Key to all Mythologies," a unifying understanding of all worldviews in light of Christian belief. The hubris manifested in this ambition is matched by his timidity, specifically his fear of being exposed as a failure. He squanders his life in endless note taking so as to avoid serious writing, all the while disregarding the overwhelming evidence showing his lack of progress.

Like Bulstrode, Casaubon has moments of doubt and suspicion that, if honestly pursued, would expose his illusions. But, for the most part, he refuses to confess to himself the import of these reservations (419). Again, like Bulstrode, he carefully manages others' access to information about himself. Never does he reveal to others the paucity of actual accomplishment.

When Dorothea discovers the problem and urges him to start writing, he responds with anger in lecturing her about lack of qualifications to assess the status of his work.

Much of Casaubon's energy is spent in maintaining his illusions by combining "a melancholy absence of passion in his efforts at achievement" with "a passionate resistance to the confession that he had achieved nothing" (417). His motives include fear of the self-revelation inherent in publishing, but ultimately that motive is linked to his terror of death. Reflection on death would seem part of being a minister, but only when his health fails does he do so honestly: "When the commonplace 'We must all die' transforms itself suddenly into the acute consciousness 'I must die—and soon', then death grapples us, and his fingers are cruel" (424). An earlier confrontation with his mortality might have forced him to readjust his scholarly goals in a more realistic direction. Instead, he squanders his life and dampens the joy of people around him, especially that of Dorothea. Obsessed with maintaining his self-image as a great thinker, he throws away his last opportunity for happiness in loving Dorothea, treating her as little more than an assistant. Callousness turns to cruelty when he writes a will denying Dorothea an inheritance if she marries his younger rival, Will Ladislaw. There, too, he conceals from himself his "irritated jealousy and vindictiveness" by rationalizing that he is protecting Dorothea from an irresponsible gigolo.

Casaubon's vindictiveness suggests he was motivated by something more insidious than jealousy (fear or anger at the prospect of losing something we value). He is corrupted by envy. The envy, of course, is not the admiration and desire expressed in the colloquial "I envy you." It is the envy we would rarely confess to and indeed conceal from ourselves through self-deception.[13] Envy is malicious hatred of others for their good fortune, together with feeling inferior because we lack what they have. In addition to assaulting the well-being of others, envy erodes self-respect and can cause unremitting self-torture of the sort Casaubon experiences.

The primary occurrence of envy in the novel is Casaubon's animosity toward Ladislaw, but Eliot hints at the much wider role of envy in the professions. She identifies the rancor felt by the lesser-skilled medical community toward Dr. Lydgate. She also hints that Casaubon's "melancholy embitterment" at not receiving the recognition he feels he deserves may emerge from envy of more recognized thinkers.

Regret, Shame, Guilt

To betray ideals central to our identity threatens self-respect. The threat is experienced as regret, shame, or guilt. All three involve mental anguish in response to bad things, but the focus of the response differs. *Regret* is a painful response to misfortune, our own or of people we care about, centered on the desire that the misfortune had not occurred. We might regret failing to live up to the ideals defining our vocation. We might regret failing to find our vocation in the first place. And we might regret harming others during the pursuit of our profession. The latter regret is normally accompanied by *guilt:* the painful sense of being responsible for harming others and for other instances of failing to meet responsibilities. In contrast, *shame* is the pained emotion of demeaning ourselves. As a "sense of shame," it is also a self-protective fear of self-diminishment and a tendency to avoid threats to our sense of self-worth.

All the main characters in *Middlemarch* suffer some damage to their (character-) self-respect, though the damage varies in its severity and permanence. Eliot insists that character is not cut in marble; instead it "is a process and an unfolding" (149). It is "living and changing, and may become diseased as our bodies do," but it can also "be rescued and healed" (735). All this applies to how we respond to regrets, shame, and guilt, especially because the objects of these emotions indicate what we care about—on what we base our self-respect and self-esteem.

As might be expected, Casaubon's regrets remain entirely self-centered. They include regrets about the failure of his peers to appreciate his published works (279), about not finding marriage joyous when his wife judges his magnum opus as a fruitless ambition (418), and about his inability to gain literary immortality by writing his planned "Key to all Mythologies." His reputation preoccupies him, not his scholarship. Never is he able to transcend his "melancholy embitterment" (280) and morbid self-pity, except in one rare moment of sympathetic communion with Dorothea (427). In the end, he refuses Dorothea's compassionate and supportive love, responding to her as a threat rather than a helpmate. As death approaches he is roused by envy to write a will that denies Dorothea an inheritance if she marries Ladislaw.

In contrast to Casaubon, Bulstrode undergoes some change, even though he remains more concerned with his public reputation than with what is right. Upon being exposed as a moral fraud and guilty of malfeasance in the death of Raffles, he angrily denounces his accusers as being no better than he is. If he experiences guilt for his past wrongs, it remains largely unrepented. He does, however, experience remorse for the suffering he causes his wife, Harriet. He seeks her forgiveness and makes some amends by helping Fred Vincy and Mary Garth. Most important, he is able to submit to Harriet's judgment and to accept her forgiveness. Unlike Casaubon, he reveals a capacity to love at least one other human being.

Lydgate, like Levinson's biologist, "always regarded himself as a failure: he had not done what he once meant to do" (835). He suffers deep regrets and shame about abandoning his aspiration to make major innovations in science and medical practice. These emotions seem justified, but perhaps he should feel little guilt. He does not seriously harm others, and his suffering leads him to become a morally better person by replacing his arrogance with humility. If there is guilt, surely there is also a basis for self-forgiveness. He assumed responsibility for making the best of an unhappy marriage, wrote a book on gout, and achieved success as a doctor. Interestingly, even before he is forced to leave Middlemarch, his misfortunes and suffering make him a better physician, more sympathetic toward his patients: "By the bedside of patients the direct external calls on his judgment and sympathies brought the added impulse needed to draw him out of himself . . . serving better than any opiate to quiet and sustain him under anxieties" (668). Nevertheless, his regrets never disappeared, and he "accepted his narrowed lot with sad resignation" (800).

Placed in the brief "Finale," the comment that Lydgate always viewed himself as a failure is not an expression of fatalism, even about regret itself. For, if character is an ongoing process, he surely had options for transforming his regrets, either by changing attitudes about the source of his suffering, controlling the intensity or frequency of painful emotions, or changing his life.[14] For example, even though it was impossible to radically alter his profession or his marriage, he might have refocused his energies on fulfilling aspects of his work, as well as made compromises that allowed a healthy balance. The Reverend Farebrother illustrates this possibility of transcending painful regrets.

As a vicar, Farebrother "felt himself not altogether in the right vocation," and confesses that he is "not a model clergyman—only a decent makeshift" (172, 176). It is unclear why he made the wrong choice: possibly a lack of courage or too little self-confidence. What is clear is that he modifies his attitudes and makes creative adjustments: "'I used often to wish I had been something else than a clergyman' . . . 'but perhaps it will be better to try and make as good a clergyman out of myself as I can'" (511). Farebrother makes adjustments and compromises that enable him to serve as a caring and helpful counselor, far more so than the other clergy in the novel. He does so by allowing his other interests to be expressed, especially his dominant love of biology and other natural sciences (172).

Here we might recall Wittgenstein's advice to a former student who expressed regrets and self-doubts about choosing to become a physician: "The thing now is to live in the world in which you are, not to think or dream about the world you would like to be in. Look at people's sufferings, physical and mental, you have them close at hand, and this ought to be a good remedy for your troubles."[15] Lydgate does move in that direction, but he never fully appreciates its moral significance. Certainly, creative compromises are important in our culture of rapid change, as identities become increasingly protean.[16]

Dorothea also has regrets. She feels "that there was always something better which she might have done, if she had only been better and known better" (835). But she has few grounds for shame and guilt. Even her regrets are largely transcended through the love she found in marriage, in raising her child, and in continuing to help others. Her sympathy and kindness remain unchanged, while one aspect of her character undergoes change: She gains greater practical wisdom about how to help others. She accepts her lot with joyful affirmation, unlike Lydgate's sad resignation. As Eliot concludes, some may regret "that so substantive and rare a creature should have been absorbed into the life of another," but "no one stated exactly what else that was in her power she ought rather to have done" (836). Feminist objections are better directed at the constraining circumstances, not her choices. If anything, those circumstances made her choice to marry Ladislaw reasonable, even daring.

In contrast to Lydgate's sad resignation, Casaubon's embittered self-pity, Bulstrode's crushing humiliation, and even Farebrother's prudent compromise, Dorothea illustrates how regrets can be creative rather than corrosive. Some regrets are perhaps inevitable when ideals are seriously pursued, for it is in the nature of ideals rarely to be perfectly achievable. As Dorothea becomes a practical idealist, her regrets serve as reminders of possible goods yet to be achieved.

To conclude, the consensus paradigm, with its exclusive focus on codified duties and public dilemmas, eclipses or marginalizes the topics dealt with in this chapter, including self-fulfillment and self-betrayal, realism and illusion, self-respect and self-deception, regrets and shame, guilt and self-acceptance, envy and self-righteousness. These topics in moral psychology become legitimate, however, once we rethink professional ethics to include personal commitments in professional life. That rethinking also carries implications for understanding the integrity of professionals, implications touched on throughout this book and unfolded more fully in the next chapter.

13

INTEGRITY AND INTEGRATION

Not long ago, professionals and other workers in industrialized nations could reasonably look forward to shorter workweeks and expanded leisure. That has changed. Relentless economic pressures have extended many workweeks to fifty hours or more, not counting time spent commuting to work, unwinding after stressful days, and meeting continuing education requirements. According to one estimate, from 1969 to 1987 the average American employee's yearly work increased by 163 hours, roughly one extra month per year.[1] In addition, the 1990s brought intensified global competition and worsened bargaining positions for workers, leaving them little choice but to meet expectations for greater involvement with work. Those who were even less fortunate were fired during the waves of layoffs that, for the first time, hit hard at white-collar workers and later forced many to take substantially-lower-paid jobs. On a more positive note, many professions continue to be deeply engaging in ways that evoke personal commitments. Whatever the cause of increasing involvement with professions, integrating work with family and other commitments is now a major moral challenge. So is avoiding burnout.

My emphasis on personal ideals in professional life may seem to make matters worse by encouraging excessive zeal at work, compounding the dangers of burnout and harm to families. But excessive zeal is just that—a lack of reasonable proportion and balance. Realistic ideals of caring bring resources for avoiding burnout and for integrating professional and other commitments by keeping moral imperatives clear. To see this, we need a conception of professionals' overall integrity that is wider than the usual idea of integrity within a professional role. We also need a pragmatic view of moral reasoning that cautions against rigid hierarchies among commitments, while being sensitive to the need for setting priorities in specific contexts where work and family compete. These are large topics, and in this concluding chapter I can only say enough to invite their inclusion in the study of professional ethics.

Professionals' Integrity

According to the consensus paradigm, burnout and family life are either irrelevant to understanding professional integrity or pose threats to it. The consensus paradigm limits professional ethics, in terms of which professional integrity is defined, to the duties accepted as a consensus within a profession and incumbent on all its members. These duties are specified as independent of family situations. Should family or other personal matters conflict with codified duties, it is assumed that the latter alone specify one's duty as a professional. In turn, this duty is taken to be what one ought to do, all things considered, in professional contexts. Family considerations are either irrelevant or a threat to that duty.

At the very least, however, it is ironical to fragment integrity according to separate roles and spheres: integrity as a professional, as a spouse, as a parent, as a citizen, and so on. Even more than most virtues, integrity resists fragmentation into insulated domains, as its very etymology suggests: *integritas* means wholeness and suggests unity, interrelatedness, integration, harmony among aspects of character. Admittedly, virtues can be manifested in varying degrees and in some contexts but not others.[2] Life is complex, and we must admit that there can be genuine subunities and limited integrity within particular domains of life, without unity overall. An engineer might be honest at work but dishonest with his spouse, and a police officer might be courageous on the job but a coward when she invests in stocks. At the same time, this "gappiness" of character calls for some accounting. If virtue appears here, why not there? Is it perhaps only a hypocritical posture that conceals other motives?

Integrity provokes us to seek wider unities. If we are to establish a framework for connecting professional with other major dimensions of life, we need to attend to a professional's wider integrity, integrity defined by professional duties and roles and much more.

Role integrity is integrity within a professional (or other) role. Using the consensus paradigm, professionals' role integrity consists in regularly meeting their professional responsibilities specified in codes of ethics. Using the widened view of professional ethics set forth in this book, role integrity also includes meeting professional responsibilities connected with supererogatory personal commitments that are not incumbent on all members of a profession. All these responsibilities are encompassed by the broader idea of a professional's *overall integrity:* the global integrity of a person who is a professional, taking into account all major aspects of his or her life rather than solely role behavior within in a profession. A professional's overall integrity considers all of an individual's central commitments, including those to family and to oneself, as well as those defining professional role integrity. My suggestion is that professional ethics should include the study of professionals' overall integrity—wherever nonprofessional commitments require integration with professional ones.

Integrity, by which I now mean overall integrity, is coherence of character and conduct as formed around a core of reasonable and authentic commitments to moral values. As such, integrity combines three distinct, though overlapping, types of unity: personal integration, moral decency, and authenticity. Each type of unity has personal variations in style and emphasis, and each is open to alternative philosophical conceptions.[3]

(1) *Personal integration* is the (rough) consistency and harmony among one's major commitments. Unlike wantons, who act willy-nilly on passing desires, persons with integrity struggle to maintain ongoing coherence in their lives around a core of basic commitments.[4] More than implying logical consistency, integration means that all major commitments are pursued in tandem without excessive disruption and anxiety. Conflicts and tensions among commitments are inevitable, and the only way to avoid them is to drastically narrow commitments to the point of leading an impoverished life. Nevertheless, integration implies habits of interweaving commitments so as to reduce and resolve conflicts. Even when values apply within narrow domains, such as in the context of a particular job, they remain values of the whole person rather than of isolated fragments of the person.

(2) *Moral decency* is unity between conduct and fundamental moral values. Persons of integrity are reliable in meeting their responsibilities and commitments. They are decent, honest, and fair. They make a genuine effort to be mindful of relevant moral values. With varying degrees of success, they achieve moral understanding (in a sense that leaves much room for differences among reasonable persons).

Moral decency is salient in everyday conceptions of integrity, but it is downplayed in some philosophical theories. Most notably, John Rawls suggests that integrity is a formal virtue that "allows for most any content," as long as a person manifests "truthfulness and sincerity, lucidity and commitment, or, as some say, authenticity": "A tyrant might display these attributes to a high degree."[5] But it is jarring to say that tyrants like Hitler and Stalin had moral integrity because of the fervor of their commitments. Moral integrity is built around a core of at least minimal moral reasonableness and decency. And when authenticity reduces to mere affirmation of and action on our desires, it is not a moral virtue.

Moral integrity contrasts with nonmoral forms: artistic integrity (devotion to artistic ends), intellectual integrity (devotion to inquiry), religious integrity, (devotion to religious values), and personal integrity (unified action in living up to whatever values one believes in). Nevertheless, these other forms of integrity usually have moral dimensions. That is obvious in the case of religious integrity, because religious outlooks typically have substantial moral content. Intellectual integrity, too, implies the virtues of honesty, both truthfulness and trustworthiness in pursuing truth and courage in speaking the truth as one sees it.

What about artistic integrity? Paul Gauguin was devoted to his craft, imposed stringent demands on it, and refused to "sell out" for more lucrative commercial offers.[6] He also abandoned his wife and children (raising questions about his overall integrity) and the humdrum job that supported them, in order to pursue an impoverished but enormously creative life in Tahiti centered around his art. He manifested several nonmoral excellences: artistic integrity (commitment to art), integrity of purpose (devotion to his plans), and personal integrity (fidelity to his personal ideals). But there is an additional moral dimension in how his art enriched our lives, leading us to appreciate beauty in other cultures in ways that evoke a sense of shared humanity. Gauguin's life was morally complex.

(3) *Authenticity* is unity among self-conception, social identity, motivation, and conduct. As authentic persons, we identify with our commitments, affirming them as central to who we are. We do not hold our commitments grudgingly or with regret.[7] We are significantly autonomous in that we sustain commitments on the basis of honest reflection. Authenticity does not imply forming values from scratch, ex nihilo—none of us do that, contrary to the hyperbole of the existentialist Jean-Paul Sartre.[8] Sartre also suggested that authenticity requires avoiding all self-deception, but as a moral virtue it only requires avoiding objectionable forms of self-deception that distort moral understanding.

In addition, as authentic persons we present to the world an identity that reflects our commitments. Other people might misperceive us, but we are not hypocrites. Because authenticity implies publicly standing for the values to which we are committed, we want our identity to be manifested openly.[9] Of course, countervailing reasons may override this wish. For example, privacy may be essential to survival when there is a threat of violence against people voicing minority views and practices.

Authenticity implies having appropriate motives for commitments. In particular, professional integrity implies heeding professional standards for the right reasons or at least not entirely for the wrong reasons. Completely selfish individuals lack moral integrity, not only because of their irresponsible conduct but because of their absence of caring about other people. In contrast, morally concerned professionals care about their clients and the public and, to that extent, their professional motivation connects with their moral motivation in private life.

To act on professed values (to "walk the talk") is the most familiar aspect of authenticity. The requisite fidelity means sincerely trying to live up to moral commitments, in the teeth of many obstacles.[10] Some obstacles are internal: lack of persistence or moral initiative, emotional instability, self-deception, weakness of will, and envy (discussed in chapters 11 and 12). Other obstacles are external: economic pressures, employers' authority, interpersonal conflicts, and conflicting responsibilities. Especially these external obstacles frequently require reasonable compromises.

"Compromise" has two senses: (i) betray one's fundamental principles or (ii) work out a reasonable accommodation, whether through mutual concessions between conflicting parties or by reasonably modifying and adjusting one's principles in order to work effectively within groups. Compromise in the first sense betrays integrity by violating basic commitments that ought to guide conduct. Compromise in the second sense often preserves integrity, enabling us to go further in meeting our commitments than we could by refusing involvement altogether.[11] In practice, drawing the line between the two types of compromise can be difficult. It also has a highly personal dimension.

Consider Secretary of State Cyrus Vance's agreement to lie as part of a 1980 attempt to rescue American hostages being held by Iran.[12] Vance openly told European allies that the United States would not use force to rescue the hostages if they would participate in an economic boycott of Iran. In fact, he knew the military strike was already underway, and his lies were designed to deceive Iran so they would not anticipate a rescue attempt. It was hoped the deception might work, because Vance was especially admired for his honesty. Most of us would find deception to save lives an acceptable compromise, certainly permissible and possibly obligatory. A sincere apology to European allies would suffice to preserve integrity. But Vance regarded the lie as a necessary evil, one that betrayed his exceptional commitment to honesty. In his eyes, the evil was sufficiently great to require him to submit a letter of resignation prior to the deception and effective after the rescue attempt occurred. He agreed to dirty his hands for a worthy cause but felt he was doing something wrong in one serious respect—hence his resignation. Critics might see him as overly conscientious, even self-indulgent, but his conduct was understandable as an effort to maintain integrity.

Integration, moral reasonableness, and authenticity are the primary forms of unity defining integrity. A professional's integrity, then, is the moral reasonableness, authenticity, and integration of a person who works as a professional. This conception enables us to recognize issues about burnout and family as significant matters for professional integrity.

Burnout and Balance

Burnout poses a more or less severe threat to professionals: severe, because it can cause (or constitute) a general loss of commitment; more or less, because it occurs in many degrees and can be temporary or more lasting. Burnout is a complex phenomenon manifested in symptoms such as exhaustion, chronic anger and frustration, unremitting stress, depression, despair (loss of hope and meaning), and a premature desire to stop working altogether.

A familiar stereotype portrays burnout as caused by excessive caring about clients, and, hence, my emphasis on ideals of caring may seem to worsen the threat of burnout. That stereotype has its origin in the early studies by psychologists that targeted care-oriented professions such as nursing, social work, counseling, high school teaching, and public-defense law. According to those studies, empathetic professionals become so caught up in their clients' suffering that they themselves suffer "compassion fatigue." Now, obviously personal ideals of caring often do cause burnout when pursued fanatically, without due attention to other important goods. Even then, however, it is unclear whether excessive caring is the primary cause, rather than horrific workloads and lack of social recognition. In fact, personal ideals can strengthen personal commitments by providing unifying forms of caring that bridge personal and professional life.

Identifying the causes of burnout is a task for science, and more work needs to be done. Nevertheless, we can at least challenge the official stereotype by citing several examples from literature, the implications of which are borne out by recent scientific studies.

Graham Greene's *A Burnt-Out Case* was published in 1960, a decade before burnout became a major interest in psychology.[13] Querry, the novel's protagonist, is a wealthy and world-renown architect who is devoted to the aesthetic aspects of his craft but who cares little about people—including his clients, the public who use his structures, and individuals in his private life. When asked about why his indifference to people does not render his buildings unreliable in such simple matters of adequate plumbing, he explains: "A writer doesn't write for his readers, does he? Yet he has to take elementary precautions all the same to make them comfortable. My interest was in space, light, proportion. . . . Materials [and plumbing] are the architect's plot. They are not his motive for work. Only the space and the light and the proportion."[14]

Burnout ends Querry's career. Its immediate cause is not excessive caring about people, but just the opposite. He is forced to realize how he harmed people closest to him. A related cause is his lack of caring about people his work affected: "To build a church when you don't believe in a god seems a little indecent, doesn't it?"[15] Despairing about his life and especially about his relationships with others, he abandons architecture and wanders aimlessly until he settles in an African mission. There he encounters a compassionate physician who helps lepers cope as their disease "burns out" by destroying limbs and skin. Gradually, life reengages him as he makes a modest contribution to the physician's work by doing errands and routine construction.

In an episode that initiates a process of healing his despair, he rescues his African aide who had become lost and injured in the jungle. Later, a deeper peace comes when he resolves "never again from boredom or vanity to involve another human being in my lack of love. I shall do no more harm, he thought, with the kind of happiness a leper must feel when he is freed at last by his seclusion from the fear of passing on contagion to another."[16] Religious symbols permeate the novel; for example, the name of the African helper is Deo Gratias ("Thanks be to God"), the words Querry calls out to locate his aide in the jungle. Querry himself is not religious, however, and the transformation he experiences is largely moral in nature.

Loss of caring about the technical aspects of craft is an additional source of burnout. Thomas Buddenbrooks, in Thomas Mann's *Buddenbrooks*, undergoes a gradual dissolution, in contrast to Querry's sudden snap. The process begins with increasing fatigue in his late thirties, deepens into depression during his early forties, and culminates with a paralyzing listlessness and inner emptiness. Buddenbrooks is a successful businessperson who no longer feels challenged: "He was empty inside, and he could see no exciting project or absorbing task into which he could throw himself with joy and satisfaction."[17] His substantial community involvements had also peaked. Prominent as a senator, his lack of advanced degrees prevented him from running for mayor, despite having the talent to succeed in politics.

The previous examples might lead us to expect that risks of burnout double when there is a dual lack of caring, about clients and craft. That occurs with Andrei Ragin in Chekhov's "Ward No. 6." Dr. Ragin has an intellectual and religious bent, so much so that he originally planned to enter a theological academy to become a priest. His father, who was a surgeon, sneered at the plan and threatened to disown him if he pursued it. Ragin buckled to the father's pressure and became a physician, even though he lacked any calling for medicine or the sciences.

His career begins well enough. Working diligently in a hospital, he shows due consideration for patients, although he has difficulty asserting himself in directing his hospital staff. Gradually, however, he is overwhelmed and then bored with the routineness of suffering. Chekhov casts the problem in general terms, as one of overdistancing (as noted in chapter 6): "People who have official, professional relationship with someone else's suffering—judges, authorities, physicians, for example—become so inured in the course of time, from force of habit, that even should they want to be sympathetic, they are incapable of any but a formal concern for their clients."[18] Ragin's problem is not excessive emotional involvement, but the bureaucratic regimen and demanding schedule that deaden his impulses to become emotionally involved. Eventually he finds his work senseless and simply stops caring: "Why keep people from dying if death is the normal, legitimate end for everyone? What difference does it make if some peddler or official lives an extra five or ten years?"[19]

Ragin is forced to resign from the hospital, not only because of his incompetency but because his peers object to the extensive time he spends discussing the meaning of life with a patient in psychiatric Ward No. 6. Without the discipline provided by work, Ragin's condition deteriorates to the point where he becomes a patient himself, living in the same ward alongside patients he had once treated. Brutalized by a hospital attendant, he is literally beaten into the awareness that throughout his twenty-year career "he had not known and had not wanted to know" that his patients had undergone the same torment that he now suffered.[20] He also acknowledges that his intellectualizing about religion and philosophy had inhibited compassion for his patients and concealed his terror about death.

Professionals who succeed better than Dr. Ragin in finding a career suited to their interests must still contend with the danger of cynicism, the forms of which include despair (hopelessness), contempt for humanity, and callousness. Its core belief, however, is that humans are unworthy of compassion because they are entirely or primarily motivated by selfishness. Cynicism can be the product of a cruel upbringing, but just as likely it emerges from disillusionment that is preceded by an unrealistic and sentimental view of our own or others' motives.

Return once more to Jean-Baptiste Clamence in Camus's *The Fall*. When he worked as a successful and respected attorney, he was convinced that his noble acts of defending the poor were motivated by generosity and justice. His self-satisfaction was punctured by a cowardly act of failing to risk his life to save a drowning woman. "After prolonged research on myself, I brought out the fundamental duplicity of the human being. Then I realized, as a result of delving in my memory, that modesty helped me to shine, humility to conquer, and virtue to oppress."[21] In another person, this insight might catalyze reform, self-forgiveness, and humility. Instead, Clamence grows cynical, abandons his career as an attorney, and becomes a "judge-penitent" who confesses his duplicity in order to force others to recognize their own hypocrisy. If he could not be morally pure, he can at least evade judgment by holding up a mirror to others so that they have to judge themselves instead of him.

Clamence's role as judge-penitent is more than a literary mirror that Camus uses to disclose his readers' self-deceptions. Camus reminds us that cynicism has moral consequences. Far from being the admirable toughness it is often taken to be, cynicism provides a convenient rationale for apathy: If humanity is thoroughly corrupt, why assume the burdens of moral responsibility for helping others? Clamence's cynicism enables him to be utterly irresponsible, while foreclosing criticism from others, whom he causes to judge themselves rather than him: "I have accepted duplicity instead of being upset about it. On the contrary, I have settled into it and found there the comfort I was looking for throughout life. . . . The essential [thing] is being able to permit oneself everything, even if, from time to time, one has to profess vociferously one's own infamy."[22]

Taken together, Querry, Buddenbrooks, Ragin, and Clamence suggest that burnout is often due to the absence, not the presence, of ideals of caring. It is true, however, that having ideals is a backdrop to burnout, even if it is not its cause. According to Ayala M. Pines, burnout is the special form of depression that results from the failure to find the meaning which individuals seek in and through work.[23] At least often, burnout is the affliction of professionals who begin with high ideals and with exceptionally strong motivation, but who become disillusioned when they feel unable to achieve the ideals to a satisfactory degree. The ideals may be to help people or to excel in their craft. Either way, "in order to burn out, one has to first be 'on fire.'"[24] When commitments prove unfulfilling, the ensuing sense of futility and fatigue can cause burnout.

Nonetheless, Pines suggests that burnout is usually overcome not by abandoning ideals, but instead by adjusting them to make them more realistic and in balance with other goods. The requisite balance and realism take several forms. One form is balance among the various rewards from work. In my terms, meaningful work provides satisfactions through craft, moral caring, and compensation. Craft satisfactions come through participating skillfully in the technical aspects of a profession. Caring relationships include both interactions with clients and with colleagues. And compensations take the form of money, authority, and recognition. There is wide variation in the combination of these goods that proves satisfying, but most of us need a balance among them all.

Another form is balance among different tasks at work. Most professions involve multiple tasks that are challenging and satisfying in different degrees. For example, college professors engage in teaching (at different levels), research (of varied kinds), and service (to campus and community). One of the most effective ways to recover from burnout, short of changing jobs, is changing the emphasis given to various tasks—emphasis in terms of effort, energy, and time. Thus, a professor burned out by unrelenting publication pressures may find renewal through greater attention to teaching, and a professor burned out by teaching may find renewal through engaging in research. Or, a professor preoccupied with the technical skills in teaching (communicating knowledge) might pay more attention to its human dimension (counseling, empathy). Even within these dimensions, there are further ways to focus. For example, contrary to the platitude that professionals must treat all clients identically, the fact is that professionals find meaning by giving competent service to all clients while extending themselves with special concern to clients who reciprocate with appreciation or other reward.[25]

Yet another form of balance is between work and private life. Burnout can result from reducing one's life to being a professional. When work fails to provide sufficient meaning, happiness, and fulfillment, then self-esteem and self-respect collapse. Much recent literature suggests that the best antidote to burnout is a balance between work, family life, leisure, and community involvement.[26] I will return to this idea in a moment.

"Balance" is a normative term. Contrary to the image of a scale for measuring weights, it does not mean giving identical amounts of time or resources to the items balanced. Nor is it "just a negative matter of not falling over; it is a positive one of attaining one's full growth."[27] "Balance" means giving commitments *due* attention, the attention deserved as important ingredients of a meaningful life. And it implies integration and harmony, as well as reasonable distribution of time and emotional energy. There must be meaning-giving integration, balance, and mutual reinforcement among major commitments.

Pragmatism and Priorities

Maintaining integrity is an ongoing process rather than a final achievement. In addition to effort and self-control, it requires habits of moral reasoning in discerning possibilities, setting desirable priorities, and appreciating the need for compromises. This reasoning implies struggling to see one's life in its entirety. Because work and family are intersecting and interacting, their ongoing integration is an important part of responsible moral reasoning. Once again we must reject the consensus paradigm insofar as it suggests that reasoning about professional ethics is restricted to the duties incumbent on all professionals.

A familiar model of moral reasoning is *hierarchical:* We identify moral principles relevant to a situation and then apply them according to their place within a ranking of their general importance. Integrity consists in acting on the most important principle. John Kekes defends this model: "Integrity is to adhere, in the face of difficulties, to the pattern of hierarchically organized commitments that compose our moral perspectives."[28] Kekes abandons the traditional idea of socially given rankings. For him, integrity is a more personal matter of working out and abiding by an autonomously chosen hierarchy of principles. Having a moral perspective means sorting out, according to our own preferences, three types of commitments: unconditional, defeasible, and loose. At the top of the hierarchy are a few unconditional commitments, such as a commitment to God, that we regard as absolute and virtually exceptionless. Next in importance are defeasible (overridable) commitments, such as to particular intimate relationships such as marriage or friendship. Less important are additional loose commitments to variable customs and conventions.

Kekes develops this hierarchical model by focusing on extreme situations, for example, Socrates choosing death over betrayal of his philosophical mission, and Antigone accepting death as a punishment for placing family above patriotism. Kekes also provides an insightful discussion of Thomas More as someone who had unconditional commitments to obey God, defeasible commitments of loyalty to his country and loyalty to his family, and looser commitments of obeisance to the local conventions in showing respect to his monarch. When ordered to violate his unconditional commitment to his church, which required obeying the Pope's prohibition against King Henry VIII marrying Ann Boleyn, More maintained his integrity at the cost of his life.

Contrary to Kekes's description, however, the hierarchical model does not capture the varied ways in which sound moral reasoning takes place in everyday contexts. To be sure, there are tragic situations that force a sweeping sacrifice of some important commitments in order to meet another one. But tragedies are not sound models for routine situations. Using Kekes's hierarchical model, the first thing to decide is whether work commitments have general priority over family and other commitments, or vice versa. Few of us proceed in that manner, and it is questionable whether we should.

Fundamental professional duties, such as maintaining confidentiality and avoiding conflicts of interest, generally should override personal matters. Moreover, moral decisions routinely require us to set priorities among conflicting commitments and clashing goods. But the priorities are context oriented and situation forced, rather than general fixed rankings of principles. We should not confuse (a) setting priorities in particular contexts, with (b) ranking principles and commitments in general and in the abstract. In some situations work commitments do and should override family obligations; in other situations, the reverse is true. Good moral resoning is aimed at discerning which is which.

Consider Bernard William's example of a chemist, George, who is having great difficulty finding a job after completing his Ph.D. degree.[29] He is under considerable pressure to find work because he and his wife have several young children. An acquaintance offers to help him obtain a financially rewarding job in a laboratory doing research in biological and chemical warfare, but George is strongly opposed to such research on moral grounds. The acquaintance points out that, if George does not take the job, it is likely that another person with far more zealousness for the work will take the job, and hence it is better in terms of overall consequences that he take the job.

Using the hierarchical model, the chemist would reflect calmly on whether his family or his opposition to biochemical warfare is most important to him, or simply apply the general ranking of commitments he worked out on other occasions. Most likely, however, both commitments are deeply and profoundly important to him, so that a general ranking of them would be impossible. Whichever way he decides will involve elements of compromise and balancing commitments under conditions of uncertainty and change, rather than simply opting for one commitment as having greatest overall importance in his life. Perhaps in his immediate situation he will choose to take the job temporarily but leave as soon as other jobs become available. Or perhaps he will negotiate with his wife an acceptable temporary sacrifice of income. Either way, he will struggle to sustain both major commitments, rather than endorse one as always paramount.

A *pragmatic* model of moral reasoning seeks to make sense of how sound moral reasoning can take place without rigid rankings of commitments. Pragmatism is not crass expediency. It refers to the practical reasonableness articulated by classical American pragmatists, especially John Dewey. According to Dewey, rigid rankings of abstract principles are usually not possible, given the complexity of both values and the world. Values are too intimately linked to the means needed for achieving them, and those means are in turn linked to details about situations in which we make decisions. In resolving moral dilemmas, one must exercise "creative intelligence" in order to find a practical solution that "coordinates, organizes and functions each factor of the situation which gave rise to conflict, suspense and deliberation."[30]

Rules play an important role, but more as general guides rather than recipes for resolving dilemmas:

> A moral principle, such as that of chastity, of justice, of the Golden Rule,
> gives the agent a basis for looking at and examining a particular question

that comes up. It holds before him certain possible aspects of the act; it warns him against taking a short or partial view of the act. It economizes his thinking by supplying him with the main heads by reference to which to consider the bearings of his desires and purposes; it guides him in his thinking by suggesting to him the important considerations for which he should be on the lookout.[31]

This passage overstates matters somewhat, elevating flexibility to the point where the authority of shared rules is underappreciated. Nevertheless, Dewey reminds us that any established set of rules (made central in the consensus paradigm) is far less than the full substance of morality.

Rankings among values should occur in particular contexts of action or policy formation, not in the abstract. The pragmatic model replaces cut-and-dried, once-and-for-all, rankings, with limited rankings that are unavoidable in particular situations. As James Wallace writes in developing Dewey's ideas, pragmatism "stresses the importance of intelligent, calculated improvisation and the virtue of resourceful inventiveness in adapting our practical knowledge to unprecedented difficulties."[32] Wallace also quotes George Eliot, who acknowledged the importance of moral principles while warning against abstract rankings of principles: "No formulas for thinking will save us mortals from mistake. . . . We must be patient with the inevitable makeshift of our human thinking, whether in its sum total or in the separate minds that have made the sum."[33]

Pragmatic moral reasoning is also a central feature of Carol Gilligan's feminist "ethics of care." It is a feature distinct from the separation of caring and justice critiqued in chapter 5. Gilligan criticizes the hierarchical approach to moral thinking embedded in Lawrence Kohlberg's stages of moral development that culminate with a ranking of universal moral principles. Recall that Heinz's Dilemma was whether Heinz should steal a drug needed to save his wife from a pharmacist who refuses to lower its prohibitive cost. According to Kohlberg, whose studies were conducted solely on males, the correct way to reason consists in ranking principles: "value human life" over "do not steal." In the course of her investigations, Gilligan heard women express greater sensitivity to searching contextually for caring responses that tried to sustain human relationships, including that with the pharmacist, and avoidance of abstract ranking of principles.

Gilligan's approach to moral reasoning envisions integrity as the search to maintain all moral relationships relevant to particular contexts. What is needed is not absolute ranking of principles, but skill in reconciling competing legitimate demands. That is what Mary Catherine Bateson discovered in her study of successful professional women: skill in undertaking an ongoing "struggle to combine multiple commitments, always liable to conflict or interruption" as well as a "search in ambiguity for her own kind of integrity, learning to adapt and improvise."[34] Our broadened conceptions of overall integrity and pragmatic reasoning provide a framework for undertaking this struggle and search.

Work and Family

Let us think through what is involved in attempting a general ranking of commitments to profession versus family. One possibility would be to make work paramount, in a systematic and thoroughgoing manner. George de Mare interviewed a vice president of a multibillion-dollar chemical corporation who sacrificed two marriages for work before opting permanently to avoid family involvements that threaten work. He regrets having to make the sacrifices, but he would make them again if necessary. For him, work is paramount, and not merely for selfish reasons.

> Our world does require single-mindedness and strong motivation to succeed. What we call single-mindedness, will to give of oneself and sacrifice for our enterprise, others call ambition, love of power and ruthlessness. I wouldn't go along with that. If you want to succeed anywhere, you must pay a price. . . . I still look forward every morning to my work in the corporation and to the years I'll be spending there.[35]

The man's career supports his claims about motives. Most of his management positions were in human resources, and his accomplishments included many community-building programs such as integrating a black-white assembly line in a southern factory. He was driven by the excitement and challenge of the work, in addition to the enormous pressures to spend long and intense hours at the office. Yet the source of the excitement and challenge included opportunities to make a difference in the lives of corporate employees and community members.

To be sure, many professionals who make work paramount are more narrowly focused on self-oriented compensations, although they may not fully admit it to themselves. Seemingly overzealous service to clients, community, and craft can mask a primary drive for money, authority, prestige, and other perquisites of career advancement. In this way, professional success becomes a rationalization for ignoring the moral demands of family life. Witness the workaholic attorney who leaves home for work at seven-thirty in the morning, returns at six-thirty for dinner and to see his two small children, and then at eight o'clock returns to the office for several more hours of work.[36] Perhaps early in his career the long hours were needed to keep his highly competitive job, but well into his marriage the work becomes a way to escape the responsibilities of emotional involvement in his family.

Some professionals are preoccupied with longer-term fame, rather than advancements within their immediate jobs. In *To the Lighthouse*, Virginia Woolf describes such a man, whose prototype was her father, Leslie Stephen. Mr. Ramsay has a distinguished teaching position, literary reputation, and colleagues and students who admire him. He is not a genius, however, and he is painfully aware that his accomplishments will dim with time. His admirable concern for craft goods, including excellence in his profession, was tainted by self-preoccupation: "He would always be worrying about his own books—will they be read, are they good, why aren't they better, what do people think of me?"[37] We are repelled by how Mr. Ramsay's self-absorption results in withholding himself from his family. He makes his wife feel she is the source of his suffering, that if he had not married her he might have achieved more lasting fame, when in fact he needed her support to make the accomplishments he did. There is also something pitiful about his inability to appreciate his genuine accomplishments and about his preoccupation with fame and praise.

Turning to the other general possibility, we might make private life paramount. Writing from a religious perspective, Gilbert C. Meilaender suggests that we should work in order to live, rather than live in order to work. He charges contemporary society with perverting the Protestant work ethic. Properly understood, the Protestant ethic centered on the idea of each person having a calling from God to serve others within a specific type of work. The modern perversion degrades the idea of a calling into work that is personally fulfilling. Work has become yet another selfish idol: "When work as we know it emerges as the dominant idea in our lives—when we identify ourselves to others in terms of what we do for a living, work for which we are paid—and when we glorify such work in terms of self-fulfillment, it is time for Christian ethics to speak a good word for working simply in order to live."[38] By living, Meilaender means sustaining meaningful personal relationships with family, friends, and community.

What does Meilaender's view amount to in practice? It implies that when opportunities at work substantially threaten personal relationships, there is a presumption against embracing the work opportunities. The opportunities might be promotions or increased salary by putting in longer hours, or they might offer relocation to another part of the country or world. It is not clear, however, that such a presumption is always reasonable. If work becomes too secondary, it can result in the loss of a job and, in difficult economies, wreak havoc with one's family. And while employers have increasingly made the claim that they are accommodating to family needs, in practice they tend to promote employees whose priorities favor the company's bottom line.[39] Moreover, we should not assume that individuals who make work enormously important in their lives, even paramount, are acting from selfish reasons, as we noted in discussing de Mare's executive.

For a great many professionals, both of the above options—work as paramount or family as paramount—are equally unappealing. Global rankings of work and family simply distort the moral reality of their lives:

"Which is more important to you, your field or your children?" the department head asked.
    She replied, "That's like asking me if I could walk better if you amputated my right leg or my left leg."[40]

Most professionals find the goods made possible through work and family mutually fulfilling and complementary. More than personal preference is at stake, however. At least where families are involved, we are considering situations where commitments have already been made and responsibilities undertaken. Hence, at issue is the task of achieving integration and balance, which means that time, energy, and overall involvement with work and family must be juggled on a daily basis.

Fortunately, there are strong tendencies toward interaction and mutual reinforcement of professionals' role integrity with their overall integrity. Habits of moral concern, of trying to act on moral values from genuine concern and to stand for that concern in public, tend to have carryover effects. Role integrity is more than simply acting rightly within one's profession. It implies doing so from appropriate motives, and those motives at least tend to have a wider influence and also depend for their sustenance on wider habits.

The physician-poet William Carlos Williams called for a medical ethics that was wider in scope than a focus on dilemmas created when professional duties clash. He was concerned, for example, with the harm done by physicians who are competent but arrogant, conscientious but condescending. Such physicians lack the sensitivity essential in helping vulnerable patients find a way to cope with frightening situations. In general, "A doctor's general attitude toward people, his personal decency and his view of what life means, can influence the way he practices medicine."[41]

The same applies to managers. In *Women in Love*, D. H. Lawrence describes a coal-mine executive whose attitudes toward his workers and toward his spouse are interwoven. Gerald Crich reduced his workers to their roles in contributing to the one thing that mattered, the "great social productive machine." In his eyes, workers were tools: "What mattered was the pure instrumentality of the individual.... Everything in the world has its function, and is good or not good in so far as it fulfils this function more or less perfectly. Was a miner a good miner? Then he was complete. Was a manager a good manager? That was enough."[42] Similar attitudes carried over into his private life. Crich is unable to feel grief at the death of his sister and later his father. He demands submission from his sexual partner Gudrun Brangwen, while maintaining his own unqualified freedom.[43]

Destructive attitudes toward other people are only one example of how attitudes toward work and nonwork are connected. Another example is when professionals center their lives around the American dream of money, status, and consumerism. Economist Juliet B. Schor cites studies showing that most workers want more time with their families, and yet they do not act on opportunities offered them to do so.[44] She explains this dissonance between stated preference and actual conduct to the consumerism deeply embedded in the American dream. In practice, many workers choose work over leisure in order to gain money to spend during leisure. The endless cycle of getting in order to spend is frequently driven by self-defeating motives. One motive is status seeking in keeping up with Joneses, when the Joneses in turn are keeping up with you in an endless rivalry. Another motive is pleasure which promises something substantial but yields something ephemeral.

Arlie Russell Hochschild found the same paradox in workers, including the majority of women workers, not taking advantage of opportunities to spend more time with their families.[45] She suggests that several factors are at play. Some people meet the need for extra money by working more. Others have reasonable worries about job security. They believe that companies with family-friendly policies do not genuinely support the policies and that working fewer hours would make them vulnerable to layoffs during economic downturns. In general, work is often more satisfying than workers acknowledge, especially given the increasing tensions within families and the fact that friends and community are primarily found at the workplace rather than their local neighborhood. Perhaps most important, women are just like men in finding that they receive most social recognition through their work rather than at home.

To conclude, I have sketched a pragmatic conception of moral reasoning in forming and balancing commitments so as to sustain overall integrity. This conception provides a framework for coping with moral complexity, though nothing like a moral algorithm. At present, meaningful work and viable families are equally at risk amidst the swirl of economic, technological, and cultural revolutions we are undergoing. Perhaps the greatest danger is the eclipse of ideals as we hunker down simply to survive. Rethinking professional ethics to include personal commitments might illuminate prospects for creative social change. My goal has been the more modest aim of understanding moral values in their full context, as bridging professional and personal life, as giving meaning to work and contributing to self-fulfillment.

NOTES

Preface

1. A notable example of a recent shift from viewing professional virtues solely as tendencies to meet professional duties to encompassing the full richness of the inner life of motives, emotions, and reasoning is the difference between the first two and next two editions of Tom L. Beauchamp and James F. Childress's classic text, *Principles of Biomedical Ethics* (New York: Oxford University Press, 1979, 1983, 1989, 1994).

2. Thinkers who have recently paid attention to ideals include Nicholas Rescher, *Ethical Idealism: An Inquiry into the Nature and Function of Ideals* (Berkeley: University of California Press, 1987); Albert Flores, ed., *Professional Ideals* (Belmont, Calif.: Wadsworth, 1988) (although his emphasis is on generic professional ideals); and Wibren Van Der Burg, "The Importance of Ideals," *The Journal of Value Inquiry* 31 (1997): 23–37.

Chapter 1

1. David Hilfiker, *Not All of Us Are Saints* (New York: Ballantine Books, 1994), 19.

2. The case for paying greater attention to religion in thinking about professionalism is made in Michael Goldberg, ed., *Against the Grain: New Approaches to Professional Ethics* (Valley Forge, Pa.: Trinity Press International, 1993); Stephen E. Lammers and Allen Verhey, eds., *On Moral Medicine,* 2nd ed. (Grand Rapids, Mich.: William B. Eerdmans, 1998); Eric Mount, Jr., *Professional Ethics in Context: Institutions, Images and Empathy* (Louisville, Ky.: Westminster/John Knox Press, 1990); and Stephen V. Monsma, ed., *Responsible Technology: A Christian Perspective* (Grand Rapids, Mich.: William B. Eerdmans, 1986).

3. Bernard Williams, "Persons, Character and Morality," in Bernard Williams, *Moral Luck* (New York: Cambridge University Press, 1981), 1–19. In many additional essays and books, Williams argues for the relevance of personal commitments in ethical theory. Surprisingly, he fails to connect those discussions to professional ethics in the one essay devoted to that topic: "Professional Morality and Its Dispositions," in *Making Sense of Humanity* (Cambridge: Cambridge University Press, 1995), 192–202.

4. Rescher, *Ethical Idealism*, 115.

5. John Kultgen, *Ethics and Professionalism* (Philadelphia: University of Pennsylvania Press, 1988), 347.

6. Albert Flores, "What Kind of Person Should a Professional Be?" in *Professional Ideals*, (Belmont, Calif.: Wadsworth, 1988) 9. Italics deleted.

Chapter 2

1. Akira Kurosawa, *Ikiru* (the movie script for *To Live*), ed. Donald Richie (New York: Simon and Schuster, 1968), 48.

2. Adam Smith, *An Inquiry Into the Nature and Causes of the Wealth of Nations*, R. H. Campbell and A. S. Skinner, eds., (New York: Oxford University Press, 1976), 26–27.

3. Adam Smith, *The Theory of Moral Sentiments*, D. D. Raphael and A. L. Macfie, eds., (New York: Oxford University Press, 1976), 267.

4. Smith, *Wealth of Nations*, 456.

5. George Bernard Shaw, *The Doctor's Dilemma* [1913].

6. Smith, *Wealth of Nations*, 123.

7. Ibid., 454.

8. Smith, *The Theory of Moral Sentiments*, 235; and specifically on seeking wealth, 83.

9. Ibid., 137.

10. See Patricia H. Werhane, *Adam Smith and His Legacy for Modern Capitalism* (New York: Oxford University Press, 1991).

11. Smith, *The Theory of Moral Sentiments*, 184, 236.

12. Milton Friedman, "The Social Responsibility of Business Is to Increase Its Profits," *The New York Times Magazine* (September 13, 1970); reprinted in most business ethics anthologies, including Joseph R. Des Jardins and John J. McCall, eds., *Contemporary Issues in Business Ethics*, 3d ed. (Belmont, Calif.: Wadsworth, 1996), 8–12. Friedman adds several elusive caveats, in particular that business should maximize profits within the bounds of law and "ethical custom," notions that seemingly imply respect for persons and the wider community. For alternative ways of interpreting Friedman, see Thomas Carson, "Friedman's Theory of Corporate Social Responsibility," *Business and Professional Ethics Journal* 12 (1993): 3–32. Norman Bowie identifies the self-defeating aspect of narrow profit seeking in "The Profit Seeking Paradox," in N. Dale Wright, ed., *Ethics of Administration* (Provo, Utah: Brigham Young University Press, 1988).

13. Smith, *The Theory of Moral Sentiments*, 184–85.

14. Robert Nozick, *The Examined Life* (New York: Simon and Schuster, 1989), 287.

15. Albert Schweitzer, *The Philosophy of Civilization* [1923], trans. C. T. Campion (Buffalo, N.Y.: Prometheus, 1987), 79.

16. Ibid., 321; Albert Schweitzer, *Out of My Life and Thought*, trans. A. B. Lemke (New York: Henry Holt, 1990), 91, and *Reverence for Life: Sermons 1900–1919*, trans. Reginald H. Fuller (New York: Irvington Publishers, 1993), 141. On p. 255 of *The Philosophy of Civilization* he writes: The *ego* which has reached the farthest heights of willing and representing enlarges itself by over-lapping other human existences. Self-devotion [i.e., devotion to others] is, therefore, not a surrender of the self, but a manifestation of its expansion.

17. Henry Clark, *The Ethical Mysticism of Albert Schweitzer* (Boston: Beacon Press, 1962), 70. Cf. Schweitzer, *The Philosophy of Civilization*, 304. Also see Os-

kar Kraus, *Albert Schweitzer: His Work and His Philosophy* (London: Adam and Charles Black, 1944), and Gabriel Langfeldt, *Albert Schweitzer: A Study of His Philosophy of Life* (London: George Allen and Unwin, 1960).

18. Schweitzer, *Out of My Life and Thought*, 157. I develop and defend my interpretation of Schweitzer in "Rethinking Reverence for Life," *Between the Species* 9 (1993): 204–13; and "Good Fortune Obligates: Gratitude, Philanthropy, and Colonialism," *Southern Journal of Philosophy* 37 (1999): 57–75.

19. Albert Schweitzer, *Memoirs of Childhood and Youth*, trans. C. T. Campion (New York: Macmillan, 1961), 60–61.

20. Schweitzer, *Out of My Life and Thought*, 82.

21. Herbert Spiegelberg, "Good Fortune Obligates: Albert Schweitzer's Second Ethical Principle," *Ethics* 85 (1975): 229. Spiegelberg offers little argument for his view.

22. Schweitzer, *The Philosophy of Civilization*, 320.

23. Schweitzer, *Reverence for Life*, 141.

24. Albert Schweitzer, "On the Edge of the Primeval Forest," in *The Primeval Forest*, trans. C. T. Campion (New York: Pyramid Books, 1961), 128–30.

25. Schweitzer, *Reverence for Life*, 139.

26. Schweitzer, *The Philosophy of Civilization*, 9.

27. Having sketched the contrasts between Schweitzer and Smith rather starkly, I should note some similarities. Not only were they both somewhat unconventional Christians; both were enormously influenced by Stoics such as Seneca, Epictetus, Marcus Aurelius, and Cicero. This influence is clear in Smith's emphasis on prudence, self-command, and frugality (*The Theory of Moral Sentiments*, 5–10). It is equally clear in Schweitzer's view that ethics centers on self-perfection, albeit through humanitarian concern. Indeed, sometimes he mistakenly portrays the motive for helping others as a concern for self-perfection: "It is not from kindness to others that I am gentle, peaceable, forbearing, and friendly, but because by such behaviour I prove my own profoundest self-realization to be true" (*The Philosophy of Civilization*, 315). Smith and Schweitzer also share the Stoics' convictions that morality is rooted in natural dispositions of empathy and sympathy and that each of us is a citizen in a world of shared humanity.

28. Brian O'Connell, Introduction to *America's Voluntary Spirit*, ed. Brian O'Connell (New York: Foundation Center, 1983), xi.

29. Madeleine M. Kunin, *Living a Political Life* (New York: Vintage Books, 1994), 78.

30. Ibid., 79–80.

31. Sharon Bertsch McGrayne, *Nobel Prize Women in Science* (New York: Birch Lane Press, 1993), 297.

32. Ibid., 299.

33. Sara Lawrence-Lightfoot, *I've Known Rivers: Lives of Loss and Liberation* (New York: Penguin, 1994), 21.

34. Robert MacNeil, *The Right Place at the Right Time* (New York: Penguin, 1992), 312.

35. Meryle Secrest, *Frank Lloyd Wright* (New York: HarperPerennial, 1993); and Frank Lloyd Wright, *An Autobiography* (New York: Duell, Sloan and Pearce, 1943).

36. Anthony T. Kronman, *The Lost Lawyer: Failing Ideals of the Legal Profession* (Cambridge, Mass.: Harvard University Press, 1993), 371–74.

37. John Rawls, *A Theory of Justice* (Cambridge, Mass.: Harvard University Press, 1971), 426.

38. Robert Nozick, *Philosophical Explanations* (Cambridge, Mass.: Harvard University Press, 1981), 597.

39. Mihaly Csikszentmihalyi, *Creativity: Flow and the Psychology of Discovery and Invention* (New York: HarperCollins, 1996), 110–13, and *Flow: The Psychology of Optimal Experience* (New York: HarperCollins, 1990).

40. Michele Lamont, *Money, Morals, and Manners: The Culture of the French and the American Upper-Middle Class* (Chicago: University of Chicago Press, 1992), 69.

41. Ibid., 72.

42. Denise Hamilton, "Fighting Abuse Is Job, Pet Project," *Los Angeles Times* (August 27, 1996), E1 and E4.

43. Gregory S. Kavka, *Hobbesian Moral and Political Theory* (Princeton, N.J.: Princeton University Press, 1986), 64–65. Kavka also offers an extensive criticism of psychological egoism.

44. See Alfie Kohn, *The Brighter Side of Human Nature* (New York: Basic Books, 1990); Morton Hunt, *The Compassionate Beast* (New York: William Morrow, 1990); and Lawrence Kohlberg, *The Psychology of Moral Development*, vol. 2 of *Essays on Moral Development* (New York: Harper and Row, 1984).

45. Mary Midgley, *Beast and Man: The Roots of Human Nature*, rev. ed. (New York: New American Library, 1995), 331.

46. Daryl Koehn, *The Ground of Professional Ethics* (New York: Routledge, 1994), 120.

47. Ibid., 119.

48. Ibid., 118.

49. Albert Camus, *The Fall*, trans. Justin O'Brien (New York: Vintage, 1956), 84.

50. John Kekes, *The Examined Life* (Lewisburg, Pa.: Bucknell University Press, 1988), 161–73.

51. Robert N. Bellah, Richard Madsen, William M. Sullivan, Ann Swidler, and Steven M. Tipton, *Habits of the Heart: Individualism and Commitment in American Life* (Berkeley: University of California Press, 1985), 66.

52. Stephen L. Darwall, *Impartial Reason* (Ithaca, N.Y.: Cornell University Press, 1983), 164–65; cf. Jeffrey Blustein, *Care and Commitment: Taking the Personal Point of View* (New York: Oxford University Press, 1991), 47–48; and Victor E. Frankl, "Self-Transcendence as a Human Phenomenon," in Anthony J. Sutich and Miles A. Vich, eds., *Readings in Humanistic Psychology* (New York: Free Press, 1969), 113–25.

53. Robert Nozick, *Anarchy, State, and Utopia* (New York: Basic Books, 1974), 42–45.

54. Charles Taylor, *The Ethics of Authenticity* (Cambridge, Mass.: Harvard University Press, 1992), 28–29. Also see Lawrence A. Blum, *Vocation, Friendship, and Community: Limitations of the Personal-Impersonal Framework* (Cambridge: Cambridge University Press, 1994), 98–123, and Alan Gewirth, *Self-Fulfillment* (Princeton, N.J.: Princeton University, 1998).

55. Cf. Alasdair MacIntyre, *Dependent Rational Animals* (Chicago: Open Court, 1999), 119.

Chapter 3

1. However, I agree with Jeffrey Stout's assessment that moral disagreements are not as extensive as the Tower-of-Babel metaphor suggests. *Ethics after Babel: The Languages of Morals and Their Discontents* (Boston: Beacon Press, 1988).

2. Randall Collins, *The Credential Society* (New York: Academic Press, 1979).

3. John A. Robertson, "Eggs, Embryos, and Professional Ethics," *The Chronicle of Higher Education* (January 5, 1996), A64. Subsequent related scandals raise worries about entrenchment of lax ethical standards: Goldie Blumenstyk, "U. of California at Irvine Is under Fire Again over Research Ethics," *The Chronicle of Higher Education* (January 8, 1999), A52.

4. Some may prefer to follow Alan Gewirth in speaking of "rational morality" rather than "ordinary morality," as a way of emphasizing that the relevant standards are morally justified rather than merely customary. See "Professional Ethics: The Separatist Thesis," *Ethics* 96 (1986): 287. But it is clear that writers, including myself, who have used the expression "ordinary morality" in this context intend to refer to justified principles. See Mike W. Martin, "Rights and the Meta-Ethics of Professional Morality" and "Professional and Ordinary Morality: A Reply to Freedman," *Ethics* 91 (1981): 619–25, 631–33.

5. *People v. Belge*, 376 N.Y.S.2d 771 (4th Dept. 1975). The case became classic, owing to Monroe H. Freedman's spirited defense of the attorneys in *Lawyers' Ethics in an Adversary System* (Indianapolis, Ind.: Bobbs-Merrill, 1975), 1–8.

6. Daryl Koehn, *The Ground of Professional Ethics* (New York: Routledge, 1994), 56, also 153.

7. Ibid., 54–56, 61–67.

8. Ibid., 63. Koehn prefaces this claim with the remark that individuals cannot lessen their responsibilities "by saying, 'My colleagues may be bound by this pledge, but I personally never swore an oath to act for the benefit'" of clients. This statement is inconsistent with her earlier emphasis on individual pledges as the ground of professional duties.

9. Koehn notes that public trust in professionals must be established, at least tentatively, before clients seek services from professionals. Yet she never explains how a pledge that clients know nothing about can play that role. Ibid., 38.

10. Ibid., 110.

11. Michael Davis, "Thinking Like an Engineer: The Place of a Code of Ethics in the Practice of a Profession," *Philosophy and Public Affairs* 20 (1991): 153. Also see his *Thinking Like an Engineer* (New York: Oxford University Press, 1998).

12. Michael Davis, "The Special Role of Professionals in Business Ethics," *Business and Professional Ethics* 7 (1988): 55. Also see "Do Cops Really Need a Code of Ethics?" *Criminal Justice Ethics* 10 (1991): 14–28.

13. John Kultgen, *Ethics and Professionalism* (Philadelphia: University of Pennsylvania Press, 1988). For an example of how codes can be misused, see Edwin T. Layton, "Engineering Ethics and the Public Interest: A Historical View," in Albert Flores, (ed.), *Ethical Problems in Engineering*, 2nd ed. (Troy, N.Y.: Rensselaer Polytechnic Institute, 1980), 26–29. Davis's inversion of priorities—emphasizing fairness to colleagues more than duties to the public—has some puzzling consequences. For example, he writes that a code enables a practitioner to pursue the goals of her profession at "minimal cost to herself and those she cares about (including the public, if looking after the public is part of what she cares about)." ("Thinking Like an Engineer," 161) Why the *if?* Why not instead *because* professionals should care directly about the persons affected by their work?

14. See, e.g., *Zauderer v. Office of Disciplinary Counsel*, 471 U.S. 626 (1985) and *Peel v. Attorney Registration and Disciplinary Commission of Illinois*, 110 S.Ct. 2281 (1990).

15. Michael Davis, "The Moral Authority of a Professional Code," in J. Roland Pennock and John W. Chapman, eds., *Authority Revisited: NOMOS XXIX* (New

York: New York University Press, 1987), 332. Davis begins this essay with a false dilemma: Either codes state what all decent persons know (and hence have no moral authority of their own), or they go beyond ordinary morality (and hence violate universal moral requirements). But "moral authority" need not mean creating new moral requirements. It can also refer to official interpretations (by professional societies and organizations) that accurately identify what ordinary morality requires with regard to professional contexts. In "Is There a Profession of Engineering?" Davis goes some way toward remedying the problems I see in his earlier essays. He stipulates that there are moral constraints on the conventions (codes of ethics) that groups of professions may adopt, but he does not retract the earlier work and even refers to is as clarifying his view. In this essay his concern is to rule out the possibility of gross immorality, as among a group of thieves or Nazi engineers. To do so he stipulates that "*Professional standards are always morally permissible*" and that professions serve a moral ideal "in a morally-permissible way" (*Science and Engineering Ethics* 3[1997]: 417, 419). These stipulations, however, again raise concerns about idealizing what a profession is, just as before he conflated ideal with actual codes. My point is that any actual profession and code can have specific aspects that are morally objectionable and hence that professional ethics must make reference to moral values beyond what any actual group of professionals sets forth as its standards.

16. Ibid., 321, 325, 332. Cf. Davis, "Thinking Like an Engineer," 157, 163ff. His use of "rational persons" is ambiguous between (1) morally responsible and (2) self-interested. His interest in sense (2) is indicated by his endorsement of a version of psychological egoism—"people act only to maximize their own welfare"—although he construes personal welfare as enlightened self-interest that links one's good to that of others. Michael Davis, "The Use of Professions," *Business Economics* 22 (October 1987): 6.

17. Paul F. Camenisch, *Grounding Professional Ethics in a Pluralistic Society* (New York: Haven, 1983), 58–61; also 91–109.

18. Ibid., 104.

19. See Robert Jay Lifton, *The Nazi Doctors: Medical Killing and the Psychology of Genocide* (New York: Basic Books, 1986), and Charles E. McClelland, *The German Experience of Professionalization* (Cambridge: Cambridge University Press, 1991).

20. Camenisch admits as much at the end of *Grounding Professional Ethics in a Pluralistic Society*, 136–37.

21. Of course, differences arise at the level of detail, but those details shape variations within each type of ethical theory, as much as different types of theories. Thus, David Ross's version of duty ethics set forth in *The Right and the Good* (Oxford: Clarendon, 1930) is in many ways closer to Richard Brandt's rule-utilitarianism in *A Theory of the Good and the Right* (Oxford: Clarendon, 1979) than to Kant's absolutistic version of duty ethics; A. I. Melden's rights ethics in *Rights and Persons* (Berkeley: University of California Press, 1977) has less in common with libertarian rights theories than it does with John Rawls's *A Theory of Justice* (Cambridge, Mass.: Harvard University Press, 1971); John Stuart Mill's version of utilitarianism in *On Liberty* [1859], ed. Elizabeth Rapaport (Indianapolis, Ind.: Hackett Publishing, 1978) (though not in *Utilitarianism*) is closer to libertarian rights ethics than it is to many other utilitarian theories. Cf. Mike W. Martin, *Everyday Morality*, 3rd ed. (Belmont, Calif.: Wadsworth, 2001), ch. 2.

22. Examples of this general approach include Alan H. Goldman, *The Moral Foundations of Professional Ethics* (Totowa, N.J.: Rowman and Littlefield, 1980);

and Gewirth, "Professional Ethics." The issue of the relationships between professional and ordinary morality should not be reduced to whether the ethics of everyday personal life is the source of professional ethics, since more general moral principles may govern both personal and professional life. In my view, they do. For example, principles of justice apply to both everyday personal relationships and also enter into the justification of professional ethics, but with different implications because of relevant differences in context. Cf. Thomas Nagel, "Ruthlessness in Public Life," in Stuart Hampshire, ed., *Public and Private Morality* (Cambridge: Cambridge University Press, 1978), 79; and Peter A. French, *Ethics in Government* (Englewood Cliffs, N.J.: Prentice-Hall, 1983), 19.

23. Koehn, *The Ground of Professional Ethics*, 148.

24. Melden, *Rights and Persons* 122–65.

25. John Rawls, *A Theory of Justice.* The inevitability of moral pluralism in thinking about goods is emphasized, among others, by Michael Philips, *Between Universalism and Skepticism: Ethics as Social Artifact* (New York: Oxford University Press, 1994).

26. Relevant excerpts of the American Bar Association's "Model Rules of Professional Conduct" are printed in Rena A. Gorlin, ed., *Codes of Professional Responsibility*, 3rd ed. (Washington, D.C.: Bureau of National Affairs, 1994), 471–91.

27. *Tarasoff v. Regents of the University of California*, California Supreme Court, 1 July 1976. 131 *California Reporter*, 14–33.

28. Anthony T. Kronman, *The Lost Lawyer: Failing Ideals of the Legal Profession*, (Cambridge, Mass.: Harvard University Press, 1993), 1. Also see David Luban, *Lawyers and Justice: An Ethical Study* (Princeton, N.J.: Princeton University Press, 1988), esp. ch. 8. For an insightful discussion of differences among attorneys regarding the custody case, see Rand Jack and Dana Crowley Jack, *Moral Vision and Professional Decisions: The Changing Values of Women and Men Lawyers* (New York: Cambridge University Press, 1989), esp. 78–85.

29. Robert M. Veatch, "Is Trust of Professionals a Coherent Concept?" in Edmund D. Pellegrino, Robert M. Veatch, and John P. Langan, eds., *Ethics, Trust, and the Professions: Philosophical and Cultural Aspects* (Washington, D.C.: Georgetown University Press, 1991), 168.

30. The quote and the case are taken from Suzanne Gordon, "Hippocratic or Hypocritic Oath?" *Los Angeles Times* (January 21, 1996), M5.

31. For an interesting personal anecdote, see Gene Moriarty, "Ethics, *Ethos* and the Professions: Some Lessons from Engineering," *Professional Ethics* 4, no. 1 (1995): 75–93.

32. Cf. Mike W. Martin, *Virtuous Giving: Philanthropy, Voluntary Service, and Caring* (Bloomington: Indiana University Press, 1994), 73–80.

33. Glenn G. Griener makes this point in a related context, "Moral Integrity of Professions," *Professional Ethics* 2, nos. 3 and 4 (1993): 15–38.

Chapter 4

1. I offer a fuller rationale for this definition in *Virtuous Giving: Philanthropy, Voluntary Service, and Caring* (Bloomington: Indiana University Press, 1994), 7–14.

2. Hippocrates, *Precepts*, trans. W. H. S. Jones (Loeb Classical Library), ch. 6.

3. David Luban, *Lawyers and Justice: An Ethical Study* (Princeton, N.J.: Princeton University Press, 1988), 277–89.

4. Eliot Wigginton, *Sometimes a Shining Moment: The Foxfire Experience* (New York: Anchor Books, 1985).

5. Studs Terkel, *Working* (New York: Avon, 1975), 694–95.

6. Bill Berkowitz, *Local Heroes* (New York: D. C. Heath, 1987), 61–77.

7. Kent Mellerstig, "Medical Missionary Experience in Ecuador," in Bill McMillon, *Volunteer Vacations*, 2nd ed. (Chicago: Chicago Review Press, 1989), 75–83.

8. Anne Colby and William Damon, *Some Do Care: Contemporary Lives of Moral Commitment* (New York: Free Press, 1992), 230–58.

9. Robert L. Payton, *Philanthropy: Voluntary Action for the Public Good* (New York: Macmillan, 1988), 119–21.

10. Ibid., 41.

11. Ibid., 32.

12. Cf. Robert H. Bremner, *American Philanthropy*, 2nd ed. (Chicago: University of Chicago Press, 1988); Brian O'Connell, ed., *America's Voluntary Spirit* (New York: Foundation Center, 1983); and Susan J. Ellis and Katherine H. Noyes, *By the People: A History of Americans as Volunteers*, rev. ed. (San Francisco: Jossey-Bass, 1990).

13. Cf. James T. Bennett and Thomas J. DiLorenzo, *Unhealthy Charities* (New York: Basic Books, 1994).

14. Robert L. Payton, *Philanthropy: Voluntary Action for the Public Good*, 71–88.

15. Colby and Damon, *Some Do Care: Contemporary Lives of Moral Commitment*, 139.

16. J. O. Urmson, "Saints and Heroes," in A. I. Melden, ed., *Essays in Moral Philosophy* (Seattle: University of Washington Press, 1958), 198–216.

17. Michael S. Pritchard, "Good Works," *Professional Ethics* 1 (1992): 155–77.

18. Gregory Mellema, *Beyond the Call of Duty: Supererogation, Obligation, and Offence* (Albany: State University of New York Press, 1991).

19. David Heyd, *Supererogation* (Cambridge: Cambridge University Press, 1982).

20. Martin, *Virtuous Giving*, 62–93.

21. Marcia W. Baron, *Kantian Ethics Almost without Apology* (Ithaca, N.Y.: Cornell University Press, 1995); Susan C. Hale, "Against Supererogation," *American Philosophical Quarterly* 28 (1991): 273–85.

22. Owen Flanagan, *Varieties of Moral Personality: Ethics and Psychological Realism* (Cambridge, Mass.: Harvard University Press, 1991).

23. W. D. Falk, "Morality, Self, and Others," in Hector-Neri Castaneda and George Nakhnikian, eds., *Morality and the Language of Conduct* (Detroit, Mich.: Wayne State University Press, 1965), 25–67.

24. Albert Schweitzer, *Out of My Life and Thought*, trans. A. B. Lemke (New York: Henry Holt, 1990), 82.

25. A. I. Melden, "Saints and Supererogation," in Ilham Dilman, ed., *Philosophy and Life: Essays on John Wisdom* (The Hague: Martinus Nijhoff, 1984).

Chapter 5

1. Jeffrey Blustein, *Care and Commitment: Taking the Personal Point of View* (New York: Oxford University Press, 1991), 160.

2. Ibid., 159.

3. Albert Camus, *The Fall*, trans. Justin O'Brien (New York: Vintage, 1956), 48.

4. Jeffrey Blustein, *Care and Commitment*, 160.

5. Ibid., 158.

6. Ibid.

7. Peggy Anderson, *Nurse* (New York: Berkley Publishing, 1979), 100–103.

8. Edmund D. Pellegrino and David C. Thomasma, *The Virtues in Medical Practice* (New York: Oxford University Press, 1993), 76.

9. Herbert Kohl, *Growing Minds: On Becoming a Teacher* (New York: Harper Torchbooks, 1988), 64–66.

10. Lawrence A. Blum, *Moral Perception and Particularity* (New York: Cambridge University Press, 1994), 109.

11. Cf. ibid., 103–104.

12. Carol Gilligan, *In a Different Voice: Psychological Theory and Women's Development* (Cambridge, Mass.: Harvard University Press, 1982). The discussion of Jake and Amy is on p24–63, and the quote from Jake on 26. Also see Nel Noddings, *Caring* (Berkeley: University of California Press, 1984); and Sara T. Fry, "The Role of Caring in a Theory of Nursing Ethics," in Helen Bequaert Holmes and Laura M. Purdy, eds., *Feminist Perspectives in Medical Ethics* (Bloomington: Indiana University Press, 1992), 93–106.

13. Cf. Owen Flanagan, *Varieties of Moral Personality: Ethics and Psychological Realism* (Cambridge, Mass.: Harvard University Press, 1991), 204–17; Joan C. Tronto, *Moral Boundaries: A Political Argument for an Ethic of Care* (New York: Routledge, 1993), 138.; and Lawrence A. Blum, *Moral Perception and Particularity*, 215–67.

14. Carol Gilligan, "Moral Orientation and Moral Development," in Eva Feder Kittay and Diana T. Meyers, eds., *Women and Moral Theory* (Totowa, N.J.: Rowman and Littlefield, 1987), 19–33.

15. Cf. John Stuart Mill, *On Liberty* [1859], ed. Elizabeth Rapaport (Indianapolis, Ind.: Hackett Publishing, 1978).

16. William K. Frankena, "Moral-Point-of-View Theories," in Norman E. Bowie, ed., *Ethical Theory in the Last Quarter of the Twentieth Century* (Indianapolis, Ind.: Hackett Publishing, 1983), 74.

17. A. I. Melden, *Rights and Persons* (Berkeley: University of California Press, 1977), 145.

18. Herbert Kohl, *Growing Minds*, 66.

19. Michael D. Bayles, *Professional Ethics*, 2nd ed. (Belmont, Calif.: Wadsworth, 1989), 70.

20. Ibid., 79.

21. Cf. Virginia L. Warren, "Feminist Directions in Medical Ethics," *Hypatia* 4 (1989):73–87.

22. Michael D. Bayles, *Professional Ethics*, 88.

23. The distinction is set forth by Stephen L. Darwall in "Two Kinds of Respect," reprinted in Robin S. Dillon, ed., *Dignity, Character, and Self-Respect* (New York: Routledge, 1995), 181–97.

24. Robin Dillon, "Care and Respect," in Eve Browning Cole and Susan Coultrap-McQuin, eds., *Explorations in Feminist Ethics: Theory and Practice* (Bloomington: Indiana University Press, 1992), 73.

Chapter 6

1. Insightful studies of excessive detachment under the influence of authority include Stanley Milgram, *Obedience to Authority* (New York: Harper and Row, 1974), and Robert Jay Lifton, *The Nazi Doctors: Medical Killing and the Psychology of Genocide* (New York: Basic Books, 1986).

2. Perri Klass, *A Not Entirely Benign Procedure: Four Years as a Medical Student* (New York: Plume, 1994), 76.

3. Thomas Nagel, "Ruthlessness in Public Life," in Stuart Hampshire, ed., *Public and Private Morality* (Cambridge: Cambridge University Press, 1978), 77.

4. Klass, *A Not Entirely Benign Procedure*, 149.

5. Nagel, "Ruthlessness in Public Life," 76.

6. E.g., Gerald J. Postema, "Self-Image, Integrity, and Professional Responsibility," in David Luban, ed., *The Good Lawyer: Lawyers' Roles and Lawyers' Ethics* (Totowa, N.J.: Rowman and Allanheld, 1983), 286–314, esp. 291–93, 301–302.

7. Edward Bullough, "'Psychical Distance' as a Factor in Art and an Aesthetic Principle," in George Dickie and Richard J. Sclafani, eds., *Aesthetics* (New York: St. Martin's Press, 1977), 759.

8. Allan Casebier, "The Concept of Aesthetic Distance," in Dickie and Sclafani *Aesthetics*, 794.

9. Robert Klitzman, *In a House of Dreams and Glass: Becoming a Psychiatrist* (New York: Ivy Books, 1995), 95.

10. Melvin Konner, *Becoming a Doctor* (New York: Penguin Books, 1987), 365.

11. Anton Chekhov, "Ward No. 6," in *Seven Short Novels by Chekhov*, trans. Barbara Makanowitzky (New York: W. W. Norton, 1963), 113.

12. R. S. Lazarus, "Cognitive and Coping Processes in Emotion," in A. Monat and R. S. Lazarus, eds., *Stress and Coping* (New York: Columbia University Press, 1977), 150.

13. Howard J. Curzer, "Is Care a Virtue for Health Care Professionals?" *Journal of Medicine and Philosophy* 18 (1993): 63, also 55.

14. Lawrence Blum, *Friendship, Altruism, and Morality* (London: Routledge and Kegan Paul, 1980), and A. J. Vetlesen, *Perception, Empathy, and Judgment* (University Park: Pennsylvania State University, 1994).

15. Jacqueline Zalumas, *Caring in Crisis: An Oral History of Critical Care Nursing* (Philadelphia: University of Pennsylvania Press, 1995), 101, 113, 128, 139, 151.

16. Peggy Anderson, *Nurse* (New York: Berkley Publishing, 1979), 39. This is a theme, too, in Ruth Purtillo and Amy Haddad's excellent discussion of distance in *Health Professional and Patient Interaction*, 5th ed. (Philadelphia: W. B. Saunders, 1996), 230–49.

17. Eric J. Cassell, *The Nature of Suffering and the Goals of Medicine* (New York: Oxford University Press, 1991), 74.

18. Samuel Gorovitz, *Doctors' Dilemmas: Moral Conflict and Medical Care* (Oxford: Oxford University Press, 1982), 198.

19. Cf. Robert Coles, *The Call of Stories: Teaching and the Moral Imagination* (Boston: Houghton Mifflin, 1989), 102–29, esp. 109–10. Similar slipperiness and ambiguity surround detachment in other contexts, including aesthetics and religion where value differences may also be involved. Consider religion: Hindus, Muslims, Christians, Stoics, and Buddhists disagree about how much detachment from worldly concerns is desirable. For example, Theravada Buddhists understand religious detachment and enlightenment as leading to a separation from the world, whereas Mahayana Buddhists see the goal of detachment as deepening compassionate service to humanity. Note, too, that Mahayanas illustrate how selective detachments further rather than threaten compassion and caring. See Hsueh-li Cheng, "Buddhist Ethics," in Lawrence C. Becker, ed., *Encyclopedia of Ethics*, vol. 1 (New York: Garland, 1992), 103–109.

20. John Kultgen develops a scalar concept in *Autonomy and Intervention: Parentalism in the Caring Life* (New York: Oxford University Press, 1995).

21. Frederic G. Reamer, *Social Work Values and Ethics* (New York: Columbia University Press, 1995), 35. To my horror I read as this book goes to press that my personal physician humiliated a lesbian patient. According to a *Los Angeles Times* article (June 21, 1999, pp. S1 and S8), while performing a routine physical, which included a pelvic exam, the doctor learned from the patient she was gay. At the end of the exam, the doctor suggested that she make her next appointment with one of the other doctors in the office. When questioned why, "the doctor told her he didn't approve of her gay 'lifestyle.'" The patient is now suing the doctor and his health maintenance organization. The case reminds us that when and how health professionals make referrals can matter greatly as they exercise their personal "consciences." In my view, the case also illustrates the need for physicians to receive continuing education sessions on appreciating diversity. Certainly we might hope that of all professionals, physicians would avoid the homophobia that the American Psychiatric Association officially renounced over two decades ago.

22. "Code of Ethics of the National Association of Social Workers," printed in Reamer, *Social Work Values and Ethics,* 190–99.

23. Cf. Marc A. Rodwin, *Medicine, Money, and Morals: Physicians' Conflicts of Interest* (New York: Oxford University Press, 1993).

24. Cf. Elizabeth Wolgast, *Ethics of an Artificial Person: Lost Responsibility in Professions and Organizations* (Stanford, Calif.: Stanford University Press, 1992), 20–21.

25. Gerald J. Postema, "Moral Responsibility in Professional Ethics," *New York University Law Review* 55 (1980): 73.

26. Rand Jack and Dana Crowley Jack, *Moral Vision and Professional Decisions: The Changing Values of Women and Men Lawyers* (New York: Cambridge University Press, 1989), 78.

27. David Luban, *Lawyers and Justice: An Ethical Study* (Princeton, N.J.: Princeton University Press, 1988).

28. Wolgast, *Ethics of an Artificial Person,* 144.

29. On the two dimensions of honesty see Mike W. Martin, "Honesty with Oneself," in Mary I. Bockover, ed., *Rules, Rituals, and Responsibility: Essays Dedicated to Herbert Fingarette* (La Salle, Ill.: Open Court, 1991), 115–36.

30. William Broad and Nicholas Wade, *Betrayers of the Truth: Fraud and Deceit in the Halls of Science* (New York: Simon and Schuster, 1982). Also see William Maker, "Scientific Autonomy, Scientific Responsibility," and Joan C. Callahan, "Professions, Institutions, and Moral Risk," both in Daniel E. Wueste, ed., *Professional Ethics and Social Responsibility* (Totowa, N.J.: Rowman and Littlefield, 1994), 219–41, 243–70; Robin Levin Penslar, ed., *Research Ethics: Cases and Materials* (Bloomington: Indiana University Press, 1995); and Deni Elliott and Judy E. Stern, eds., *Research Ethics: A Reader* (Hanover, N.H.: University Press of New England, 1997).

31. Edmund Gosse, *Father and Son* [1907] (New York: Penguin, 1983), 102–3. Lorraine Code provides an illuminating discussion in *Epistemic Responsibility* (Hanover, N.H.: University Press of New England, 1987), 23.

32. David E. White, "Objectivity as a Journalistic Virtue," *Journal of Social Philosophy* 16 (fall 1985): 13–19.

33. Stephen Klaidman and Tom L. Beauchamp, *The Virtuous Journalist* (New York: Oxford University Press, 1987), esp. chs. 2 and 3.

34. Theodore R. Schatzki, "Objectivity and Rationality," in Wolfgang Natter, Theodore R. Schatzki, and John Paul Jones, III, eds., *Objectivity and Its Other* (New York: Guilford Press, 1995), 137–60.

35. For discussions of issues surrounding objectivity in journalism, see Elliot D. Cohen, ed., *Philosophical Issues in Journalism* (New York: Oxford University Press, 1992), 156–217.

36. Edward W. Said, *Representations of the Intellectual* (New York: Vintage Books, 1994), 11.

37. Alan H. Goldman, *The Moral Foundations of Professional Ethics* (Totowa, N.J.: Rowman and Littlefield, 1980), esp. ch. 2.

38. John Rawls drew attention to this distinction in a related context in "Two Concepts of Rules," *Philosophical Review* 64, no. 1 (1955).

39. Quoted by Mortimer R. Kadish and Sanford H. Kadish, *Discretion to Disobey: A Study of Lawful Departures from Legal Rules* (Stanford, Calif.: Stanford University Press, 1973), 86. Ronald Dworkin discusses the occasional relevance of judges' political views to their rulings in *A Matter of Principle* (Cambridge, Mass.: Harvard University Press, 1985), 9–32. The difficult question of whether religious views should enter into judges' rulings is debated by Kent Greenawalt, *Religious Convictions and Political Choice* (New York: Oxford University Press, 1988), and Kenneth I. Winston, "The Religious Convictions of Public Officials," *Canadian Journal of Law and Jurisprudence* 3, no. 1 (1990): 136, as I discuss in chapter 10.

40. Andrea Gabor, *Einstein's Wife* (New York: Viking, 1995), 272–73.

41. Michael D. Bayles, *Professional Ethics*, 2nd ed. (Belmont, Calif.: Wadsworth, 1989), 88–89.

Chapter 7

1. As useful overviews of culture-war issues, see John Arthur and Amy Shapiro, eds., *Campus Wars: Multiculturalism and the Politics of Difference* (Boulder, Colo.: Westview Press, 1995); James Davison Hunter, *Culture Wars: The Struggle to Define America* (New York: Basic Books, 1991); and Jeffrey Williams, ed., *PC Wars: Politics and Theory in the Academy* (New York: Routledge, 1995).

2. John R. Searle, "Two Concepts of Academic Freedom," in Edmund L. Pincoffs, ed., *The Concept of Academic Freedom* (Austin: University of Texas Press, 1972), 89.

3. "Statement on Professional Ethics," *AAUP Red Book: Policy Documents and Reports* (Washington, D.C.: American Association of University Professors, 1990), 75–76.

4. Edmund L. Pincoffs, "On Avoiding Moral Indoctrination," in James F. Doyle, ed., *Educational Judgments* (London: Routledge and Kegan Paul, 1973), 68–69.

5. Richard T. De George, *The Nature and Limits of Authority* (Lawrence: University Press of Kansas, 1985).

6. Hugh T. Wilder, "The Philosopher as Teacher: Tolerance and Teaching Philosophy," in Peter J. Markie, ed., *A Professor's Duties* (Totowa, N.J.: Rowman and Littlefield, 1994), 129.

7. Ibid., 139. Wilder adds a caveat concerning areas where professors lack knowledge: "Teachers do not know enough about their fields to demand agreement from students on all issues; honest tolerance—tolerance based on ignorance rather than cowardice—is a virtue" (140).

8. Edward A. Langerak, "Values Education and Learning How to Disagree," in Carlton T. Mitchell, ed., *Values in Teaching and Professional Ethics* (Macon, Ga.: Mercer University Press, 1989), 144.

9. Amy Gutmann, *Multiculturalism and "The Politics of Recognition"* (Princeton, N.J.: Princeton University Press, 1992), 14. Also see her *Democratic Education* (Princeton, N.J.: Princeton University Press, 1987).

10. Robert L. Simon, ed., *Neutrality and the Academic Ethic* (Lanham, Md.: Rowman and Littlefield, 1994), 22–23. Also see Robert L. Simon, "A Defense of the Neutral University," in Steven M. Cahn, ed., *Morality, Responsibility, and the University* (Philadelphia: Temple University Press, 1990), 24–25.

11. Simon, *Neutrality and the Academic Ethic*, 243–70.

12. Ibid., 80.

13. Ibid., 26, 47.

14. Ibid., 20.

15. Ibid., 90. Cf. Edward Shils, *The Academic Ethic* (Chicago: University of Chicago Press, 1983), 50–51.

16. Cf. John Kleinig, *Philosophical Issues in Education* (New York: St. Martin's, 1982), 62.

17. Rosellen Brown, Interview, in Alexander Neubauer, ed., *Conversations on Writing Fiction* (New York: Harper Perennial, 1994), 55.

18. For a sampling of value commitments that guide philosophers' careers, see David D. Karnos and Robert G. Shoemaker, eds., *Falling in Love with Wisdom: American Philosophers Talk about Their Calling* (New York: Oxford University Press, 1993). Martha C. Nussbaum illuminates the vitality of multicultural commitments in *Cultivating Humanity: A Classical Defense of Reform in Liberal Education* (Cambridge, Mass.: Harvard University Press, 1997).

19. Cf. Jaroslav Pelikan, *The Idea of the University* (New Haven, Conn.: Yale University Press, 1992), 43–56, and Michael Goldman, "On Moral Relativism, Advocacy, and Teaching Normative Ethics," *Teaching Philosophy* 4 (1981): 1–11.

20. Michael Oakeshott, *The Voice of Liberal Learning*, ed. Timothy Fuller (New Haven, Conn.: Yale University Press, 1989), 61. See also R. S. Peters, *Authority, Responsibility and Education*, 2nd ed. (London: George Allen and Unwin, 1963), 83–95, and R. S. Downie, "Professions and Professionalism, *Journal of Philosophy of Education* 24 (1990): 147–59.

21. Sidney Hook, "Morris R. Cohen—Fifty Years Later," in Joseph Epstein, ed., *Masters: Portraits of Great Teachers* (New York: Basic Books, 1981), 24.

22. Robert Adams, "The Problem of Total Devotion," in Robert Audi and William J. Wainwright, eds., *Rationality, Religious Belief, and Moral Commitment* (Ithaca, N.Y.: Cornell University Press, 1986), 189–93.

23. John Kleinig, *Philosophical Issues in Education*, 76, 149; Jane Roland Martin, *Changing the Educational Landscape* (New York: Routledge, 1994), 75, 202; Elizabeth Kamarck Minnich, *Transforming Knowledge* (Philadelphia: Temple University Press, 1990).

24. Israel Scheffler, "In Praise of the Cognitive Emotions," *Teachers College Record* 79 (1977): 171–86; D. N. Perkins, *The Mind's Best Work* (Cambridge, Mass.: Harvard University Press, 1981), 114–21. Also see Douglas Walton, *The Place of Emotion in Argument* (University Park: Pennsylvania State University Press, 1992).

25. Cf. David A. Garvin, "A Delicate Balance: Ethical Dilemmas and the Discussion Process," in C. Roland Christensen, David A. Garvin, and Ann Sweet, eds., *Education for Judgment* (Boston: Harvard Business School Press, 1991), 287–303.

26. This view permeates John Dewey's and R. S. Peter's writings on education. It is also defended by William K. Frankena, "The Concept of Education Today," in James F. Doyle, ed., *Educational Judgments*, 19–32; R. S. Downie, "On Having a Mind of One's Own," in Roger Straughan and John Wilson, eds., *Philosophers on Education* (London: Macmillan, 1987), 79–92; and Charles W. Anderson, *Prescribing the Life of the Mind* (Madison: University of Wisconsin Press, 1993), 79–95.

27. Cf. Michael Goldman, "On Moral Relativism, Advocacy, and Teaching Normative Ethics"; Michael Scriven, "Professorial Ethics," *Journal of Higher Education* 53 (1982): 314–15.

28. Elias Baumgarten, "Ethics in the Academic Profession: A Socratic View," *Journal of Higher Education* 53 (1982): 290.

29. Bertrand Russell, *The Problems of Philosophy* (New York: Oxford University Press, 1959), 168.

30. Gloria Albrecht and Leonard J. Weber, "Personal Commitments, Privileged Positions and the Teaching of Applied Ethics," *Professional Ethics* 3 (1994): 143.

31. For helpful teaching strategies, see Grant H. Cornwell, "From Pluralism to Relativism and Back: Philosophy's Role in an Inclusive Curriculum," *Teaching Philosophy* 14 (1991): 143–53.

32. Regarding the levels of importance of moral convictions, see John Kekes, *Moral Tradition and Individuality* (Princeton, N.J.: Princeton University Press, 1989).

33. For example, Allan Bloom, *The Closing of the American Mind: How Higher Education Has Failed Democracy and Impoverished the Souls of Today's Students* (New York: Simon and Schuster, 1987); Roger Kimball, *Tenured Radicals: How Politics Has Corrupted Our Higher Education* (New York: Harper and Row, 1990); and Dinesh D'Souza, *Illiberal Education: The Politics of Race and Sex on Campus* (New York: Random House, 1991).

34. Examples of moderate positions on the goals in teaching ethics include Daniel Callahan, "Goals in the Teaching of Ethics," in Daniel Callahan and Sissela Bok, eds., *Ethics Teaching in Higher Education* (New York: Plenum, 1980), 61–80; W. B. Carnochan, *The Battleground of the Curriculum* (Stanford, Calif.: Stanford University Press, 1993), 117; Steven M. Cahn, *Saints and Scamps: Ethics in Academia*, rev. ed. (Totowa, N.J.: Rowman and Littlefield, 1994), 64–70; and Shils, *The Academic Ethic*.

35. Few philosophers have played major roles in the culture wars. Even John Searle, the philosopher most prominently involved, has said little about ethical values during his spirited defense of objective standards of truth. See, e.g., "The Storm over the University," *The New York Review of Books* (December 6, 1990): 34–42, and "Rationality and Realism, What Is at Stake?" *Daedalus* 122 (fall 1993): 55–83.

36. Laura M. Purdy, "Politics and the College Curriculum," in Simon, *Neutrality and the Academic Ethic*, 236–64.

37. Stanley Fish argues that it is not clear that sophisticated forms of conceptual relativism have any direct practical consequences. See *There's No Such Thing as Free Speech: And It's a Good Thing, Too* (New York: Oxford University Press, 1994).

38. See, e.g., Diana T. Meyers, *Self, Society, and Personal Choice* (New York: Columbia University Press, 1989).

39. Richard Mohr, "Teaching as Politics," *Report from the Center for Philosophy and Public Policy* 6 (winter 1986): 8. Cf. Henry A. Giroux, *Schooling and the*

Struggle for Public Life: Critical Pedagogy in the Modern Age (Minneapolis: University of Minnesota Press, 1988).

40. Cf. Gerald Graff, *Beyond the Culture Wars: How Teaching the Conflicts Can Revitalize American Education* (New York: W. W. Norton, 1992).

Chapter 8

1. These terms are used roughly in the ways set forth by Richard T. De George, *The Nature and Limits of Authority* (Lawrence: University Press of Kansas, 1985), 22.

2. *The Presidential Commission on the Space Shuttle* Challenger *Disaster* (Washington, D. C.: U. S. Government Printing Office, 1986). The literature on *Challenger* is enormous. I find the following sources especially helpful: Russell P. Boisjoly, Ellen Foster Curtis, and Eugene Mellican, "Roger Boisjoly and the *Challenger* Disaster: The Ethical Dimensions," *Journal of Business Ethics* 8 (1989): 217–30; Patricia H. Werhane, "Engineers and Management: The Challenge of the *Challenger* Incident," *Journal of Business Ethics* 10 (1991): 605–16; Maureen Hogan Casamayou, *Bureaucracy in Crisis: Three Mile Island, the Shuttle* Challenger, *and Risk Asssessment* (Boulder, Colo.: Westview Press, 1993); and Rosa Lynn B. Pinkus, Larry J. Shuman, Norman P. Hummon, and Harvey Wolfe, *Engineering Ethics: Balancing Cost, Schedule, and Risk—Lessons Learned from the Space Shuttle* (Cambridge: Cambridge University Press, 1997).

3. Michael Bayles provides an overview of standard models of professional-client relationships in chapter 4 of *Professional Ethics*, 2nd ed. (Belmont, Calif.: Wadsworth, 1989). Joseph A. Raelin provides an early and helpful discussion of professional-manager relationships, although one that does not view managers as professionals, in *The Clash of Cultures: Managers Managing Professionals* (Boston: Harvard Business School Press, 1991).

4. William Lowrance equates safety with acceptable risk in *Of Acceptable Risk* (Los Altos, Calif.: William Kaufmann, 1976). In doing so, he departs too far from common usage, according to which we say products or activities are not altogether safe even though we judge their risks acceptable—that is, they are worth the risk.

5. Joseph R. Herkert, "Management's Hat Trick: Misuse of 'Engineering Judgment' in the *Challenger* Incident," *Journal of Business Ethics* 10 (1991): 618.

6. Ibid., 619.

7. Samuel C. Florman, *Blaming Technology: The Irrational Search for Scapegoats* (New York: St. Martin's, 1981).

8. Samuel C. Florman, *The Civilized Engineer* (New York: St. Martin's, 1987), 164. For a related argument see Michael Davis, "Thinking Like an Engineer: The Place of a Code of Ethics in the Practice of a Profession," *Philosophy and Public Affairs* 20 (1991): 150–167.

9. Ibid., 165.

10. Versions of the shared-agency model are developed in most texts on engineering ethics, including Charles E. Harris, Jr., Michael S. Pritchard, and Michael J. Rabins, *Engineering Ethics: Concepts and Cases* (Belmont, Calif.: Wadsworth, 1995); Eugene Schlossberger, *The Ethical Engineer* (Philadelphia: Temple University Press, 1993); Stephen H. Unger, *Controlling Technology: Ethics and the Responsible Engineer,* 2nd ed. (New York: John Wiley and Sons, 1994); some authors in James H. Schaub and Karl Pavlovic, eds., *Engineering Professionalism and Ethics* (New York: John Wiley and Sons, 1983), and in Deborah G. Johnson, ed.,

Ethical Issues in Engineering (Englewood Cliffs, N.J.: Prentice-Hall, 1991); and Mike W. Martin and Roland Schinzinger, *Ethics in Engineering*, 3rd ed. (New York: McGraw-Hill, 1996).

11. Michael Davis, "Technical Decisions: Time to Rethink the Engineer's Responsibilities?" *Business and Professional Ethics Journal* 11 (1992): 51.

12. On the penalties for whistleblowing, see Myron Peretz Glazer and Penina Migdal Glazer, *The Whistleblowers: Exposing Corruption in Government and Industry* (New York: Basic Books, 1989).

13. Cf. Michael Davis, "Avoiding the Tragedy of Whistleblowing," *Business and Professional Ethics Journal* 8, no. 4 (winter 1989): 10 n. 20.

14. William H. Starbuck and Frances J. Milliken, "*Challenger:* Fine-Tuning the Odds until Something Breaks," *Journal of Management Studies* 25 (1988): 333. Also see Henry Petroski, *To Engineer is Human* (New York: St. Martin's, 1985).

15. Lon Fuller, "The Philosophy of Codes of Ethics," in Bernard Baumrin and Benjamin Freedman, eds., *Moral Responsibility and the Professions* (New York: Haven Publications, 1983), 79–84.

16. Alasdair MacIntyre, *After Virtue*, 2nd ed. (Notre Dame, Ind.: University of Notre Dame Press, 1984), 194.

17. Albert Flores also invokes this dichotomy in "What Kind of Person Should a Professional Be?" in *Professional Ideals* (Belmont, Calif.: Wadsworth, 1988), 8.

18. MacIntyre allows as much when he says (without elaboration) that "the making and sustaining of forms of human community—and therefore of institutions—itself has all the characteristics of a practice." (*After Virtue,* 194) Robert C. Solomon develops the idea of corporations as communities in *Ethics and Excellence* (New York: Oxford University Press, 1992).

19. Cf. Michael D. Smith, "The Virtuous Organization," *The Journal of Medicine and Philosophy* 7 (1982): 35–42.

20. The same is true of professional responsibilities: Physicians' duty of confidentiality, for example, must be rethought in terms of contemporary medical organizations, where as many as seventy-five hospital staff may have access to a patient's medical files. Mark Siegler, "Confidentiality in Medicine—A Decrepit Concept," *The New England Journal of Medicine* 307 (1982): 518–21.

21. Francis J. Aguilar, *Managing Corporate Ethics* (New York: Oxford University Press, 1994), 131. For additional cases, see Lynn Sharp Paine, "Managing for Organizational Integrity," *Harvard Business Review* (March/April 1994): 106–17.

22. Howard E. McCurdy, *Inside NASA: High Technology and Organizational Change in the U.S. Space Program* (Baltimore, Md.: Johns Hopkins University Press, 1993), 62.

23. Herbert A. Simon, *Administrative Behavior,* 3rd ed. (New York: Free Press, 1976), 126–27.

24. Ibid., 228.

25. Ibid., 129.

26. Ibid., 141, 11.

27. Ibid., 134–38.

28. Cf. William Lowrance, *Of Acceptable Risk,* ch. 3.

29. Robert Baum, "The Limits of Professional Responsibility," in Albert Flores, ed., *Ethical Problems in Engineering,* 2nd ed., vol. 1 (Troy, N.Y.: Rensselaer Polytechnic Institute, 1980), 48–53.

30. Paul Eddy, Elaine Potter, and Bruce Page, *Destination Disaster* (New York: Quandrangle, 1976).

31. K. Vandivier, "Engineers, Ethics and Economics," *Conference on Engineering Ethics* (New York: American Society of Civil Engineers, 1975), 20–24. For a cautionary note on Vandivier's account, see John Fielder, "Give Goodrich a Break," *Business and Professional Ethics Journal* 7 (1988): 3–25.

32. Ralph Nader, Peter J. Petkas, and Kate Blackwell, eds., *Whistleblowing: The Report of the Conference on Professional Responsibility* (New York: Grossman Publishers, 1972), 148–51.

33. For an analysis of the concept of "organizational disobedience," see James Otten, "Organizational Disobedience," in Flores, *Ethical Problems in Engineering*, 182–86.

34. *Conference on Engineering Ethics* (New York: American Society of Civil Engineers, 1975), 99, 101.

35. Ronald Dworkin, *Taking Rights Seriously* (Cambridge, Mass.: Harvard University Press, 1977), 184–205.

36. Carl W. Houston, "Experiences of a Responsible Engineer," in *Conference on Engineering Ethics*, (New York: American Society of Civil Engineers, 1975) 25–30.

37. Thomas Donaldson, *Corporations and Morality* (Englewood Cliffs, N.J.: Prentice-Hall, 1982).

Chapter 9

1. Cf. Mike W. Martin and Roland Schinzinger, *Ethics in Engineering*, 3rd ed. (New York: McGraw-Hill, 1996), 247.

2. Frederick Elliston, "Anonymous Whistleblowing," *Business and Professional Ethics Journal* 1, no. 2 (winter 1982): 39–58.

3. Roger M. Boisjoly, "The *Challenger* Disaster: Moral Responsibility and the Working Engineer," in Deborah G. Johnson, ed., *Ethical Issues in Engineering* (Englewood Cliffs, N.J.: Prentice-Hall, 1991), 6–14.

4. Paul Eddy, Elaine Potter, and Bruce Page, *Destination Disaster* (New York: Quandrangle, 1976), 185.

5. Frank Camps, "Warning an Auto Company about an Unsafe Design," in Alan F. Westin, ed., *Whistle-Blowing!* (New York: McGraw-Hill, 1981), 119–29.

6. See, e.g., Myron Peretz Glazer and Penina Migdal Glazer, *The Whistleblowers: Exposing Corruption in Government and Industry* (New York: Basic Books, 1989).

7. Michael Davis, "Avoiding the Tragedy of Whistleblowing," *Business and Professional Ethics Journal* 8, no. 4 (winter 1989): 3–19. Davis also draws attention to the potentially negative aspects of laws, as does Sissela Bok in "Whistleblowing and Professional Responsibilities," in Daniel Callahan and Sissela Bok, eds., *Ethics Teaching in Higher Education* (New York: Plenum, 1980), 277–95. Those aspects, which include violating corporate privacy, undermining trust and collegiality, and lowering economic efficiency, are indeed significant. But I am convinced that well-framed laws to protect whistleblowers can take these things into account. The laws should protect only whistleblowing that meets the conditions for the prima facie obligation I state at the beginning of the section entitled "Personal Life."

8. Robert Nozick drew attention to the general symbolic importance of government actions when he expressed serious reservations about the libertarian position he had previously defended. *The Examined Life* (New York: Simon and Schuster, 1989), 286–88.

9. The quotations are from Richard T. De George, *Business Ethics*, 3rd ed. (New York: Macmillan, 1990), 208–12. They parallel his view as first stated in "Ethical Responsibilities of Engineers in Large Organizations," *Business and Professional Ethics Journal* 1, no. 1 (fall 1981): 1–14. As an example of placing a far higher demand on engineers, see Kenneth D. Alpern, "Moral Responsibility for Engineers," *Business and Professional Ethics Journal* 2, no. 2 (winter 1983): 39–47.

10. Gene G. James, "Whistle Blowing: Its Moral Justification," in W. Michael Hoffman and Jennifer Mills Moore, eds., *Business Ethics*, 2nd ed. (New York: McGraw-Hill, 1990), 332–44.

11. David Theo Goldberg, "Tuning in to Whistle Blowing," *Business and Professional Ethics Journal* 7, no. 2 (summer 1988): 85–94.

12. As his reason for conditions (iv) and (v), De George cites the fate of whistleblowers who put themselves at great risk: "If there is little likelihood of his success, there is no moral obligation for the engineer to go public. For the harm he or she personally incurs is not offset by the good such action achieves." ("Ethical Responsibilities of Engineers in Large Organizations," 7). Like myself, then, De George implicitly views the personal suffering of whistleblowers as morally relevant to understanding professional responsibilities, even though, as I go on to argue, he invokes that relevance in the wrong way.

13. De George, *Business Ethics*, 214.

14. See especially Bernard Williams, "A Critique of Utilitarianism" in Bernard Williams and J. J. C. Smart, *Utilitarianism, For and Against* (Cambridge: Cambridge University Press, 1973), 77–150, and Bernard Williams, "Persons, Character, and Morality," in *Moral Luck* (New York: Cambridge University Press, 1981), 1–19. For samples of more recent discussions, see the special edition of *Ethics*, vol. 101 (July 1991), devoted to "Impartiality and Ethical Theory."

15. Cf. John Arthur, "Rights and Duty to Bring Aid," in William Aiken and Hugh La Follette, eds., *World Hunger and Moral Obligation* (Englewood Cliffs, N.J.: Prentice-Hall, 1977), 37–48.

16. Alpern, "Moral Responsibilities for Engineers," 39.

17. James, "Whistle Blowing: Its Moral Justification," 334–35.

18. See Martin and Schinzinger, *Ethics in Engineering*, ch. 3. The emphasis on engineers adopting a wide view of their activities does not imply that they are culpable for all the moral failures of colleagues and managers.

19. National Society of Professional Engineers, "Code of Ethics," reprinted in Martin and Schinzinger, *Ethics in Engineering*.

20. Cf. Thomas M. Devine and Donald G. Aplin, "Whistleblower Protection—The Gap between the Law and Reality," *Howard Law Journal* 31 (1988): 236.

21. I am glad that the NSPE and other professional codes say what they do in support of responsible whistleblowing, as long as it is understood that professional codes only state professional–not all-things-considered–obligations that automatically override personal responsibilities. As noted in chapter 3, codes provide a backing for morally concerned engineers, and they make available to engineers the moral support of an entire profession. At the same time, professional societies need to do far more than most of them have done to support the efforts of conscientious whistleblowers. Beyond moral and political support, and beyond recognition awards, they need to provide economic support, in the form of legal funds and job placement. Cf. Stephen H. Unger, *Controlling Technology: Ethics and the Responsible Engineer,* 2nd ed. (New York: John Wiley and Sons, 1994), esp. ch. 5; and Larry May, *The Socially Responsive Self: Social Theory and Professional Ethics* (Chicago: University of Chicago Press, 1996), 171–83.

22. As argued in chapter 8; also see Mike W. Martin, "Rights of Conscience inside the Technological Corporation," *Conceptus-Studien,* 4: *Wissen und Gewissen* (Vienna: VWGO, 1986): 179–91.

23. Alan F. Westin offers helpful suggestions about laws protecting whistle-blowers in *Whistle-Blowing!* For a recent overview of the still fragmented and insufficient legal protection of whistleblowers, see Rosemary Chalk, "Making the World Safe for Whistle-Blowers," *Technology Review* 91 (January 1988): 48–57, and James C. Petersen and Dan Farrell, *Whistleblowing: Ethical and Legal Issues in Expressing Dissent* (Dubuque, Iowa: Kendall/Hunt, 1986).

24. Cf. Edmund L. Pincoffs, *Quandaries and Virtues* (Lawrence: University Press of Kansas, 1986), 112–14.

25. Important discussions of the role of virtues in professional ethics include John Kultgen, *Ethics and Professionalism* (Philadelphia: University of Pennsylvania Press, 1988); Albert Flores, ed., *Professional Ideals* (Belmont, Calif.: Wadsworth, 1988); and Michael D. Bayles, *Professional Ethics,* 2nd ed. (Belmont, Calif.: Wadsworth, 1989). John Kekes insightfully discusses the virtues of self-direction in *The Examined Life* (Lewisburg, Pa.: Bucknell University Press, 1988).

26. Martin Benjamin, *Splitting the Difference: Compromise and Integrity in Ethics and Politics* (Lawrence: University Press of Kansas, 1990).

27. On the distinction between moral rules and ideals, see Bernard Gert, *Morality* (New York: Oxford University Press, 1988), 160–78.

28. Boisjoly, "The *Challenger* Disaster," 14.

29. Camps, "Warning an Auto Company," 128.

30. Harry Frankfurt draws attention to this felt "must" as a sign of deep caring and commitment in *The Importance of What We Care About* (New York: Cambridge University Press, 1988), 86–88.

Chapter 10

1. Anson Shupe, *In the Name of All That's Holy: A Theory of Clergy Malfeasance* (Westport, Conn.: Praeger, 1995).

2. Religious ethics need not be Divine Command Ethics, that is, ethical theories that locate the meaning or justification of all moral principles in God's commandments. Religious ethics does, however, include some moral principles that transcend or modify secular morality.

3. Cf. Richard T. De George, *The Nature and Limits of Authority* (Lawrence: University Press of Kansas, 1985), 217–43.

4. Deborah Fernhoff, "The Valued Therapist," in Michael Goldberg, ed., *Against the Grain: New Approaches to Professional Ethics* (Valley Forge, Pa.: Trinity Press International, 1993), 64.

5. Associated Press, "Architect Finds New Blueprint for His Life," *Los Angeles Times* (September 28, 1996), B8.

6. As mentioned in chapter 2, there are questions about whether Albert Schweitzer's faith played a role in supporting colonial paternalism.

7. *Paw Prints* (Capistrano Valley High School student paper), vol. 15, issue 9 (June 14, 1991), 1, 3, and Diane Seo, "High Court Refuses to Hear Teacher's Suit over Evolution," *Los Angeles Times* (1995), B1, B9.

8. Sissela Bok, *Secrets: On the Ethics of Concealment and Revelation* (New York: Pantheon Books, 1982), 131–33.

9. Larry May, *The Socially Responsive Self: Social Theory and Professional Ethics* (Chicago: University of Chicago Press, 1996), 166–67.

10. John Rawls, *A Theory of Justice* (Cambridge, Mass.: Harvard University Press, 1971), 215.

11. Kent Greenawalt, *Religious Convictions and Political Choice* (New York: Oxford University Press, 1988), 240. Also see his *Private Consciences and Public Reasons* (New York: Oxford University Press, 1995).

12. Greenawalt, *Religious Convictions*, 241.

13. Kenneth I. Winston, "The Religious Convictions of Public Officials," *Canadian Journal of Law and Jurisprudence* 3, no. 1 (1990): 141. Additional limitations on legislators arising from the need for continual compromises are discussed by Dennis F. Thompson in *Political Ethics and Public Office* (Cambridge, Mass.: Harvard University Press, 1987). .

14. Page references in parentheses are to Margaret P. Battin, *Ethics in the Sanctuary* (New Haven, Conn.: Yale University Press, 1990).

15. For an engaging study of how moral disagreements within a religion can have fundamental importance to both the religion and to American politics, see James Davison Hunter, *Culture Wars: The Struggle to Define America* (New York: Basic Books, 1991).

16. Battin acknowledges Karen Lebacqz's *Professional Ethics: Power and Paradox* (Nashville, Tenn: Abingdon, 1985), which focuses on confidentiality issues in the mainstream ministry.

17. As an analogy, suppose we were interested in the ethics of voluntary organizations whose aim was to preserve the environment or relieve world hunger. There are professionals involved, for example, professional development officers, whom we (the public) want to hold accountable in terms of professional standards (for development officers). Others involved in voluntary associations are nonprofessional volunteers who are accountable in terms of ordinary moral standards.

18. Battin also discusses organized religion as a profession in "Applied Professional Ethics and Institutional Religion: The Methodological Issues," *The Monist* 67 (1984): 569–88. Perhaps what Battin intended to say is that engaging in practices of providing religious services is a profession, not that religions are themselves professions. Yet even that analogy is stretched when religious services are provided by nonprofessional laypersons.

19. If there is an analogy here, it is not between religions and professions, but between religions and those professional societies which individuals join and leave at their discretion, such as the Institute of Electrical and Electronics Engineers.

20. Indeed, the free and gossip-rich flow of information often contributes to communities. Cf. John Sabini and Maury Silver, "A Plea for Gossip," in *Moralities of Everyday Life* (New York: Oxford University Press, 1982), 89–106.

21. Indeed, most Mormons have affirmed the attempt by their authorities to keep information about temple rituals secret. That attempt has been frustrated by recent books such as Deborah Laake, *Secret Ceremonies: A Mormon Woman's Intimate Diary of Marriage and Beyond* (New York: William Morrow, 1993). However, in defending the permissibility of membership-approved confidentiality conventions, I am not suggesting that the Mormon religion is admirable in other areas such as free speech. For an indication of disagreement within the church about freedom of speech in a matter involving university professors, see the report by the American Association of University Professors (AAUP), "Academic Freedom and Tenure: Brigham Young University," *Academe* (September/October 1997): 52–71. This report was followed by formal censure of Brigham Young University by AAUP for free speech violations.

22. Margaret P. Battin, "Reading Religions: A Reply to Callahan, Martin, and Quinn," *Professional Ethics* 3, no. 2 (1994): 71.

23. A related problem is the belief in a scripture as literally the word of God, a tenet central to fundamentalist sects. This doctrine gives the church authorities enormous leeway in claiming O-level status for virtually any scripture-based doctrine.

24. Sterling M. McMurrin, *Religion, Reason, and Truth: Historical Essays in the Philosophy of Religion* (Salt Lake City: University of Utah Press, 1982), xii. At the same time, given the prominent role of religious authority in Mormonism, it is perhaps harder to maintain a Mormon identity after rejecting theism than it is to maintain, say, a Jewish identity after rejecting beliefs in the supernatural, as, for example, Albert Einstein did. McMurrin's relationship with church officials was occasionally rocky, and on at least one occasion some church officials sought to excommunicate him.

Chapter 11

1. Character explanations of actions should not be confused with explanations of how character is formed. The latter include psychological theories of moral development, sociobiological theories about the evolution of human capacities, anthropological theories, religious explanations, and some social explanations.

2. In the criminal justice literature, James Q. Wilson is a notable exception. See *The Moral Sense* (New York: Free Press, 1993) and *On Character* (Washington, D.C.: AEI Press, 1995).

3. Donald Davidson, *Essays on Actions and Events* (Oxford: Oxford University Press, 1980); Robert Audi, *Action, Intention, and Reason* (Ithaca, N.Y.: Cornell University Press, 1993). On the role of folk psychology as a touchstone for more abstruse psychological theories, see Jerome Bruner, *Acts of Meaning* (Cambridge, Mass.: Harvard University Press, 1990).

4. With modifications of terminology, the categories (though not the examples) are those set forth by Ronald D. Milo in *Immorality* (Princeton, N.J.: Princeton University Press, 1984). For example, I use "perverse immorality" for his "perverse wickedness," and "moral indifference" for his "lack of moral concern."

5. Of course, the evil of Nazi professionalism took many forms. See Robert Jay Lifton, *The Nazi Doctors: Medical Killing and the Psychology of Genocide* (New York: Basic Books, 1986), and Charles E. McClelland, *The German Experience of Professionalization* (Cambridge: Cambridge University Press, 1991).

6. For an insightful discussion of refusal, see Jean Hampton's conception of "defiance explanations" in "The Nature of Immorality," *Social Philosophy and Policy*, 7 (1989): 22–44. I disagree, however, with Hampton's attempt to reduce other types of explanation of wrongdoing to this category. Regarding degrees of sociopathy, see the classic text by Hervey Cleckley, *The Mask of Sanity*, 5th ed. (Saint Louis, Mo.: C. V. Mosby, 1976).

7. Mary Midgley also views this as a prejudice in *Wickedness: A Philosophical Essay* (London: Routledge and Kegan Paul, 1984), 2.

8. Cf. Owen Flanagan, *Varieties of Moral Personality: Ethics and Psychological Realism* (Cambridge, Mass.: Harvard University Press, 1991).

9. Quoted by Joan C. Callahan, "Professions, Institutions, and Moral Risk," in Daniel E. Wueste, ed., *Professional Ethics and Social Responsibility* (Totawa, N.J.: Rowman and Littlefield, 1994), 246–47.

10. Ibid., 262.

11. Ibid., 248–49.

12. Michael Davis, "Explaining Wrongdoing," *Journal of Social Philosophy* 20 (1980): 74–90. Quotations are from p83, 78–79. Davis also discusses the *Challenger* case in "Thinking Like an Engineer: The Place of a Code of Ethics in the Practice of a Profession," *Philosophy and Public Affairs* 20 (1991): 150–67.

13. Joan S. Lockard and Delroy L. Paulhus, eds., *Self-Deception: An Adaptive Mechanism?* (Englewood Cliffs, N.J.: Prentice-Hall, 1988); Shelley E. Taylor, *Positive Illusions: Creative Self-Deception and The Healthy Mind* (New York: Basic Books, 1989); Mike W. Martin, *Self-Deception and Morality* (Lawrence: University Press of Kansas, 1986), 109–37.

14. Alasdair MacIntyre, *After Virtue*, 2nd ed. (Notre Dame, Ind.: University of Notre Dame Press, 1984), 194. Cf. Albert Flores, ed., *Professional Ideals* (Belmont, Calif.: Wadsworth, 1988), 6–10.

15. Ibid.: (a), (b), and (d) on p189–90; (c) on 197.

16. Ibid., 190–91.

17. To be fair, MacIntyre recognizes that "the making and sustaining of forms of human community—and therefore of institutions—itself has all the characteristics of a practice," (*After Virtue*, 194). He also recognizes that communities contribute to fostering or undermining virtues. And he writes, "Institutions and practices characteristically form a single causal order."

18. For examples, see Francis J. Aguilar, *Managing Corporate Ethics* (New York: Oxford University Press, 1994), and Joseph A. Raelin, *The Clash of Cultures: Managers Managing Professionals* (Boston: Harvard Business School Press, 1991).

19. Robert Jackall, *Moral Mazes: The World of Corporate Managers* (Oxford: Oxford University Press, 1988), 105–11.

20. The idealization began with Plato in *The Republic*, pt. 1, ch. 3.

21. Cf. Banks McDowell, *Ethical Conduct and the Professional's Dilemma: Choosing between Service and Success* (New York: Quorum Books, 1991).

22. Marc A. Rodwin, *Medicine, Money, and Morals: Physicians' Conflicts of Interest* (New York: Oxford University Press, 1993).

23. Elizabeth Wolgast, *Ethics of an Artificial Person: Lost Responsibility in Professions and Organizations* (Stanford, Calif.: Stanford University Press, 1992), 144. Cf. David Luban, *Lawyers and Justice: An Ethical Study* (Princeton, N.J.: Princeton University Press, 1988).

24. Hard determinism, the view that all of us are entirely determined by influences outside ourselves, would seem to excuse wrongdoing in the professions and elsewhere. It would also seem to favor social explanations and dismiss character explanations as wrongheaded. In fact, hard determinism leaves no room for our ordinary moral concept of responsible agency or even for our full-blooded notion of wrongdoing. In thereby overthrowing the ordinary concept of "wrongdoing," hard determinism undermines social as well as character explanations of wrongdoing.

Chapter 12

1. Alan Mintz, *George Eliot and the Novel of Vocation* (Cambridge, Mass.: Harvard University Press, 1978).

2. Parenthetical page references are to George Eliot, *Middlemarch* (New York: Penguin, 1994).

3. George Levine, "Determinism and Responsibility," in Gordon S. Haight, ed., *A Century of George Eliot Criticism* (Boston: Houghton Mifflin, 1965), 349–60.

4. Stephen L. Darwall drew the distinction as "recognition" versus "appraisal" self-respect, *Impartial Reason*, (Ithaca, N.Y.: Cronell University Press, 1983), 149. Also see Robin S. Dillon ed., *Dignity, Character, and Self-Respect* (New York: Routledge, 1995).

5. The term "inner hypocrisy" is borrowed from Joseph Butler, "Upon Self-Deceit," in W. E. Gladstone, ed., *The Works of Joseph Butler*, vol. 2 (New York: Macmillan, 1896), 180. I discuss Butler in *Self-Deception and Morality* (Lawrence: University Press of Kansas, 1986).

6. John Rawls, *A Theory of Justice* (Cambridge, Mass.: Harvard University Press, 1971), 440.

7. Alan Mintz, *George Eliot and the Novel of Vocation*, 104.

8. Bert G. Hornback, *Middlemarch, A Novel of Reform* (Boston: Twayne, 1988).

9. Joshua Halberstam, "Fame," *American Philosophical Quarterly* 21 (January 1984): 93–99.

10. Daniel J. Levinson, *The Seasons of a Man's Life* (New York: Knopf, 1978), 268.

11. Jean-Paul Sartre, *Being and Nothingness*, trans. Hazel E. Barnes (New York: Washington Square Press, 1966), 86–116. The literature on self-deception is considerable. The best single work on self-deception is Herbert Fingarette, *Self-Deception* (New York: Humanities Press, 1969), a work that resonates with Eliot's talk of "two [sub-]selves" in self-deception. Also see his "Self-Deception Needs No Explaining," *The Philosophical Quarterly* 48 (1998): 289–301. For a sample of the recent literature, see Mike W. Martin, ed., *Self-Deception and Self-Understanding* (Lawrence: University Press of Kansas, 1985); Brian P. McLaughlin and Amelie Oksenberg Rorty, eds., *Perspectives on Self-Deception* (Berkeley: University of California Press, 1988); and Roger T. Ames and Wimal Dissanayake, eds., *Self and Deception: A Cross-Cultural Philosophical Enquiry* (Albany: State University of New York Press, 1996).

12. Contrary to Alfred R. Mele, "Real Self-Deception," *Behavioral and Brain Sciences* 20 (1997): 91–102.

13. See Henry Fairlie, *The Seven Deadly Sins Today* (Notre Dame, Ind.: University of Notre Dame, 1979), 61. For a justly famous case study, see Peter Shaffer, *Amadeus* (New York: New American Library, 1984).

14. Janet Landman, *Regret: The Persistence of the Possible* (Oxford: Oxford University Press, 1993), 210.

15. Ludwig Wittgenstein, quoted by M. O' C. Drury, "Some Notes on Conversations with Wittgenstein," in Rush Rhees, ed., *Recollections of Wittgenstein* (Oxford: Oxford University Press, 1984), 95–96.

16. Robert Jay Lifton, *The Protean Self: Human Resilience in an Age of Fragmentation* (New York: Basic Books, 1993), and Kenneth J. Gergen, *The Saturated Self: Dilemmas of Identity in Contemporary Life* (New York: Basic Books, 1991).

Chapter 13

1. Juliet B. Schor, *The Overworked American: The Unexpected Decline of Leisure* (New York: BasicBooks, 1991), 29.

2. On the "gappiness" of character, see Owen Flanagan, *Varieties of Moral Personality: Ethics and Psychological Realism* (Cambridge, Mass.: Harvard University Press, 1991).

3. For especially interesting discussions, see Gabriele Taylor, "Integrity," in *Pride, Shame, and Guilt: Emotions of Self-Assessment* (Oxford: Clarendon, 1985), 108–41; Lynne McFall, "Integrity," *Ethics* 98 (1987): 4–20; and Mark S. Halfon, *Integrity: A Philosophical Inquiry* (Philadelphia: Temple University Press, 1989), 32.

4. Harry G. Frankfurt, *The Importance of What We Care About* (Cambridge: Cambridge University Press, 1988).

5. John Rawls, *A Theory of Justice* (Cambridge, Mass.: Harvard University Press, 1971), 519.

6. Bernard Williams made the example familiar in the philosophical literature. His partly fictional Gaugin makes his decision after engaging in moral reasoning that took seriously his obligations to his family, even though ultimately he made the artistic commitment paramount. "Moral Luck," in *Moral Luck* (Cambridge: Cambridge University Press, 1981), 20–39.

7. Harry G. Frankfurt understands this idea in terms of second-order desires: one desires to have moral desires. *The Importance of What We Care About* 80–94.

8. See Mary Midgley, "Creation and Originality," in *Heart and Mind: The Varieties of Moral Experience* (New York: St. Martin's, 1981), 43–58.

9. Cheshire Calhoun, "Standing for Something," *The Journal of Philosophy* 92 (1995): 235–60.

10. This "motivational internalism" is defended by Thomas E. Wren in *Caring About Morality* (Cambridge: Massachusetts Institute of Technology Press, 1991) and Michael Smith in, *The Moral Problem* (Oxford: Blackwell, 1994).

11. Martin Benjamin, *Splitting the Difference: Compromise and Integrity in Ethics and Politics* (Lawrence: University Press of Kansas, 1990), 32–38.

12. Peter A. French, *Ethics in Government* (Englewood Cliffs, N.J.: Prentice-Hall, 1983), 5–6.

13. Cf. W. B. Schaufeli, C. Maslach, T. Marek, eds., *Professional Burnout: Recent Development in Theory and Research* (Washington D.C.: Taylor and Francis, 1993), 3.

14. Graham Greene, *A Burnt-Out Case* (New York: Penguin, 1960), 44.

15. Ibid., 114.

16. Ibid., 118.

17. Thomas Mann, *Buddenbrooks*, trans. John E. Woods (New York: Vintage, 1993), 595.

18. Page references are to Anton Chekhov, "Ward No. 6" in *Seven Short Novels by Chekhov*, trans. Barbara Makanowitzky (New York: W. W. Norton, 1963), 113.

19. Ibid., 120.

20. Ibid., 156.

21. Page references are to Albert Camus, *The Fall*, trans. Justin O'Brien (New York: Vintage, 1956), 84.

22. Ibid., 141.

23. Ayala M. Pines, "Burnout: An Existential Perspective," in Wilmar B. Schaufeli, Christina Maslach, and Tadeusz Marek, eds, *Professional Burnout: Recent Developments in Theory and Research* 33–51; Cary Cherniss, *Beyond Burnout* (New York: Routledge, 1995), 181–89.

24. Pines, "Burnout" 41.

25. Cherniss, *Beyond Burnout*, 63–75.

26. Christina Maslach, *Burnout: The Cost of Caring* (Englewood Cliffs, N.J.: Prentice-Hall, 1982).

27. Mary Midgley, *Beast and Man: The Roots of Human Nature,* rev. ed. (New York: Routledge, 1995), 192.

28. John Kekes, *Moral Tradition and Individuality* (Princeton, N.J.: Princeton University Press, 1989), 230, and on Thomas More, 167–72.

29. Bernard Williams, " A Critique of Utilitarianism" in Bernard Williams and J. J. C. Smart, *Utilitarianism, For and Against* (Cambridge: Cambridge University Press, 1973), 97–98.

30. John Dewey, *Human Nature and Conduct* [1922] (New York: Modern Library, 1957), 183.

31. John Dewey, *Theory of the Moral Life* [1908] (New York: Holt, Rinehart and Winston, 1960), 141.

32. James D. Wallace, *Moral Relevance and Moral Conflict* (Ithaca, N.Y.: Cornell University Press, 1988), 93–94. The spirit of Dewey's thinking is also powerfully conveyed by Arthur E. Murphy in *The Theory of Practical Reason,* ed. A. I. Melden (La Salle, Ill.: Open Court, 1964).

33. George Eliot, *Daniel Deronda* [1876] (New York: Penguin, 1974), p. 572.

34. Mary Catherine Bateson, *Composing a Life* (New York: Plume, 1990). Also see Myra Dinnerstein, *Women between Two Worlds: Midlife Reflections on Work and Family* (Philadelphia: Temple University, 1992), and Robert Jay Lifton, *The Protean Self: Human Resilience in an Age of Fragmentation* (New York: Basic Books, 1993).

35. George de Mare, *Corporate Lives* (New York: Van Nostrand Reinhold, 1976), 145.

36. Arlie Hochschild, with Anne Machung, *The Second Shift* (New York: Avon, 1985), 110.

37. Virginia Woolf, *To the Lighthouse* (San Diego: Harcourt Brace Jovanovich, 1927), 118.

38. Gilbert C. Meilaender, *Friendship: A Study in Theological Ethics* (Notre Dame, Ind.: University of Notre Dame Press, 1981), 97.

39. Betsy Morris, "Is Your Family Wrecking Your Career? (and Vice Versa)," *Fortune* (March 17, 1997), 71–90.

40. Cited in Deborah J. Swiss and Judith P. Walker, *Women and the Work/Family Dilemma* (New York: Wiley, 1993), 63.

41. Quoted from conversation by Robert Coles, *The Call of Stories: Teaching and the Moral Imagination* (Boston: Houghton Mifflin, 1989), 116. For an interesting contemporary study, see Michael F. Myers, *Doctors' Marriages,* 2nd ed. (New York: Plenum Medical, 1994).

42. D. H. Lawrence, *Women in Love* (New York: Penguin, 1982), 295–300.

43. Ibid., 542.

44. Schor, *The Overworked American.*

45. Arlie Russell Hochschild, *The Time Bend: When Work Becomes Home and Home Becomes Work* (New York: Henry Holt, 1997), esp. 197–203.

INDEX

Beauchamp, Tom L., 96, 219 n.1
Bellah, Robert, 28
benevolence. *See* altruism
Benjamin, Martin, 237 n.26
Bloom, Allan, 232 n.33
Blum, Lawrence A., 74–75, 222 n.54
Blustein, Jeffrey, 70–73, 222 n.52
Boisjoly, Roger, 139, 146, 150, 182
Bok, Sissela, 155
Bowie, Norman, 220 n.12
Brand, Cabell, 55
bribes, 43
Bullough, Edward, 85
Burg, Wibren Van Der, 219 n.2
burnout, xi, 87–89, 202, 206–210

Cahn, Steven M., 232 n.34
Callahan, Daniel, 232 n.34
Callahan, Joan C., 180–82, 187,
    229 n.30
Calhoun, Cheshire, 242 n.9
Camenisch, Paul F., 39–41, 43
Camps, Frank, 140, 150
campus wars, ix, 113–15
Camus, Albert, 27, 71, 209
Cannon, Katie, 10–20, 21, 152
caring
    and justice, 76–79
    meanings of, 70
    motives of, ix, 23, 69
    pretense of, 69, 75, 89
    and professional distance, 82
    as sustaining professionals, 79,
        89–90, 206–210
Carson, Thomas, 220 n.12
case studies, 4, 189
Casebier, Allan, 85
Cassell, Eric, 90
Catholics, 6, 155, 159, 166–67
Chalk, Rosemary, 237 n.23
Challenger, x, 120–28, 139–40, 146,
    182–84
character gaps, 203. *See also* virtues
Chekhov, Anton, 88, 208
chemist, 212. *See also* Elion, Ger-
    trude B.
Childress, James F., 219 n.1
Christian Fundamentalists, 95–96,
    154
Christian Scientists, 6, 155–56,
    163–64

Clamence, Jean-Baptiste, 27, 71, 75,
    209
Clinton, President Bill, 4
codes of ethics, 6, 32–35, 37–39, 138,
    236 n.21
Cohen, Elliot D., 230 n.35
Coleman, Jack, 58–59
Coles, Robert, 67, 243 n.41
collegiality, 87–88
communal goods, 26, 31. *See also*
    public goods
community, 3, 16–17, 27, 59, 117,
    126, 149, 208, 234 n.18
Community Boards, 54
community standards, 39–40
compartmentalizing motives, 14
compensation motives, 22, 24, 31,
    210
competitive advertising, 38
compromise, 156–57, 205–206, 212
confidentiality, 35, 39–40, 44–45,
    160–63, 166, 211, 234 n.20
conflict resolution, 54. *See also*
    compromise
conflicts of interest, 99–100, 187–88
consensus paradigm
    and abuse of codes, 50
    and compartmentalized ethics,
        121
    in conventional versus critical ver-
        sions, 6, 32
    defined, 4
    and family, 203
    and professional distance, 82
    and responsibilities, 32–50
    and right of conscience, 136
    and self-betrayal, 201
    truth in, 32–43, 102
    and voluntary service, 51, 59
    and whistleblowing, 138, 147,
        150
    and wrongdoing, x, 173
Cornwell, Grant H., 232 n.31
craft motives, 22, 210. *See also*
    motives
Csikszentmihalyi, Mihaly, 24
Curzer, Howard J., 89–91

Darwall, Stephen L., 222, n.52,
    227 n.23, 241 n.4
Davidson, Donald, 239 n.3

Davis, Michael, xi
  on codes of ethics, 38–39, 43,
      223 nn.13,15–16
  on whistleblowing, 141–42,
      235 n.7
  on wrongdoing, 182–84, 187
DC-10 airplane, 140
De George, Richard T., 143, 144,
    233 n.1, 236 n.12
De Mare, George, 214
decency, 35, 153, 204
decorum, professional, 87
democratic values, 105, 154
determinism, 240 n.24
Dewey, John, 212–13, 232 n.26
Dillon, Robin, 81
dirty hands, 34
distance, professional
  compared to aesthetic distance,
      84–86
  moral versus psychological, 83
  over- and under-, ix, 82, 84–85, 91
  supports coping, 86–89
  and explaining wrongdoing, 177–78
Donaldson, Thomas, 235 n. 37
Downie, R. S., 231 n.20, 232 n.26
downsizing, 59, 130, 202
Dworkin, Ronald, 133, 230 n.39

economics and ethics, 12–16
Eddy, Mary Baker, 155
egotism, 191–93, 215
Elion, Gertrude B., 19, 21, 48, 64, 97
Eliot, George, 189–201, 213
engineers
  as caring, 75
  in relationships to managers, 119–37
  and safety, 44, 124–25, 131–32
  and whistleblowing, 138–50
  who are pacifists, 48
envy, 198
ethical relativism, 38, 40, 41, 111
ethical theories, 41–43, 62–63, 76,
    97–98, 111–12, 210–13
Ethics in the Sanctuary, x, 151, 158–68
euthanasia, xiii. See also suicide,
    physician-assisted
experience machine, 30

fairness, 34, 38
false consciousness, 165

The Fall, 27, 71, 209
family, xi, 3, 55, 93–94, 144, 147,
    190–200, 202, 211–12, 214–17
fanatics, 7
feminism, 106, 113–15, 181, 193, 201.
    See also Gilligan, Carol
Fernhoff, Deborah, 153–54
fertility clinic scandal, 34
fiduciary model, 80
Fish, Stanley, 232 n.37
Flanagan, Owen, 241 n.2
Flores, Albert, 5–6, 219 n.2, 234 n.17,
    237 n.25
Florman, Samuel C., 122–23
flow experiences, 24
Foxfire Magazine, 54
Frankfurt, Harry, 237 n.30, 242 n.7
French, Peter, 242 n.10
Friedman, Milton, 15
Friedman, Monroe H., 223 n.5
Fry, Sara T., 227 n.12
Fuller, Lon, 125

Garrow, Robert, 34
Gewirth, Alan, 222 n.54, 223 n.4,
    224 n.22
Gilligan, Carol, 76–78, 213–14
Goldberg, Michael, 219 n.2
Goldman, Alan, 224 n.22
Goldman, Michael, 231 n.19,
    232 n.27
good fortune obligates, 17
good works, 59–60
goods
  communal, 26, 31
  internal versus external, 125–26,
      184–86
  profession-specific, 26–27, 73–76, 80
  public versus private, 21, 26, 29,
      31, 126–27, 131
Gorovitz, Samuel, 90
Gosse, Edmund, 95–96
Gosse, Philip, 95
Graff, Gerald, 233 n.40
gratitude, 17–18
greed, 4, 15, 176, 196
Greenawalt, Kent, 157–58, 230 n.39
Greene, Graham, 207
Griener, Glenn G., 225 n.33
guilt, 199. See also wrongdoing
Gutmann, Amy, 231 n.9

motives of, 24, 58, 216
and personal commitments,
11–12, 55
as supervising professionals,
120–24
Mann, Thomas, 207–208
May, Larry, 155–56, 236 n.21
McAuliffe, Christa, 120
McFall, Lynne, 242 n.3
McMurrin, Sterling M., 168, 239 n.24
meaningful work, vii, 29
intrinsic satisfactions in, 21–24
and public goods, 29, 73, 76
See also motives; profession-specific
goods
Meilaender, Gilbert C., 215
Melden, A. I., 64, 78, 107, 224 n.21
Mellerstig, Kent, 55
membership consent, 158–64
Mellema, Gregory, 61–62
Meyers, Diana T., 232 n.38
Michel, Anneliese, 155
Middlemarch, 189–201
Midgley, Mary, 26, 171, 239 n.7,
242 n.8, 243 n.27
Milgram, Stanley, 227 n.1
Mill, John Stuart, 92, 224 n.21,
227 n.15
Milliken, Frances J., 124
Milo, Ronald D., 239 n.4
mixed motives, 21–28, 184–88
Mohr, Richard, 232
money, 13, 21–23, 24, 28, 210
Monsma, Stephen, 219 n.2
moonlighting, 99
moral concern, 23–24
moral psychology, vii, 82, 84, 201
moral reasoning, 144, 202, 210–13
moral schizophrenia, 16
More, Sir Thomas, 211
Mormons, 159, 161–63, 167–68,
238 n.21
Morton Thiokol, 120–24, 139,
182–84
motives
for acts versus habits, 79
for caring, 70
mixed, 21–28, 184–88
three types of, viii, 22–23, 126, 195,
210, 214, 216–17
for wrongdoing, 175, 194–98

Mount, Eric, 219 n.2
Mulloy, Lawrence, 120, 122
Murphy, Arthur E., 243 n.32
mysticism, ethical, 16

Nagel, Thomas, 83–84, 91,
225 n.22
NASA. *See Challenger*
National Society of Professional
Engineers, 146
Nazi Germany, 29, 40, 84, 97, 204,
223–24 n.15, 239 n.5
Newmark, Colin, 155–56
Noddings, Nel, 227 n.12
nonprofit organizations, 18, 55–59
Nozick, Robert
experience machine of, 30
and libertarianism, 15–16,
235 n.8
on meaningful work, 22
nurses, 73–74, 90, 206
Nussbaum, Martha, 231 n.18

Oakeshott, Michael, 107
objectivity
in adjudication, 97–98
and conflicts of interest, 99–100
in evaluation, 98–99
and perspectivism, 113–15
and professional distance, 94–99
skepticism about, 96–97
and truth seeking, 95–97
O'Connor, Sandra Day, 98
ordinary morality, 34–35, 39–40,
162–63, 223 n.4, 223 n.15
Otten, James, 235 n.33
oxymorons, 65

paradox
economic, 31
of not taking leisure time, 217
of professional distance, 86, 90
of reason-compatibility, 128–32
of self-deception, 195–96
of service, 31
volunteer, 60
paternalism, 20, 78–79, 80–81,
91–93, 153
Payton, Robert, 56–58
Pelligrino, Edmund D., 74
Peloza, John, 154

personal commitments
  and confidentiality, 44–45
  as neglected in professional ethics,
    vii, 4, 6
personal style
  in architecture, 20
  in teaching, 108–113
perspectivism, 113–15, 168–69
Peters, R. S. 231 n.20, 232 n.26
pharmacists, 77, 213
philanthropy
  of Albert Schweitzer, 16–18
  corporate, 15
  defined, 51–52, 56
  of Dorothea Brooke, 190
  and hypocrisy, 196
philosophers, 231 n.18. *See also*
  professors
physicians
  as assisting suicide, 49–50, 91
  as caring, 23, 74, 208, 216
  and Christian Science, 155–56,
    163–64
  and do no harm, 33
  in fertility clinic scandal, 34
  in health maintenance organiza-
    tions, 47, 188
  as hired guns, 93
  and homophobia, 229 n.21
  integrity of, 192–94
  and professional distance, 83,
    86–90
  regrets of, 199–200
  and teamwork, 88
  trust in, 37
  voluntary service by, 3–4, 16–18,
    52–53, 55
Pincoffs, Edmund L., 230 n.4,
  237 n.24
Pines, Ayala M., 209–210
Pinkus, Rosa Lynn B., 233 n.2
Pinto automobiles, 140
pleasures, 21–28, 30
pluralism, 40, 112, 225 n.25
police officers, 25, 203
politicians, 18, 83, 94, 158
polygamy, 162
Postema, Gerald J., 228
power, 23–24, 28
pragmatism, 202, 210–13, 217
predominant egoism, 26

Pritchard, Michael S., 59–60, 233 n.10
pro bono service, viii, 52–55
profession-specific goods, 26–27,
  73–76, 80
professional ethics
  as compartmentalized, 121
  and everyday morality, 34–35,
    39–40, 162–63
  senses of, 6–7
professionals
  career choices of, 18–19, 48
  independence of, 119
  interactions among, 121
  personal ideals of. *See* ideals,
    personal
professors
  as advocating values, 19–20,
    101–115
  and burnout, 210
  as caring, 75
  as grading fairly, 99, 104
  teaching styles of, 108–113
  as truth seekers, 101–105
promises, 36–37, 60–62
psychiatrists. *See* therapists
psychological egoism, 25–26
public goods, 21, 26, 29, 31, 51–52,
  126–27, 131
Purdy, Laura, 113

Rabins, Michael J., 233 n.10
Raelin, Joseph A., 233 n.3
Rawls, John, 22 107, 157, 224 n.21,
  230 n.38
Reagan, President Ronald, 121, 128
realism in pursuing ideals, 7,
  190–94, 209–210
reason-compatibility paradox, 128–32
regret, 198–201
religion
  Albert Schweitzer's views of, 17
  and democratic values, 154,
    156–58
  and detachment, 228 n.19
  in education, 19–20, 154
  and grading, 104–105
  and hypocrisy, 196–97
  as motivation, 3, 5, 152–53
  and science, 95, 154
  and unconditional commitments,
    211

teaching styles, 108–113
teamwork, 87–88, 149
Terkel, Studs, 54, 56
therapists, 45, 82, 87, 153
Thomasma, David C., 74
Thompson, Dennis F., 238 n.13
tolerance, 105–106
Tower of Babel, 33
trust, 15, 33, 36–37, 79–81, 164, 188
truth
    and objectivity, 95–97
    and professors' obligations, 101–105
    responsibility, 102–103
    skepticism about, 113–15
truthfulness, 95–96, 101–102
Twitchell, Robyn, 155–56

unified good of clients, 73–76
Urmson, J. O., 59, 64

Vance, Cyrus, 206
Vandivier, Kermit, 235 n.31
Veatch, Robert M., 46
veterinarians, 23
virtues, vii, 5, 105, 148–50
vocation, 28–31, 58, 76, 190, 200
volunteer paradox, 60–65
voluntary service
    and nonprofit organizations, 55–58
    paradox of, 60
    as philanthropy, 51–55
    and supererogatory responsi-
        bilities, 59–65

Wallace, James, 213
Walton, Douglas, 231 n.24
Warren, Virginia L., 227 n.21

Watanabi, Kanji, 11
weakness of will, 174, 176–77, 205
Wealth of Nations, 12–15. *See also*
    Smith, Adam
Weber, Leonard J., 232 n.30
Werhane, Patricia H., 220 n.10,
    233 n.2
Westin, Alan F., 237 n.23
whistleblowing
    cases of, 139–40
    and character, 148–50
    defined, 139
    legal protection of, 124, 142
    life and death issues concerning,
        138
    and personal life, x, 144–48
    traditional approaches to, 141–43
Wigginton, Eliot, 54–55
Wilder, Hugh T., 104–105, 230 n.7
Williams, Bernard, xi, 5, 212, 219 n.3,
    236 n.14, 242 n.6
Williams, William Carlos, 216
Wilson, James Q., 239 n.2
Winston, Kenneth I., 158, 230 n.39
Wittgenstein, Ludwig, 200
Wolgast, Elizabeth, 94, 188, 229 n.24
Woolf, Virginia, 214–15
Wren, Thomas E., 242 n.10
Wright, Frank Lloyd, 20
wrongdoing
    and bad apples, 174, 179–84
    and blaming, 176
    explanations of, x, 171, 173–88
    global versus situational explana-
        tions of, 174
    types of character explanations of,
        176–79